The Engaged Sociologist

Connecting the Classroom to the Community

Edition 5

Kathleen Odell Korgen
William Paterson University

Jonathan M. White
Bentley University

Los Angeles | London | New Delhi
Singapore | Washington DC

Los Angeles | London | New Delhi
Singapore | Washington DC

FOR INFORMATION:

SAGE Publications, Inc.
2455 Teller Road
Thousand Oaks, California 91320
E-mail: order@sagepub.com

SAGE Publications Ltd.
1 Oliver's Yard
55 City Road
London EC1Y 1SP
United Kingdom

SAGE Publications India Pvt. Ltd.
B 1/I 1 Mohan Cooperative Industrial Area
Mathura Road, New Delhi 110 044
India

SAGE Publications Asia-Pacific Pte. Ltd.
3 Church Street
#10-04 Samsung Hub
Singapore 049483

Acquisitions Editor: Jeff Lasser
Editorial Assistant: Nick Pachelli
Production Editor: David C. Felts
Copy Editor: QuADS Prepress (P) Ltd.
Proofreader: Lawrence W. Baker
Typesetter: C&M Digitals (P) Ltd.
Indexer: Kathy Paparchontis
Cover Designer: Anupama Krishnan
Marketing Manager: Erica DeLuca

Copyright © 2015 by SAGE Publications, Inc.

All rights reserved. No part of this book may be reproduced or utilized in any form or by any means, electronic or mechanical, including photocopying, recording, or by any information storage and retrieval system, without permission in writing from the publisher.

Printed in the United States of America.

Library of Congress Cataloging-in-Publication Data

Korgen, Kathleen Odell, 1967–

The engaged sociologist : connecting the classroom to the community / Kathleen Odell Korgen, William Paterson University, Jonathan M. White, Bentley University.—Edition 5.

pages cm
Includes bibliographical references and index.

ISBN 978-1-4833-5919-9 (pbk. : alk. paper)

1. Service learning—United States. 2. Sociology—Study and teaching (Higher)—United States. I. White, Jonathan M. (Jonathan Michael) II. Title.

LC221.K68 2015
361.3'70973—dc23   2014030443

14 15 16 17 18 10 9 8 7 6 5 4 3 2 1

Contents

Preface

A Note From the Authors to the Students Reading This Book

Sociology is the coolest academic discipline. Seriously, what other area of study is better at helping you figure out how society operates and how you can use that knowledge to create social change? Both of us were drawn to sociology because we wanted to figure out how to fight injustice and promote democracy more effectively. It has also guided us in everyday life tasks, such as figuring out how to get policies passed on campus, deciding whom to vote for, and learning why it's vital to earn a college degree in a service-based economy. This book is part of our efforts to get students hooked on sociology and, in the process, help them to become engaged and effective citizens who can strengthen our democratic society.

This book is also part of a larger, national effort to "educate citizens" by encouraging students to participate in civic engagement exercises that connect the classroom to the community. Organizations such as The Democracy Imperative, Campus Compact, and the American Democracy Project are establishing movements to make civic engagement a part of the college experience for all undergraduates. College leaders all across the country realize that as educators they are obligated to give students the tools they will require to be effective citizens as well as the skills they will need in the workforce. Leaders in *all* sectors of society understand that higher education, when connected to the larger society, benefits everyone, on *and* off campus.

We believe, as leaders of the American Sociological Association have noted when promoting public sociology, that sociology is particularly suited to teaching students what they need to know to become effective and full members of our society. As the prominent sociologist Randall Collins has pointed out, the two core commitments of sociology are (a) to understand how society works and (b) to use that knowledge to make society better. We believe that helping students learn how to think sociologically and use sociological tools is, in effect, enabling them to become better citizens. No doubt, the professors who assigned this book to you also share this belief. They will gladly tell you why *they* think sociology is an incredibly useful and practical academic discipline.

We also know that sociology is fun to learn and to teach. That's why we created a book that we hope will be enjoyable to use for both students and teachers. The exercises throughout the chapters allow students to connect the sociological knowledge that they are learning to their campus and the larger community. So as soon as you develop your sociological eye, you will make use of it! *Please note that you will need to make sure you follow the rules for research on human subjects and get approval from the Institutional Review Board on your campus before carrying out some of these exercises.* (Your professor will tell you how to do so.) This book will also help you to connect your own life to the larger society, as you learn about the "sociological imagination" and the power it has to positively affect your community. The Sociologist in Action sections in each chapter will give you powerful examples of how sociology students and professional sociologists (both professors and applied sociologists) use sociology in myriad ways in efforts to improve society. By the end of the book, you can create your own Sociologist in Action section, in which you'll show how you used sociological tools in efforts to influence society. If you want to see more examples of sociologists in action please check out our other books, *Sociologists in Action: Sociology, Social Change, and Social Justice* and *Sociologists in Action on Inequalities: Race, Class, Gender, and Sexuality.*

We look forward to seeing your Sociologist in Action pieces and featuring many of them in future editions of this book and on the website for *The Engaged Sociologist* (http://study.sagepub.com/korgen5e). In the meantime, we hope you enjoy the book and use the knowledge and skills you gain from it to make yourself a more effective citizen, strengthen our democracy, and work for a more just and civil society. We think that you will discover what we discovered when we began our journey as sociologists—that sociology is a cool and powerful tool. And, of course, we hope that you have a lot of fun in the process!

Acknowledgments

This fifth edition would not have been possible without the very able assistance of many people. We would first like to thank our very supportive editor, Jeff Lasser. We are delighted to be working with him. We would also like to thank our former editors: Dave Repetto, who brought a commitment to connecting the classroom to the community, wonderful insight, and a wealth of good judgment to this project, and Ben Penner, our original editor, for his excellent work and for believing in the vision of this book. Ben's enthusiasm for *The Engaged Sociologist*, and for public sociology in general, inspired us as we conceptualized and wrote this book. We remain indebted to him for his good humor and his passion and insight regarding the powerful connections between sociology and student engagement. We also are indebted to David C. Felts and Karen Wiley, our production editors, for their strong support and ability to guide us throughout the course of this project. We would particularly like to thank Shamila Swamy, Rajasree Ghosh, Teresa Herlinger, and Patrice Sutton for their exceptionally astute and thoughtful work copyediting the book. Nick Pachelli, our editorial assistant, has done a wonderful job keeping things organized and on time. Finally, we owe a special debt of gratitude to our colleague, Howard Lune, for his contributions to this book.

Finally, we would both like to thank the following reviewers, whose thoughtful and excellent suggestions helped us make this book so much better than it otherwise would have been: Tessa le Roux, Lasell College; Meg Wilkes Karraker, University of St. Thomas; Regina Smardon, Methodist University; Sherrie Steiner, Booth University College; Beverly L. Stiles, Midwestern State University; Stephen Light, State University of New York, Plattsburgh; Ronda Copher, University of Minnesota; Kooros M. Mahmoudi, Northern Arizona University; Amy Holzgang, Cerritos College; Peter J. Stein, William Paterson University; Eric K. Leung, Los Angeles Valley College; John Lynxwiler, University of Central Florida; Jack Estes, Borough of Manhattan Community College, City University of New York; Werner Lange, Edinboro University of Pennsylvania; Rachel Bandy, Simpson College; Beverly L. Rogers, Collin County Community College District; Chiquita D. Howard-Bolstic, Virginia Polytechnic Institute and State University; Janice K. Purk, Mansfield University; Andrew Butz, Portland Community College; and Joanna Hunter, Radford University.

Kathleen would like to thank her encouraging, accommodating, and overall wonderful husband, Jeff, daughters, Julie and Jessica, and mother, Patricia Odell, for putting up with the many late nights, early mornings, and weekends this project consumed. Jeff and Patricia also read innumerable early drafts with good cheer and made many helpful suggestions. This book would never have been completed on time if we didn't live together, Mom. Thank you! Thanks also to Judy and Ben Korgen, Ann Odell, Mike Odell, John Odell, Nancy Baffa, Conor Odell, and Neway Odell.

Jonathan would like to thank his wife and best friend, Shelley, for her incredible friendship, love, and support. Our amazing partnership continues to energize me, enabling me to continue moving forward as a public sociologist and scholar-activist. I also want to thank the many students who have inspired me with their energy, intellect, and unwavering belief that social change is indeed possible, including the amazing student leaders of the Bentley Service-Learning Center. I also owe an enduring debt of gratitude to the dedicated and skilled staff of the Bentley Service-Learning Center. I remain constantly inspired by the staff of Free The Children and Me to We and by the millions of young people involved in their programs, working tirelessly for a better world. A huge thanks also goes to my family, who provide me with unwavering support, love, and happiness and who inspire me to continuously work toward creating a stronger civil society. And a very special group of people, my 13 nephews and nieces, deserve a special debt of gratitude because they are particularly inspirational in so many ways!

1

The Engaged Sociologist

The Sociological Perspective and the Connections Among Sociology, Democracy, and Civic Engagement

H ave you ever wanted to help change society? Do you want to have a voice in how things work throughout your life? If so, you've come to the right discipline. Sociology helps you to understand how society operates and, in turn, how to make society better.

Sociology is the scientific study of society. As sociologists, we see how individuals both shape and are shaped by larger social forces. By developing what is called a *sociological eye* (Collins, 1998; Hughes, 1971), we are able to look beneath the surface of society and see how it really works. For example, with a sociological eye, we can recognize the tremendous influence of culture on individuals. Imagine how different you might be if you had grown up in Sweden, Ethiopia, Bangladesh, or another country with a culture very different from your own.[1] You would still look about the same (though you'd have different mannerisms, speak a different language, and have a different haircut and clothes), but your values, norms, and beliefs would be different. Your view of the proper roles of men and women, your religious or secular values, your career goals, your education, and so forth are shaped by the society in which you grew up.

Look at the differences between your immediate family and some of your relatives who may have much more or much less money. Does social class cause the differences, or do the differences help determine the social class to which we will belong?[2] Consider the varying perspectives that your male relatives and your female relatives bring to the same questions. They all live in the same world, in close proximity perhaps, but they have had such different experiences of it that some people even joke that men and women come from different planets (Gray, 2004). By using the sociological eye, we can look at the world from a unique angle, notice what is often unobserved, and make connections among the patterns in everyday events that the average person might not notice. In doing so, we can understand how different organizations, institutions, and societies function; how social forces shape individual lives and ideas; and, in turn, how individuals shape organizations and institutions.

By viewing society through the perspective of a *social world model*, we can study different levels of social units—from small- to large-scale parts of the world—that interact with one another. For example, we can study participation in the democratic process through examining *interpersonal and local organizations* (e.g., political activism among students on your campus and your school's College Democrats and College Republicans clubs), *larger organizations and institutions* (e.g., national Democratic and Republican Parties and state boards of elections), and *nations or global communities* (e.g., the U.S. presidential electoral process and the UN Millennium Declaration implementation). No matter which of these we might choose to study, however, we would always be particularly concerned with the connections between the varying social groups. For example, using the social world model would help us see that individuals are influenced by and can influence their classmates, their political party, their nation, and their global community.

The social world model and a sociological eye also enable us to recognize persistent patterns that work to create disadvantages for certain groups in society, resulting in institutional discrimination (intentional or unintentional structural biases). For example, U.S. society functioned in such a way for over 200 years that there were no female Supreme Court justices before President Ronald Reagan appointed Sandra Day O'Connor in 1981. Sociologists, using the sociological eye, recognize that the long-standing all-male makeup of the Supreme Court was part of a larger pattern of sex discrimination. Some of the discrimination was deliberate and based on people's ideas about gender. Some of it was political, based on a calculation of how the public would respond to the nomination of a woman to such a post. Some of it even had to do with the fact that our culture tends to use similar language and ideas to describe both *leadership qualities* and *masculinity*. Thus, when people think of leadership, they tend to associate it with the qualities that men often bring to the table (Schein, 2001).[3] Social science research on the connections among gender roles, socialization, and sex discrimination, such as Betty Friedan's book *The Feminine Mystique* (1963), which shattered the myth that women could find fulfillment only as wives and homemakers, became part of public knowledge and was used to make the case for the women's movement in the 1960s and 1970s. Ultimately, with many other feminist scholars contributing research, this movement paved the way for a political environment conducive to the appointment of Sandra Day O'Connor and, eventually, Ruth Bader Ginsburg, Sonia Sotomayor, and Elena Kagan.

Use of the sociological eye also helps efforts to persuade governmental officeholders to initiate social policies that address social inequities. By looking beneath the surface of governmental operations, we can answer the following questions: To whom do office holders tend to respond the most? Why? How can we use this information to make sure that they respond to us? What social forces compelled Ronald Reagan, one of our most conservative presidents and not known as a women's rights advocate, to become the first president to choose a female Supreme Court justice?

The Two Core Commitments of Sociology

According to Randall Collins (1998), using the sociological eye is one of two "core commitments" of sociology. The second is *social activism*. Once we understand how society operates, we are obligated to participate actively in efforts to improve it.

The sociological eye and social activism go hand in hand. The sociological eye helps us to uncover social patterns in society, and our use of those findings leads us to become effective, engaged citizens. Once you start seeing the world through a sociological eye, you will see social patterns all around. You can also learn how to discover more social patterns, through using sociological research methods. The more you train yourself as a sociologist, the stronger your sociological eye and ability to practice effective and constructive social activism will become.

You will see throughout this book how sociology can be used to make a positive impact on society. Each chapter contains examples of *sociologists in action*, those who have honed their sociological eye and use their sociological skills to create social change. In doing so, they fulfill the two commitments of sociology.

The Sociological Imagination

To understand how we might influence society, we must first understand how we are affected by it. C. Wright Mills (1959/2000) described this ability as the "sociological imagination." When we begin to relate personal troubles to public issues, connecting our individual lives to what's happening in our society, we are using the sociological imagination.

For instance, both of us experienced our parents divorcing. As individuals, this was a personal trouble for each of us. Using the sociological imagination, we see that we were a part of a cohort of American children who lived through the great rise in the divorce rate in the 1970s. If we had been children during the 1870s, our parents would most likely have remained married. However, the changes that our society went through in the 1960s and 1970s (legal rights and protections for women, which enabled more women to exit relationships; the decline of religiosity; cost of living increases, which required more women to join the workforce, etc.) resulted in an increase in the divorce rate and, in turn, our own parents' divorces. Our personal troubles (the divorces of our parents) were directly related to a public issue (the society-wide rise in the divorce rate).

Today, one of us is having a difficult time finding clothes for her young daughters that do not resemble those of the women on *The Real Housewives* and *Pretty Little Liars* shows. As a mother, she's horrified that anyone would expect little girls to wear such skimpy outfits (particularly *her* little girls!). As a sociologist, she can look at a sample of clothing stores and advertisements in the United States and quickly realize that her experience is part of a society-wide pattern of sexualizing girls—even very young girls (Healy, 2012). She can then start to research why a society like ours, with such a long history of public activism around "standards of moral decency," is so consistent—almost aggressive—in the sexualizing of girls. One hypothesis she might test is that this social behavior is related to the relative absence of mothers in the highest positions of fashion design and marketing. If she were to discover this to be true, she could use her findings to work for social change, trying to make these workplaces more open and inviting for fashion designers and marketers who are mothers.

One of the functions of sociology, as Mills (1959/2000) defined it, should be to "translate personal troubles into public issues" (p. 187). Once you start using your sociological imagination and looking at the world through the sociological eye and the social world model, it's impossible not to notice the connections between yourself as an individual and larger societal patterns. Consider the kind of job you hope to get after leaving college. Will you make an annual salary or an hourly wage? Will you be able to support a family? Will your job help you make a meaningful life for yourself? Will you have job security? Will your position lead to movement up or down the social class ladder? How will your job compare with those in the corner office of a major corporation or those found on the floor of a sweatshop?

Sweatshops are production sites where workers face near-slavery conditions, with few or no protections from unsafe work environments or arbitrary punishments, and where they work for below–living wage pay. Sweatshop jobs do not come with insurance, sick days, retirement plans, or protection against arbitrary termination. These sites may seem very distant from your life and from the lives of most college students. On the surface, colleges and sweatshops seemingly have nothing to do with each other. However, if you look underneath the surface (or, perhaps, at what you or your classmates are wearing), you may see a connection. The students at Duke University did: When they learned of the horrible sweatshop conditions in which most of their Duke-labeled clothes were being manufactured, they mobilized and established a United Students Against Sweatshops (USAS) group on campus. Their efforts, and those of several administrators at Duke (particularly the director of Duke Store Operations), sparked a campus-wide discussion about sweatshops and the university's responsibility to ensure that clothing with a Duke label is "sweat-free." In 1997, Duke was the first institution of higher education in the United States to adopt a code of conduct for mandating that the apparel companies with which they do business must submit to independent monitoring of the conditions in their factories. In 1999, Duke helped establish the Fair Labor Association (FLA), a collaboration of companies, civic organizations, and universities that began monitoring factories to root out abuses of workers. As of 2014, nearly 200 colleges and universities were affiliated with the FLA (FLA, 2014).

In 2000, another group of students, experts on labor rights, and university administrators established the Worker Rights Consortium (WRC) to assist in the enforcement of the codes of conduct established between colleges and universities and the companies that manufacture clothes for them. By 2014, 180 institutions of higher education and six high schools were WRC affiliates (WRC, 2014).[4] Today, students in universities around the country are creating Fair Trade Universities, working with their schools' administrators to "embed Fair Trade practices and principles into policy, as well as the social and intellectual foundations of their communities" (http://fairtradecampaigns.org/about/; go to http://fairtradecampaigns.org/campaign-type/universities to find out more about the Fair Trade Universities movement).

Sociology and the Critical Consumption of Information

In addition to having a trained sociological eye and making use of the socio-logical imagination, sociologists are informed and critical consumers of the barrage of information coming at us from all directions. Sociological research methods guide how we conduct research and how we interpret the information relayed by others. By understanding how "good" research is done, we can evaluate the information disseminated throughout society and know what news sources are trustworthy. These skills help us in our efforts to both understand and change society. In Chapter 3, we will outline in greater detail how sociological research methods can be used in this way.

Sociology and Democracy

Through reading this book and carrying out the exercises within it, you will learn how to look beneath the surface of social events, connect personal troubles to public issues, and know what information sources are trustwor-thy. You can then use these sociological tools to strengthen our society, make our nation more democratic, and work toward ensuring the rights and well-being of people all around the world. Although democracy is defined in different ways by a multitude of scholars, all point out that it is a system of governance that instills state power in citizenship rather than in government. This book shows how sociology can enable citizens (like you!) to become knowledgeable, active, and effective participants in our democratic society.

As you read the rest of this book, please think about what these sociology students have accomplished and how you, too, can use what you learn from this course to become a *sociologist in action!*

Sociologist in Action: The Social Justice League at Bridgewater State University

Joshua Warren, Bria Wilbur, Curtis Holland, and Jillian Micelli were four sociology majors at Bridgewater State University (BSU) who used their sociological eyes to make the connection between their campus and the community. Wanting to use the knowledge they learned in their courses to help effect positive social change, they created a student group called the Social Justice League. This group orga-nized many events to educate the campus community about social justice issues, raise funds, and move the college toward more just practices.

One of the Social Justice League's big events was the creation of a "Tent City"—students, faculty, and staff slept outside in tents during a cold week in November. Each day, Tent City speakers from area shelters and organizations spoke to the campus community, and faculty from all across the campus brought their classes to these lectures. Students sleeping in Tent City were not allowed to use computers or cell phones, ate their meals in a "mock soup kitchen" set up in the cafeteria, and could bathe only by using public showers during set hours. In addition to creating the educational and symbolic components of Tent City, the students also raised several thousand dollars in cash and supplies to support a local homeless shelter.

The Social Justice League launched another strategic and powerful education and awareness campaign on campus when its members organized a series of educational events and demonstrations about sweatshop labor and the clothes sold at their college bookstore. They showed videos on the topic of sweatshops to the campus community, gave talks to classes, and staged a "mock sweatshop." Through these efforts, the students created a high level of campus awareness about sweatshops.

The Social Justice League also brought the issue of sweatshops to the direct attention of Dr. Dana Mohler-Faria, the president of BSU, who worked with the group to form a campus council to research the suppliers of the clothing sold at the student bookstore. After carefully examining the issue, the president agreed that BSU should join the WRC. Bria summed up the campaign by saying, "We worked extremely hard and I never felt more proud of myself than when I got the phone call that our campaign was successful and that BSU was going to join the Worker Rights Consortium! It was through sociology that I learned about these issues." Thanks to the efforts of the skilled and passionate members of the Social Justice League, BSU joined the growing ranks of colleges committed to ensuring that their campuses are sweat-free.

Jillian described the connection between her sociological training and her actions to work for the betterment of society like this: "Within one year, my life changed dramatically. [By changing] my major to sociology the night before classes started, not only did I gain a degree in sociology, I also gained knowledge I would have never gained otherwise. The training and skills I learned from courses on genocide to courses on social inequality truly motivated me to strive for social change not only in the Social Justice League, but beyond. It taught me the connection I have with the global market and how if one pushes for something they believe in, social change will follow."

(Continued)

(Continued)

Speaking of his work as president of the Social Justice League, Joshua said, "By combining what I've learned in my studies with my passion for social justice and civic engagement, I am able to not only serve those immediately in need but also think about the reasons for why there is a need. It enables me to do more than just put a 'band-aid' on a problem. I can act proactively to find the source of the issue and uproot it!"

Curtis made his awareness of the two core commitments of sociology clear when he said, "As I began to realize that I was becoming a burgeoning sociologist, I realized simultaneously that the knowledge I was gaining from sociological inquiry came with a great responsibility."

Recently, the students of the Social Justice League joined forces with students from the Free The Children Bridgewater State University chapter to work with administrators across the campus and help BSU become one of the first universities in the country to gain Fair Trade University status.

EXERCISE 1.1   How Is Higher Education Related to Democracy?

If you live in a democracy, then you have inherited certain social obligations. What do you think they are? Is voting one of them? How about going to college? Think about the connection between democracy and higher education, and answer the following questions:

1. What do you think is the purpose of higher education?

2. Why did you decide to go to college?

3. Do you think your college education will help you become a better citizen? Why or why not?

4. Now go to the Campus Compact webpage at www.compact.org/resources-for-presidents/presidents-declaration-on-the-civic-responsibility-of-higher-education, and read the "Presidents' Declaration on the Civic Responsibility of Higher Education."

5. Did your answer to Question 1 relate to the presidents' description of the purpose of public higher education? Why do you think it did or did not?

(Continued)

(Continued)

6. Why is an educated public necessary for a strong democratic society?

7. Is a public higher education attainable for all Americans? (Be sure to look at the information in Exercise 1.4 before you answer this question.) Why or why not? If not, what are the ramifications of this situation for our democracy? How can you, using what your sociological eye has uncovered, work to make public higher education more attainable and realizable for more people?

EXERCISE 1.2   Walking Billboards

You occupy many social roles in your life: You are a student, somebody's friend, somebody's child, and perhaps a parent, sibling, employee, teammate, boss, neighbor, girlfriend or boyfriend, or mentor. To many thousands of companies out there, your main role is that of consumer. How do apparel companies market themselves, specifically, to men, women, and different racial and ethnic groups? How do members of each of these groups act as "walking billboards" for the apparel companies that make the clothing they wear?

Next time you are in one of your other classes, note the following:

1. How many students are there? How many are male, and how many are female?

2. How many of each sex are wearing visible product or company logos on their clothing, including footwear, baseball caps, and so on? (Include yourself in your answers.)

3. Are there any logos that occur more than once throughout the class?

4. Are there any logos or brands that are considered "in" on your campus?

5. Using your newly trained "sociological eye," analyze the results you have gathered. What institutional and societal forces might be at work here? Do you notice any specific trends along race or gender lines? Do people from certain sex or racial or ethnic groups, teams, or cliques exhibit trends in their dress? How about the faculty? Do you detect any trends among your teachers? What does all of this tell you about consumerism, values, norms, and the culture of your campus?

EXERCISE 1.3	What's the Connection Between College Students and Sweatshops?

1. Watch *Outside the Lines: Cowboys Clothing Controversy* at http://espn. go.com/espn/otl/story/_/id/7435424/dallas-cowboys-dip-sports-apparel-business-comes-allegations-sweatshop-labor.

2. Determine if your campus belongs to the FLA or the WRC. You can find out if your campus belongs to the FLA at http://www.fairlabor.org and the WRC at http://www.workersrights.org/.

3. Ask the manager of your campus bookstore what vendors they use to obtain the clothes sold on campus. If your campus does belong to the FLA or WRC, contact that organization, and ask about its findings on the vendors your campus bookstore uses.

4. If your school is not an FLA or WRC affiliate, do some research on your own to find information about the vendors. The USAS's Sweatfree Campus Campaign website, which you can access through http://usas.org/, is one useful site. You should also check out the websites for the Business & Human Rights Resource Centre at www.business-humanrights.org/Cate gories/Individualcompanies and Green America's Responsible Shopper at http://www.greenamericatoday.org/programs/responsibleshopper.

5. Ask the campus bookstore manager if he or she is aware of the conditions under which the vendors' employees work.

6. Write a two- to three-page paper that describes your findings and why you believe your campus should or should not be affiliated with the FLA or WRC. If it is not (and you think it should be), describe which organization you think it should join and how you could help create a movement on campus to bring about such an affiliation.

EXERCISE 1.4	Worried About the Increasingly High Cost of Tuition?

You are not alone. According to the College Board (2011), after adjusting for inflation, from 2001–2002 through 2011–2012, in-state tuition and fees increased by 56% at 4-year state colleges and universities, 38% at 2-year colleges, and 26% at 4-year private institutions. During the same decade (between 2001–2002 and 2011–2012), state funding per full-time college student declined by 23%.

(Continued)

(Continued)

In 2013–2014, the average cost of tuition and fees was $30,094 at private nonprofit 4-year colleges, $8,893 (up 4.4% from 2010–2011) at 4-year (in-state) public institutions, and $3,264 (up 8.7% from 2010–2011) at public (in-state) 2-year institutions. Keep in mind that these figures do not include room and board costs (College Board, 2014).

1. How would strategies to deal with the increase in tuition vary depending on whether it is viewed as (a) a personal trouble or (b) a public issue?

2. Go to the website "Higher Ed Not Debt" at http://higherednotdebt.org. What are some of the actions suggested on that website, or that you have thought of yourself, that you could take to convince state legislators to increase funding for public higher education in your state?

3. Choose one of the actions you've listed under Question 2 that is a manageable action for you to take. Now, carry out the plan you devised, and write a report that describes (a) what you did and (b) the outcome of your actions. Note that you might have to wait a while to complete (b), so you should start on (a) right away.

EXERCISE 1.5   Are Campus Workers Paid Enough to Be Able to Support Themselves?

Are workers on your campus paid enough to be self-sufficient?

1. Conduct research on the wages paid to cafeteria and custodial staff on your campus. You can gather this information through interviews, or if you are able to access the campus financial reports, you can use them.

2. Once you have gathered your data, read the "Self-Sufficiency Standard" at http://www.selfsufficiencystandard.org/standard.html, and look at the Self-Sufficiency wage data for your state. If your state is not listed there, you can use the Living Wage Calculator at http://www.living wage.geog.psu.edu.

3. Based on what you have read, determine whether or not the cafeteria and custodial workers on your campus are making "living or self-sufficient" wages.

(Continued)

(Continued)

4. Read "Living Wage Overview" at http://laborcenter.berkeley.edu/living
   wage/overview.shtml, and look at the USAS overview of campaigns for
   Campus Worker Justice at http://usas.org/campaigns/campus-worker-
   justice/.

5. Write a two-page paper that describes the findings for your campus and
   how students can help raise the salaries of low-wage campus workers.

DISCUSSION QUESTIONS

1. Before reading this chapter, had you ever recognized a connection between your
   own life and the lives of people working in sweatshops? Why or why not? Do
   you now see a connection? Now that you have thought about this, how will you
   proceed?

2. Think of one personal trouble in your life (e.g., struggling to pay for college or
   to find a job that pays well, a time when you were discriminated against, etc.).
   Now, use your sociological imagination, and relate it to a public issue. How
   would your attempts to deal with the problem differ depending on whether you
   view it as (a) an individual problem or (b) a societal issue?

3. Do you know what the president of the United States, your state senators, and
   your representative are doing about (a) sweatshops and (b) funding for higher
   education? If you don't know, why do you think you are unaware of their positions on these issues? Would their positions on these issues influence whether or
   not you would vote for them (or have they influenced your decision)? Why or
   why not?

4. Do you think you could use your sociological eye to do something similar to
   what the members of the Social Justice League did at BSU? Why or why not?
   What are some of the ideas you have?

5. Explain why the second core commitment of sociology (social activism) must be
   preceded by the first (use of the sociological eye). Provide an example of how you
   might fulfill both core commitments.

SUGGESTIONS FOR SPECIFIC ACTIONS

1. Join an already established campus group working against sweatshops. (You may
   substitute a different issue or campaign if you are already involved or interested
   in one, with the permission of your instructor.)

2. Establish your own campus group to fight sweatshops. Go to http://www.freethe children.com/get-involved/ and the anti-sweatshop movement's USAS website (http://usas.org) to learn how to form a local group to combat sweatshops.

3. Go to your representative's and senators' websites (you can find them at http://www.house.gov and www.senate.gov). Send them an e-mail or letter that conveys your thoughts and feelings about a public issue of concern to you.

4. Investigate the safety of the work and living environments provided for students, faculty, professional staff, and support staff on your campus. If there are clear deficiencies or inequities, organize a group of students, faculty, and professional and support staff to advocate for improved conditions for all campus workers. For the past few years, sociology students at the University of Virginia, the University of California at Berkeley, and many other colleges across the nation have carried out just this type of research and activism. You can find information on recent campaigns at http://usas.org/ and in *Berkeley's Betrayal: Wages and Working Conditions at CAL* (http://publicsociology.berkeley.edu/publications/betrayal/betrayal.pdf).

Please go to our website at http://study.sagepub.com/korgen5e to find further civic engagement opportunities, resources, peer-reviewed articles, and updated web links related to this chapter.

NOTES

1. If you did grow up in Sweden, Ethiopia, or Bangladesh, then imagine that you grew up in New Jersey.

2. It works both ways, of course. And bonus points to you for looking at the endnote.

3. We should note that this view is less prevalent today than it was at the time of Sandra Day O'Connor's appointment to the Supreme Court.

4. To learn more about the history of the sweat-free campus movement read "The Future of the Student Anti-Sweatshop Movement: Providing Access to U.S. Courts for Garment Workers Worldwide" at http://digitalcommons.wcl.american.edu/cgi/viewcontent.cgi?article=1058&context=lelb. See also the WRC website at http://www.workersrights.org.

REFERENCES

College Board. (2011). *New College Board trends reports: Price of college continues to rise nationally, with dramatic differences in pricing policies from state to state.* Retrieved from http://www.prnewswire.com/news-releases/new-college-board-trends-reports-price-of-college-continues-to-rise-nationally-with-dramatic-differences-in-pricing-policies-from-state-to-state-132594313.html

College Board. (2014). *Average published undergraduate charges by sector, 2013–14.* Retrieved from http://trends.collegeboard.org/college-pricing/figures-tables/average-published-undergraduate-charges-sector-2013-14

Collins, R. (1998). The sociological eye and its blinders. *Contemporary Sociology, 27*(1), 2–7.

Fair Labor Association. (2014). *Affiliates: Colleges and universities.* Retrieved from http://www.fairlabor.org/affiliates/colleges-universities

Friedan, B. (1963). *The feminine mystique.* New York, NY: W. W. Norton.

Gray, J. (2004). *Men are from Mars, women are from Venus: A practical guide for improving communication and getting what you want in your relationships.* New York, NY: HarperCollins.

Healy, V. O. (2012, August 29). Mature designs for young girls difficult to avoid. *Chicago Tribune.* Retrieved from http://www.chicagotribune.com/news/local/ct-met-mature-school-clothes-20120829,0,5946648.story

Hughes, E. C. (1971). *The sociological eye: Selected papers.* Chicago, IL: Aldine-Atherton.

Mills, C. W. (2000). *The sociological imagination.* New York, NY: Oxford University Press. (Original work published 1959)

Schein, V. E. (2001). A global look at psychological barriers to women's progress in management. *Journal of Social Issues, 57,* 675–688.

Worker Rights Consortium. (2014). *WRC affiliated colleges and universities.* Retrieved from http://www.workersrights.org/about/as.asp#highschool

2

Founders and Foundations of Sociology

Theory

Sociology was founded by social scientists eager to (a) understand the major social changes of the late 19th and early 20th centuries and (b) make society better. In this chapter, you will learn how six of the founders of sociology—Karl Marx, Max Weber, Émile Durkheim, George Herbert Mead, Jane Addams, and W. E. B. Du Bois—carried out the two core commitments of sociology. Each of these theorists, in his or her own way, looked beneath the surface of society to understand how it operates and used this knowledge to improve society.

Although all of these founders responded to aspects of the social forces related to industrialization, their works are myriad and focus on a variety of subjects. Marx and Weber are considered conflict theorists,[1] Durkheim was a functionalist, Mead and Addams were symbolic interactionists, and Du Bois inspired critical race theory. However, to one degree or another, all of them looked at the roots of inequality in society and the possible solutions to this social problem. They used theories to explain how society works and how it might be improved. Like all explanations, some theories are more convincing than others. As you read through the chapter, think about which theories are most helpful to you as you try to understand how society operates and how you might work to make it better.

Karl Marx

According to Marx (1818–1883), class conflict over the control of the production of goods leads to inequality in society. He maintained that in every economic age, there is a dominant class (the owners) that owns and controls the means of production and exploits the other class (the workers).

For example, in the feudal era, there were landowners and serfs, and in the industrial era, there were factory owners and factory workers. Marx believed that the workers would eventually overthrow the owners when

1. the economic means of production was sufficiently technologically advanced that it could easily support everyone in society and

2. the workers united, realizing that they, as a class, were being exploited by the owners.

Marx believed that the workers (*proletariat*) were under a "false consciousness" regarding their social class arrangements. That is, although they were conscious that there were class differences, they didn't understand why these differences existed, how those in power had manipulated the system to create these differences, or even the extent of these differences. Thus, their *consciousness* of the class differences was *false*.

Marx believed that the owners (*bourgeoisie*) owned not only the means of production for market goods but also the means for the production of *ideas* in society. In Marx's words,

> The ideas of the ruling class are in every epoch the ruling ideas, i.e., the class which is the ruling material force of society is at the same time its ruling intellectual force. The class which has the means of material production at its disposal has control at the same time over the means of mental production, so that thereby, generally speaking, the ideas of those who lack the means of mental production are subject to it. (Marx & Engels, 1970, p. 64)

The owner's ability to control the dominant ideas of society helped them stay in power. The workers were exposed primarily to ideas that promoted the status quo and maintained their false consciousness. This worked to prevent the members of the proletariat from realizing that the capitalist system was designed to exploit rather than benefit them.

To counteract this false consciousness, Marx spent much of his life trying to unite the proletariat, encouraging them to establish a "class consciousness," overthrow the ownership society, and transform the economic system from capitalism to communism. Consciousness was key to Marx's approach. As long as millions of individual workers saw themselves as struggling alone or in competition with other workers, nothing would change. Marx wanted to impart a larger, societal view of the system to the working class, in which they would understand the role of the class system in their personal lives and act collectively against the system itself. His most famous attempt was *The Communist Manifesto* (Marx & Engels, 1848/2002), which concludes, "Let the ruling classes tremble at a Communist revolution. The proletarians have nothing to lose but their chains. They have a world to win. Workingmen of all countries, unite!" (p. 258).

Conflict theory is a modern extension of Marx's insights, although many conflict theorists support democracy, not communism. In its general form, *conflict theory* begins with the assumption that at any point in time, in any society, there will be different interest groups, different strata of society that have conflicting needs, and that much of what happens politically, socially, or economically is a manifestation of this conflict. Conflict theorists maintain that at the core of society lies the struggle for power among these competing groups.

Max Weber

Whereas Marx focused on class conflict and economic systems, Max Weber (1864–1920) looked more at the combination of economic and political power. Weber expanded Marx's idea of class into three dimensions of stratification: (1) *class* (based on possession of economic resources—most important in industrial capitalist societies), (2) *status* (prestige—most important in traditional societies), and (3) *party* (organizations formed to achieve a goal in a planned manner, such as political parties, unions, and professional associations—most important in advanced industrial, highly rational societies). In most eras, there would be a great deal of overlap among the three dimensions. For example, someone high in class would also tend to be high in status and political power.

Unlike Marx, Weber was very pessimistic about attempts to eliminate inequality from society. He believed that even if one aspect of conflict and inequality could be eliminated, others would remain and perhaps become an even more important basis for inequality (e.g., the rise of the importance of difference in party position in China after status inequality had largely been eliminated). Weber's (1946) definition of *power*—"the chance of a man or a number of men to realize their own will in a communal action even against the resistance of others who are participating in the action" (as quoted in Gerth & Mills, 1958, p. 180)—remains the starting point for most modern sociological explorations of power relations.

Weber's work on bureaucratic institutions helps us understand how power is won and held within advanced industrial societies of all types (whether capitalist, communist, or anything in between). Thanks to Weber, we now comprehend how powerful bureaucratic structures can be and how much of the structure remains intact even when the individuals in charge are replaced. For example, whoever controls the governmental bureaucracy in a highly developed nation can exert tremendous power over all aspects of that society. Controlling the government bureaucracy enables one to control key institutions in society (including the military) and to define the standards by which other bureaucracies will be created, evaluated, and carried forth.

The crucial element of a power structure is its perceived *legitimacy*. Persons or institutions have legitimacy when people accept their authority and follow their orders. Because the power of lower level functionaries depends on the same system that empowers those in higher positions, it becomes difficult and dangerous, and therefore unlikely, for someone in a lower stratum to really challenge the upper strata. The bureaucracy protects itself.

When properly managed, bureaucratic structures are extremely efficient, whether they are being used well or poorly. One infamous example of this is that the same highly efficient train system that existed in Germany before Hitler came to power (to transport workers and travelers) was used to transport men, women, and children to the death camps of the Third Reich. In fact, Hitler and the Nazis used many of the mechanisms of Germany's bureaucracy to carry out one of the most efficient (albeit horrible and nearly incomprehensible) acts in human history.

Although Weber cautioned against the establishment of sociology as a science that should direct society, he did not shy away from using his knowledge to try to guide his country (Germany) in turbulent times. He may have been pessimistic about anyone's potential to eradicate inequality, but he nonetheless felt obliged to do what he could to promote democracy in his society. Weber was deeply involved in the political realm throughout his life. His greatest impact on German society, as an engaged citizen, came toward the end of his life, during and right after World War I. He wrote many newspaper articles, memos to public officials, and papers against the annexationist policies of the German government during the war, and he advocated for a strong, democratically elected parliament and against the extreme ideologies of both the right and the left (Coser, 1977, p. 242).

Émile Durkheim

Whereas Karl Marx and Max Weber were conflict theorists, Émile Durkheim (1858–1917) adopted a functionalist perspective. According to this perspective, society is like a biological organism, with each organ dependent on the others for survival. Functionalists believe that society is made up of interdependent parts, each working for the good of the whole, rather than being composed of competing interests (as conflict theorists maintain). Durkheim believed that humans are selfish by nature and must be channeled and controlled through proper socialization by institutions in society. According to Durkheim, properly functioning institutions, such as the education system, the family, occupational associations, and religion, will ensure that people work for the good of society rather than just for themselves as individuals.

Durkheim (1903/1933) maintained that society is held together by a sense of connectedness, or *solidarity,* that its members feel. This type of bond changes as society moves from simple (e.g., agrarian) to more complex (e.g., industrial and postindustrial). The simpler societies, in which almost everyone shares a common way of life, are based on what Durkheim called *mechanical solidarity.* In this type of society, there is little room for individualism. People are bound to one another through tradition and a common way of life.

The more complex societies, in which people perform different and often highly selective tasks, are founded on *organic solidarity.* In this type of society, people come together to exchange services with one another. It is the many exchanges, and the interactions during those exchanges, that bind the members of the group to one another. They rely on one another for needed goods and services and understand (to some degree) each other's different perspectives through communicating during their exchanges. In these societies, there is more room for individualism. However, while the members depend on one another to survive and prosper, the ties holding the community together are weaker.

Seeing the political and social upheaval that plagued his home country of France during his lifetime, Durkheim studied how society operates and sought ways to make improvements. According to Durkheim, at the core of a smooth-functioning society lies solidarity. Societies with increased divisions of labor can achieve stability only if their members are socialized through their institutions to believe that they are obligated to one another as members of a common community.

Durkheim argued that the existence of *external inequality* in an industrial society indicates that its institutions are not functioning properly. He divided inequalities into *internal* (based on people's natural abilities) and *external* (those forced on people). Because an organic society needs all its members to do what they do best in order for it to function most effectively, external inequality that prevents some people from fulfilling their innate talents damages all of society and should be eradicated. For example, if someone with the potential to find a cure for cancer—or just to be a good physician—never gets to fulfill this potential because she was raised in a poor neighborhood and attended a terrible school with teachers who never encouraged her to go to college, the whole society suffers.

Among Durkheim's concerns were the problems of how to reduce external inequalities and increase social consensus (solidarity). He maintained that it was up to the various institutions in society to create opportunities and incentives for all its members to become engaged citizens and share their gifts. Durkheim used his various positions in the educational system to mold France's public schools around these ideas.

George Herbert Mead

George Herbert Mead (1863–1931), the founder of symbolic interactionism, was the first sociologist to focus on how the mind and the self are created through social processes. Instead of looking at the individual as either distinct from or controlled by society, Mead saw that people are both shaped by and shapers of society. He was particularly interested in how the human self develops through communicating with others via language and other symbolic behavior (symbolic interaction).

According to Mead, humans are not truly human unless they interact with one another. In turn, the nature of our interactions with others determines how we see ourselves and our role in society. *Symbolic interactionists* maintain that society is a social construction, continually created and re-created by humans. We may not realize it, but society is maintained by our implicit agreement to interact with one another in certain ways. As we "practice" certain patterns of interaction, we reinforce the belief system that society "just works that way." Therefore, by changing how we interact with one another, we can change society.

Mead used his sociological expertise about the influence of the social environment to contribute to several social programs and movements in Chicago. For example, he served as treasurer of Hull House (the social service "settlement house" cofounded by Jane Addams and Helen Gates Starr; see below), was a member of the progressive City Club, participated in a variety of local movements and social programs in the city, and edited the journal *Elementary School Teacher*. Mead also spent much time advocating for a reform of the public school system that would provide tenure for teachers and give them greater influence over how they could teach students (Cook, 1993).

Mead spoke publicly and often on behalf of the immigrant population of Chicago, encouraging school reform to aid immigrants in the assimilation process.[2] He helped establish and, with Addams, served as vice president of the Immigrants' Protective League. The league supported studies on immigrants and pushed for legislation to protect them from exploitation. For many years, Mead was a fund-raiser and policymaker for the University of Chicago's settlement house and eventually served as president of the Settlement House Board of Directors. As a member of the board of directors, he led the effort to conduct research on social and economic conditions in the neighborhoods surrounding the stockyards in Chicago in order to advocate for social change. Mead's work to promote social scientific studies in Chicago eventually led to the creation of the Department of Public Welfare (Cook, 1993).

Jane Addams

Jane Addams (1860–1935) grew up in a time when the norm was for women to marry young and raise a family. Her father, however, a wealthy mill owner and state senator, permitted her to attend college, with the understanding that she would then marry and raise a family (Haberman, 1972). Instead, she ignored the gender norms of the time and courageously chose to become a public citizen and scholar. Addams is considered the founder of modern social work as well as one of the founders of sociology.

Addams, with her friend Ellen Gates Starr, established one of the first settlement houses in the United States. After visiting a similar neighborhood center in England during a trip after college, they returned to Chicago and created Hull House in 1888. Hull House became the model for "settlement houses" in newly developing urban areas throughout the United States. The model was based on the vision that middle- and upper-class people could move to the city and serve the poor while living among them. People in need, such as poor immigrants and women, would be exposed to the culture, values, and knowledge of the educated settlement house workers while they all resided in the same large households. Meanwhile, those who worked at the settlement houses provided social services and advocated for social policies that would empower and protect the members of these lower class and working-class groups.

Hull House also served as "an underground university for women activists focusing on questions of housing, sanitation, and public health" (Berger, 1997, para. 5). Addams believed that all members of society, not only the privileged and wealthy, deserve protection. In turn, helping those in need benefits everyone in society, for "the good we secure for ourselves is precarious and uncertain until it is secured for all of us and incorporated into our common life" (Linn, 2000, p. 107).

One of the more colorful Hull House studies involved researching garbage collection in Chicago. Lack of proper collection was allowing disease to spread, particularly in poor, immigrant communities. In response, the

Hull House Women's Club stepped out of the roles expected of them as ladies in late-19th-century Chicago and began to personally collect the garbage that was polluting the poor neighborhoods! Before doing that, however, they used their sociological eyes and research skills to carry out

> a major investigation into the city's garbage collection system. Then Addams submitted to the city government her own bid to collect garbage. The resulting public uproar forced the mayor to appoint Addams as garbage inspector for her ward. The Hull House women formed a garbage patrol, getting up at 6 a.m. to follow the garbage trucks, mapping routes and dump sites, and making citizens arrests of landlords whose properties were a health hazard. Their vigilance moved garbage reform to the top of Chicago's civic agenda, forcing industry to take responsibility for its trash. (Berger, 1997, para. 5)

This episode in the life of Hull House beautifully illustrates how Addams carried out the two core commitments of sociology. She and her colleagues used their sociological eyes to notice a pattern of inequality and then used social activism to address that inequity.

While Addams and her partners at Hull House helped initiate a grassroots social reform effort, they soon recognized that structural changes were necessary to fix the causes and not just the symptoms of inequality. She and other Hull House residents worked to improve policy regarding the juvenile justice system, secure women the right to vote, strengthen workers' rights, and establish child labor laws. Addams and her colleagues knew that people without safe places to live and employment that paid a livable wage would never escape the cycle of poverty. While social services provided by the government assisted people in need, ending inequality would require structural changes such as greater access to education, skills training, and capital. Addams devoted her life to this effort. As a scholar and engaged citizen, she remained true to the belief that "nothing could be worse than the fear that one had given up too soon, and left one unexpended effort that might have saved the world" (as quoted in Lewis, 2009, para. 2). Addams was formally recognized as a leader in reforming social policy when, in 1931, she became the second woman, and the first from the United States, to receive the Nobel Peace Prize.

W. E. B. Du Bois

William Edward Burghardt Du Bois (1868–1963) grew up as one of the few black residents in Great Barrington, Massachusetts. While Du Bois was an excellent student, whom his teachers encouraged, his classmates did not treat him as an equal. During these early years in school, Du Bois began to recognize the racial division in society. He believed, though, that empowering himself with education would allow him to better understand and help improve the situation of black citizens. When Du Bois was in college at Fisk University, a historically black university in Nashville, Tennessee, he traveled with the glee club to a summer resort in Minnesota. There, he was exposed to privileged white vacationers and was struck by how their lives contrasted with those of the rural, poor black children whom he taught during the summers he was at Fisk.

Du Bois's early experiences furthered his drive to learn more and to improve the lives of black Americans in the United States. After leaving Fisk and earning a bachelor's degree at Harvard, he won a fellowship that allowed him to travel throughout Europe while he studied with the top social scientists of the time. In 1895, Du Bois became the first black person to earn a PhD from Harvard University. He went on to teach at a number of colleges and established the Department of Social Work at what is now Clark Atlanta University in Georgia.

Despite attending and achieving great success at Harvard, Du Bois (1953) described his experience as being "in Harvard but not of it." Being surrounded by, but never connected to, the mainstream academic and public worlds was a constant theme in the lives of both Addams and Du Bois. Even though he was armed with numerous scholarly achievements and a graduate degree from Harvard, Du Bois never gained a position as a full teaching professor at a predominantly white university. There is little doubt that Du Bois's and Addams's experience with discrimination shaped their desire to help those who suffered in their societies. They collaborated on numerous projects for social justice over the course of their careers (Deegan, 1988).

Throughout his life, Du Bois documented and railed against the status of black Americans, noting that although African Americans were an integral part of U.S. society, they were not fully accepted into it. Du Bois's major achievements as a sociologist, founder of critical race theory, and activist began with his famous study *The Philadelphia Negro* (1899). This groundbreaking work was the first social scientific research to dismiss the notion of racial inferiority. It documented the negative impact of racial discrimination and segregation on the condition of African Americans in the urban North.

Like Addams, Du Bois advocated for social policy changes and pushed for efforts to improve the situation of blacks throughout the country. He used the Hull House studies of poor immigrant neighborhoods in Chicago as his research model for *The Philadelphia Negro*. Also, just as Jane Addams and her colleagues at Hull House lived among the people they studied (a technique known as ethnography), Du Bois resided with the poor blacks in Philadelphia while he carried out his research for *The Philadelphia Negro*. While he did not enjoy living in that environment (Deegan, 1988), experiencing the conditions firsthand allowed him to establish rapport with and gain the trust of the thousands of black residents of Philadelphia he surveyed and interviewed.

Throughout his long career, Du Bois advocated for the rights of black Americans, women, and workers. He lived his belief that "there is in this world no such force as the force of a person determined to rise" (Aberjhani, 2003, p. 33). In addition to cofounding (with a number of people, including Addams) and leading the National Association for the Advancement of Colored People for many years, he promoted social action by editing the organization's journal, *The Crisis*; writing several books, including *The Souls of Black Folk* (1903/2005); organizing conferences of scholars; teaching; and speaking out on behalf of those without power in society. Eventually, he became frustrated with what he viewed as a lack of social progress in the United States. He joined the (then banned) Communist Party, surrendered his U.S. citizenship, and became a renowned citizen of Ghana before his death.

The founders of sociology were deeply interested in using their knowledge for the good of society. One wonders how they might make sense of society today and what changes they would recommend to curb current systems of inequality. As we can see, their respective views of the world influenced how they perceived the social issues of the day and their proposed solutions for them.

Theory and Society

Sociologists use theory to elucidate and make sense of social patterns. Without theories, we would have little or no understanding of why society operates the way it does and how we might improve it. Looking at the world through a theoretical perspective can also help us detect social patterns that we might otherwise overlook and help us figure out where we should concentrate our focus. For instance, conflict theorists are more likely to notice discrimination, class inequality, and struggles for power in society than are those who do not view society through a similar lens. Similarly, symbolic interactionists tend to be more aware of the impact of small-group interactions and symbols. For example, such theorists are quick to observe that seemingly minor behaviors (e.g., sitting with legs crossed or uncrossed) can have serious diplomatic repercussions.[3]

The level of analysis also varies among the theoretical perspectives. Some portray the world through a wide-angle lens, looking at larger (macro and meso-) social patterns (e.g., functionalism and conflict theory), whereas others (e.g., symbolic interactionists) view society closeup, from a more detailed (micro) angle. Sometimes, as the Sociologist in Action section below illustrates, theories help us achieve important practical goals. While theory is powerful in helping us analyze the social world, it is also important to remember that whenever people use a particular theoretical lens (or any point of view), they will be more attuned to some social patterns than others.

Sociologist in Action: Brian J. Reed

Social network theory helped the U.S. Army capture Saddam Hussein. Major Brian J. Reed, a doctoral candidate in the Department of Sociology at the University of Maryland, College Park, used his sociological training in social network analysis when he was stationed in Iraq and assigned the task of devising a strategy to capture the former Iraqi dictator. He described his use of social network theory in locating Hussein in the following way:

> The intelligence background and link diagrams that we built [to capture Hussein] were rooted in the concepts of network analysis. We constructed an elaborate product that traced the tribal and family linkages of Saddam Hussein, thereby allowing us to focus on certain individuals who may have had (or presently had) close ties to [him]. (Hougham, 2005, p. 3)

Reed's expertise in network analysis allowed him and the soldiers under his command to re-create and study a detailed picture of Hussein's social network, thereby, determining where he would be most likely to hide.

Reed also maintains that his sociological training helped him comprehend the Iraqi culture and, because of this understanding, more effectively carry out military operations in that country. Recognizing the practical applications of sociological research and theory, the Army Research Institute gave $1.1 million in 2005 to the University of Maryland's Center for Research on Military Organization, of which Reed is a member, to conduct research on social structure, social systems, and social networks.

EXERCISE 2.1   What Would the Founders of Sociology Say About . . . ?

1. Consider any public issue of inequality today (e.g., the movement to privatize the world's water, the reduction of federal and state aid for state colleges and universities, the high cost of running for public office, environmental racism, the increasing gap between the wealthy 1% and the remaining 99%, the decrease in funding for housing for poor people, etc.).

(Continued)

(Continued)

2. Describe how three of the six founders of sociology discussed above might respond when told about this issue. Be sure that your answer also briefly summarizes what the issue is about.

3. Which of the responses makes the most sense to you? Why?

4. Is there anything you feel is missing from the founders' perspectives that you might want to add? If so, explain what you would like to add and why. If not, explain why you think their perspectives do not need to be expanded or revised.

EXERCISE 2.2   Going Deeper

As noted above, the founding theorists we discussed in this chapter were deeply influenced by the social problems that existed in their societies. Choose one of the theorists, and obtain more information about that person's society. How did the social issues prevalent at that time influence his or her sociological perspective (theory) and research topics? What theory would you use to analyze your society today? Why?

EXERCISE 2.3   Are You a Worker or an Owner?

1. According to Marx's perspective, do you think you were raised by workers (proletariat) or owners (bourgeoisie)? What makes you think so? Be specific.

2. Do you think most workers in the United States have developed a class consciousness? Why or why not? Be sure to provide evidence for your answer.

3. Can you see yourself encouraging workers to overcome their false consciousness and develop a class consciousness? Why or why not? How might you (or someone else) go about helping them do so?

EXERCISE 2.4   Different Perspectives Lead to Different News

This assignment will require you to watch the news for at least 1.5 hours a day for 1 week. It will also require you to have access to a wide range of stations. Watch CNN, BBC World News (now available in the United States

(Continued)

(Continued)

on most cable networks and accessible online), and Fox News, each for half an hour a day for 1 week.

As you are doing so, make notes on (a) what stories they show on the news, (b) how they portray the news events (e.g., positively or negatively), and (c) how they compare with one another. Pay attention to which stories are addressed by all three and which stories are covered only on one of the news outlets. As you do so, complete the questions below. Pick one news story that all of the networks carry, and answer the following questions:

1. How much time does CNN, BBC World News, and Fox News each give the story?

2. Are the events at the center of the story portrayed positively or negatively (or both) by each of the three networks? How do the positive and negative portrayals differ from one another?

3. How would your knowledge of the news story be different if you watched just one of the news networks?

4. How would your perception of the news story (whether the story was important, negative or positive, etc.) be different if you watched just one of the news networks?

5. After the week is over, compare the different news stations' perspectives on the world. Were you able to clearly perceive three different perspectives? If so, how did they differ? Research and analyze in detail why it is that those differences exist. What does this tell you about the objectivity of news and news stories?

Extra credit: Go to the website for the organization Fairness & Accuracy in Reporting (http://www.fair.org/index.php). Look through the articles, and identify stories you think are important but were not covered by the news stations you analyzed in Questions 1 through 5. What is your explanation for why these stories were not included, and what does this tell you about mainstream news coverage?

EXERCISE 2.5   Different Perspectives in the Online Media

Find one conservative media source (e.g., WorldNetDaily at http://www.world netdaily.com, Intellectual Conservative at www.intellectualconservative.com, or Free Republic at http://www.freerepublic.com/tag/*/index) and one

(Continued)

header

(Continued)

left-leaning source (e.g., Salon at www.salon.com, *The Nation* online at www.thenation.com, ZNet at http://www.zcommunications.org/znet, or *Mother Jones* at http://www.motherjones.com).

Read the headline stories for each at the same time of day for 5 consecutive days. Then, answer the following questions in a two- to three-page paper:

1. How similar are they in their editorial approaches? That is, to what extent do the different papers make similar decisions about which stories are most important? If they are similar, why do you think this is so? If they differ, why do you think they are different?

2. How would your perspective on society differ based on which of the media sources you read on a regular basis?

3. Discuss the possible impacts of these types of media on U.S. society.

4. What are two or three major things your answers to Questions 1 through 3 tell you about print media today?

Extra credit: Choose any two of the theorists from this chapter (Marx, Weber, Durkheim, Mead, Du Bois, and Addams). How might each of them answer Question 3?

EXERCISE 2.6   The Media and Climate Change

Read the following two overviews of climate change: "Climate Change: Basic Information" at http://www.epa.gov/climatechange/basics/ and "Global Climate Change" at http://climate.nasa.gov/scientific-consensus. Then, read "Changing the Climate Story: Competing Narratives in U.S. Television News" at http://www.yaleclimatemediaforum.org/2012/05/competing-narratives-in-us-television-news. Then, read "Communicating About Climate Change in a National Park" at http://www.yaleclimatemediaforum.org/2012/04/communicating-climate-change-in-a-national-park.

Write a two-page paper that answers the following questions:

1. What are the key points you learned from the overviews and the article about climate change news coverage?

(Continued)

(Continued)

2. How has your own perception of climate change been influenced by the media?

3. Do you think reading this information and answering these questions have altered your perception of climate change? Why or why not?

4. How might you use the information you have learned to teach students at your school about climate change?

DISCUSSION QUESTIONS

1. Sociology has always been viewed a bit warily by leaders in most societies. Why do you think this might be? What is it about a sociological perspective that might feel threatening to those in power and those benefiting from the current system?

2. Imagine you are a sociological theorist. What social issue would you choose to study first? Why? Which of the three primary sociological perspectives (functionalism, conflict theory, or symbolic interactionism) do you think you would use to explain your findings? Why?

3. If, as symbolic interactionists maintain, society is merely a social construction (that is created and re-created anew through our interactions with one another), why is it so hard to address social issues effectively? How might a symbolic interactionist respond to this question?

4. Of the sociological perspectives covered in this chapter (conflict theory, functionalism, symbolic interactionism, and critical race theory), which do you think best explains inequality in the United States today? Why do you think so?

5. While Du Bois was able to attain a higher education only through scholarships, the other founders came from middle-class to upper-class backgrounds. Why do you think this might be? Do you think that most successful scholars today come from middle-class to wealthy backgrounds? Why or why not? If so, what are the potential repercussions?

6. Describe the difference between internal and external inequality. Provide an example of how external inequality can harm a society. What can (a) society and (b) you do to curb external inequality in your society?

7. Which of the theorists described in this chapter do you think best fulfilled the two core commitments of sociology? Why?

SUGGESTIONS FOR SPECIFIC ACTIONS

1. Many sociologists note that although sociological studies have pointed out good solutions to social issues they have been largely ignored by governmental leaders and the media. Go to the American Sociological Association website at www .asanet.org or the Society for the Study of Social Problems website at www.sssp1 .org. Look around each site, and find a study that provides a good basis for the use of sociological research in public policy.

2. Write a letter to your school newspaper or another local paper describing the study and what you think would be a good public policy based on it. Go to http://www.awcnet.org/documents/WriteLettertoEditor.pdf to get tips on how to write a letter to the editor.

   Please go to the website for this book at http://study.sagepub.com/korgen5e to find further civic engagement opportunities, resources, peer-reviewed articles, and updated web links related to this chapter.

NOTES

1. Some consider Weber a functionalist.

2. See the University of Chicago Centennial Catalogue's faculty webpage on Mead at http://www.lib.uchicago.edu/e/spcl/centcat/fac/facch12_01.html.

3. In Arab nations, it is regarded as impolite to cross one's legs. In India, it is impolite to show the bottom of your shoe, as you would by crossing one foot over your knee instead of crossing your ankles.

REFERENCES

Aberjhani. (2003). *The wisdom of W. E. B. Du Bois*. Kensington, NY: Citadel.

Berger, R. M. (1997, July/August). The Good Housekeeping Award: Women heroes of environmental activism. *Sojourners*. Retrieved from http://www.sojo.net/index .cfm?action=magazine.article&issue=soj9707&article=970722

Cook, G. A. (1993). *George Herbert Mead: The making of a social pragmatist*. Urbana: University of Illinois Press.

Coser, L. A. (1977). *Masters of sociological thought: Ideas in historical and social context* (2nd ed.). New York, NY: Harcourt Brace Jovanovich.

Deegan, M. J. (1988). W. E. B. Du Bois and the women of Hull-House, 1895–1899. *American Sociologist, 19*(4), 301–311.

Du Bois, W. E. B. (1899). *The Philadelphia Negro*. New York, NY: Lippincott.

Du Bois, W. E. B. (1953). *Dr. W. E. B. Du Bois: Lecture on 23feb1953* (P. Goettlich, transcribed from a "Voices of Pacifica" recording). Retrieved http://www.mind fully.org/Reform/WEB-DuBois-23feb1953.htm

Du Bois, W. E. B. (2005). *The souls of black folk.* New York, NY: Pocket. (Original work published 1903)

Durkheim, É. (1933). *The division of labor in society* (G. Simpson, Trans.). New York, NY: Free Press. (Original work published 1903)

Gerth, H., & Mills, C. W. (Eds. & Trans.). (1958). *From Max Weber: Essays in sociology.* New York, NY: Oxford University Press.

Haberman, F. W. (Ed.). (1972). *Nobel lectures in peace 1926–1950.* Amsterdam, Netherlands: Elsevier.

Hougham, V. (2005, July/August). Sociological skills used in the capture of Saddam Hussein. *Footnotes, 33*(6), 3.

Lewis, J. J. (2009). *Jane Addams quotes* (Women's history—comprehensive women's history research guide). Retrieved from http://womenshistory.about.com/od/ quotes/a/jane_addams.htm

Linn, J. W. (2000). *Jane Addams.* Champaign: University of Illinois Press.

Marx, K., & Engels, F. (1970). *The German ideology.* London, England: Lawrence & Wishart.

Marx, K., & Engels, F. (2002). *The Communist manifesto* (G. S. Jones, Ed.). New York, NY: Penguin Classics. (Original work published 1848)

3

How Do We Know
What We Think We Know?

Sociological Methods

In one memorable scene in the iconic 1975 comedy film *Monty Python and the Holy Grail*, a group of peasants drag a woman to the center of town to be burned at the stake. Sir Bedevere, the local lord, intervenes to ensure that justice is carried out.

Sir Bedevere: What makes you think she's a witch?

Peasant 3:   Well, she turned me into a newt.

Sir Bedevere: A newt?

Peasant 3:   [pause] . . . I got better.

Crowd: [shouts] Burn her anyway![1]

How much is revealed in this simple scene!

First, this is the early Middle Ages, sometime around the mid-600s. This was a time of superstition, uncertainty, and fear for many people. It was a time before science, when religious spirituality contested with other spiritualities and forms of magic in explaining the world. Both Christians and pagans believed that witches walked the Earth and that one must be on guard against them. Certainly, there were no widely held assumptions about the nature of cause and effect or the logic of demonstrating that one thing caused another. Evidence did not need to be seen or examined; "proof" could come from the fact that a lot of people agreed on something. "Burn her anyway" is a strong argument when shouted by a large crowd of people.

The scene is carried by the self-reflective totality of its logic. Social scientists start with a belief system common during the Middle Ages that includes the existence of witches and humans being transformed by witches. We add an event: A man thinks he was turned into a newt, and those around him accuse someone of being a witch. Challenged to support the claim (*she* is a witch), they resort to the original definition of the event (there is a witch). Any evidence that worked in her favor could, of course, be interpreted to prove just how tricky those witches are. There is no space in the argument to consider counterclaims that she is not a witch or that there are no witches. You might as well light the fire. There is no way out of this logic.

Of course, things have changed a little in 14 centuries. Fewer people believe in witches,[2] most serious accusations are dealt with in the courtroom, science has considerably more support than magic does, and it rests alongside religion as a widely accepted method of explaining the world. But scientific explanations rely on the logic of cause and effect, on the careful definition of our terms and assumptions, and on the idea that evidence can be tested. Even a casual observation of U.S. society suggests that these concepts are not as widely understood or applied as we might hope. One means of finding out if the research we read about is trustworthy is to check and see if the researchers followed the basic steps of the scientific process.

The basic steps of all social science research are as follows:

1. Choose a research topic.

2. Find out what other researchers have discovered about that topic.

3. Choose a methodology (how you will collect your data).

4. Collect and analyze your data.

5. Relate your findings to those of other researchers.

6. Present the findings for public review and critique.

The Three Questions

In addition to following the basic steps of scientific research, social scientists must establish the answers to three basic questions about their work before they publicize their findings: (a) How do you know? (b) So what? (Why is it important we know this?) (c) Now what? (What do we do with this new information?) Let us consider each of these questions, from the last to the first.

The "Now What?" Question

Research is the path toward answering questions. Before we can discover new findings, we first have to raise a question. Furthermore, we like to assume that both the question and the answer are important and can influence society in some way. When we find the answer to our question, we should do something with that knowledge.

It has been popular to picture Newton "discovering" gravity as an apple fell on his head. It would be absurd to suggest that up to that point (mid-1600s, about one thousand years past the time in which the *Monty Python* skit was set), no one had noticed that things fall. But it is interesting to wonder how the observation (that things fall) became a question (How and why do things fall?).

Something in the social, political, or scientific world had changed so that it became useful to answer these questions. Did things fall any differently after Newton had named the process? No. However, he discovered new information that powerfully influenced his and future societies when he answered the questions about why and how objects fall. His general theory of gravity changed the world (Eves, 1976).

Your work does not have to change the way people view reality and the cosmos to have meaning. In the late 1950s, Harold Garfinkel (1967) attempted to explain the personal situation of a woman who had been born with male primary sexual characteristics (a penis), who in puberty had developed female secondary sexual characteristics (breasts), and who had to make a choice—accompanied by surgery—to define her sexual identity. Such cases are extremely rare and mostly unseen by the majority of our society (see Sax, 2002). One might think that sociologists would not be concerned with a lone case. Yet to appreciate and explain the case of "Agnes," Garfinkel had to address sexual norms, the power of "belonging," sanctions against deviance, and the strategies by which those with "abnormal" conditions may try to "cover" them. Agnes's biophysical condition combined with a vast and complex social world of meaning to create a problem that she had to solve. It was not, strictly speaking, the ambiguity of whether she was "really" male or female that defined the problem, but the social need for her to be unambiguous about it.

Since the time of Garfinkel's (1967) study, intersex persons have gained recognition and more acceptance. However, they still face the stigmatization that accompanies those who do not fit into the either/or characteristics most people still associate with sex categories. Garfinkel's research raises questions about (a) the social categories within which personal identities and sexual identities are constructed, (b) how norms become normal and what happens when you violate them, and (c) how we define and use notions of what is or is not "natural." Of course, once we have raised these questions, we have to start looking at everything that is considered natural and everything that is feared or hated because it is seen as unnatural, and we have to recognize how these categories are socially constructed (and can be reconstructed).

Very few people in the United States are burned at the stake anymore, but hate crimes and vigilante assaults still occur frequently. Garfinkel's research was not about Agnes. It was about what the rest of us *think* of Agnes and many other people and things that frighten or confuse us or don't fit into the norms we have constructed for our society. Answers to the "Now what?" question often challenge us, both as individuals and as a society, to rethink our most comfortable and unquestioned assumptions (norms and values) about the world.

Answers to the "Now what?" question can also help us figure out how to improve society. For example, if we can show that environmental hazards tend to be placed in predominantly minority neighborhoods (e.g., Bullard, 2000; Ewall, 2013), we can then advocate for rules that prohibit environmental racism. Likewise, if we can reveal that all parents, no matter their level of education, can increase the chances of their children attaining a high level of education by having books in their home (Evans, Kelley, Sikora, & Treiman, 2010), we can try to make that information available to all new parents.

The "So What?" Question

When we prepare our research, we have to have some idea of what new knowledge we are after and why it may be useful. The "So what?" question is like the "Now what?" question. But where the "Now what (do we do with these findings)?" question asks how we might make use of what we have learned from our research, the "So what?" question asks why sociologists need to research something in the first place.

To answer the "So what?" question, we do not need to show that lives hang in the balance. We simply need to show that there is something to be learned about our society or culture (or a different society or culture) that is worth knowing. Even abstract knowledge "for its own sake" is valuable in the quest to understand our lives, our world, and how they interact, since even seemingly inconsequential behavior adds up, collectively, to create the totality of human behavior.

Suppose we were to analyze every scene and underlying theme in *Monty Python and the Holy Grail*. (Both fans and academics have done so, though neither of us has weighed in—yet.) How would we justify all that effort on an old movie by a defunct British comedy group? Shouldn't we be putting our time to better use, like examining political regimes, industrial shifts, or responses to natural disasters? Perhaps. However, there is still a lot to learn from and about popular culture. If, for example, we concluded that the Monty Python group was a pretty funny bunch of guys, we would not be doing much. If, on the other hand, we concluded that the Monty Python players were popular and widely accepted when they were making fun of the British monarchy in general but less so when they were making fun of living members of the government, then we would be using popular culture to learn something about the political culture.

The "How Do You Know?" Question

This is the big one, and most of the rest of the chapter will address it. To put it simply, we know that our findings are well-founded if we design scientific studies that are theoretically sound and driven by data. We ask questions, determine the kinds of data needed to answer them, figure out a plan for getting the data, and define a set of clear and consistent criteria for finding the answers in the data. Only then do we actually start collecting any data. We will explain each of these steps in further detail below.

All of us can do research, but it takes special skills to conduct *social scientific* studies. Research done by social scientists (and physical scientists) seeks to answer questions for which answers are not already known. Going to AccuWeather.com on the Internet to check the forecast for tomorrow is not the same thing as conducting research on the weather. Likewise, I could do some research on what movies I should see this weekend by checking out reviews at http://www.rottentomatoes.com. However, I will not have done social scientific research.[3] Social scientific research is a tool used to discover *new* findings about our social world.

Social scientific research is not carried out exactly like studies conducted in the natural or physical sciences.[4] We study things that are always changing and always dependent on the time and place in which we are looking. A physicist can ask, "What is the boiling point of water (at a given atmospheric pressure)?" A sociologist cannot ask, "What is the boiling-over point of social unrest?" There isn't any such thing that can be nailed down. Instead, we have to ask, "How does the occurrence of a single event of great injustice contribute to the likelihood that social unrest will lead to collective social action?" The answer is not a yes or a no, or a number. It is a description of a social process in which some events lead to the possibility of other events. It's a probability estimate, but it is not a guess. We can show that our answers are reliable (consistent) and valid (accurate). Our questions are about how things work and why they work as they do. And the most interesting part is that no answer is ever final. There are always new circumstances, such as differences in history, culture, politics, economy, and geography, to take into account.

Once we have our questions, we have to figure out what data will answer them. If, for example, we wanted to know whether people in the United States generally want lower taxes, we could conduct a national *survey* with a couple of tax questions on it. You have probably seen surveys. Most are collections of short, simple questions on a set of related topics, in which you choose your answer to each question from a short list of choices. Surveys allow researchers to collect a few basic measures of something from a very large number of people, in a short amount of time, and in exactly the same way. (If you collect data from some people one way and from other people a different way, it is not appropriate to treat the data as equivalent.) The answers given by any individual *respondent* (the person who responds to the questions) are not really important to us. What we really look at is the pattern of answers across hundreds, or thousands, of cases. Surveys that contain questions followed by sets of answers from which respondents are asked to choose give us *quantitative* (or numerical) data on which we can perform statistical analyses. Statistical data give us the big picture of trends and social changes.

Perhaps we already have plenty of research that suggests that people want lower taxes. So now we might want to know what Americans are willing to give up for lower taxes (because lower taxes mean less governmental income and hence, usually, less governmental spending, meaning fewer programs). One might think that this could be done with a survey if we make the format more complex. We could, for example, identify long lists of things that the government spends money on and ask people which ones they would be willing to do without if they could have lower taxes. But then, how do we choose the list? And if we ask, "Which items would you trade?" how do we know that we aren't leading people to just identify the programs that they dislike, regardless of what they think about taxes? So just asking questions is not always the best way to find information.

Often, as researchers, we need to know more than just whether people do or do not approve of something. We need to know *why* they do or do not approve. We need to sit down and listen to people. This process is called an *interview*. Interviews can be structured, semistructured, or unstructured. Structured interviews entail asking respondents a set list of questions, often with set answer choices. Unstructured interviews involve asking people a series of *open-ended* questions on the research topic and letting them answer in whatever way they like. Semistructured interviews consist of some set questions but also allow for the interviewer to add follow-up questions as needed, and they give respondents the opportunity to answer in nonstandard ways. *Probe questions* are often used in interviews to encourage the respondents to dig deeper in their answers and analysis and also to keep them from straying too far off the topic. The data gleaned from unstructured interviews are not a pattern of "yes" or "no" opinions but the respondents' own words. This type of data collection is *qualitative* and elicits data based on words that describe "qualities," feelings, opinions, and firsthand accounts.

Unstructured and semistructured interviews allow us to listen to and question respondents at length and investigate intangibles, such as *why* they feel as they do. A survey might ask whether the respondent thinks that our nation should spend more or less than it does on loans to other nations. But we can't determine for sure *why* the individual believes that we should spend more or less by asking a survey question. An unstructured or semistructured interview gives more depth and more context than a survey, but it is longer, harder to carry out, and more expensive. Also, because time and money constraints usually mean that we can interview far fewer people in person than we could survey online or through some other means, it's difficult to make good generalizations from unstructured and semistructured interview data.

Surveys and interviews rely on *self-reported data*. This means that people tell us the answers. Yet research and common sense both tell us that people do not always know why they feel or act as they do or how they will respond to certain circumstances. Few of us want to think of ourselves as people who will walk away from someone in need of help or cause harm just because we have been so instructed. If you ask people what they would do under circumstances in which strangers need help or in which their own actions cause harm, what do you think they will tell you?[5] For this reason, sometimes you may need to observe without asking.[6]

Experiments are one technique for observing how people will react to different conditions. In experimental research, the researcher measures the relationship between two variables by manipulating one of them and observing the other. If I want to know whether people will help a stranger in need, for example, I can create a situation in which someone appears to be in need of help. That's the *cause* part of a cause-and-effect relationship (the first variable). Then, I can control circumstances so that a variety of people, one at a time, encounter the situation. Some of them will help, and others will not. That's the *effect* (the second variable). As much as possible, I would create a controlled environment in which almost nothing else can affect the outcome. For example, to control whether the *subjects* (the people being observed) were in a hurry or not, I might set up conditions in which they think they are either late or early for a meeting with me.

The classic model of an experiment, which you have probably seen acted out in movies, involves researchers (in white coats) in a lab who look through a one-way mirror while subjects respond to different *stimuli* (the *cause* part of cause and effect). *Fieldwork* provides another way of measuring how people respond to stimuli. Fieldwork is, in some respects, the opposite of experimental research. It requires the researcher to go out into the real world, where things are happening that he or she does not manipulate at all.

The place where you choose to do your experimental work is called your *field site*. Field sites might include a park on a nice day, a campaign office during the course of a political election, spring training with a baseball team, an office, a courtroom, a classroom, or any other place where the kinds of activities in which you are interested happen. As researchers, we cannot control, or really change at all, any of the many things that affect what people do. We can't create the stimulus. But, unlike in a laboratory setting, we can observe things as they actually occur in people's lives.

There are other techniques for data gathering and analysis. For example, researchers use *content analysis* when they look for patterns among cultural artifacts (e.g., television shows, commercials, newspaper articles, pictures in magazines, textbooks). *Focus groups*, or interviews conducted with a group of people, are another means of collecting data.

As you have just seen, we can use numbers to make connections between politics and the day-to-day realities of people who suffer from the effects of bad decisions. But it is ethnographic fieldwork that perhaps best embraces the lived experiences of those whose lives and circumstances we study. *Ethnography* refers to the study of cultural information, such as values and meanings, as opposed to data about structures, politics, and economics. Elliot Liebow's classic 1967 study of an American ghetto, *Tally's Corner*, for example, was praised, when it was first published, for the author's ability "to grasp the native's point of view" while emphasizing that "these 'natives' are other Americans; that their society is his society" (Rainwater, 1968, p. 431). Feminist sociologists have turned to ethnography[7] as a way of overcoming the cultural biases of research itself while conducting research on cultural biases (Ribbons & Edwards, 1997).

The Theory Problem

Recently, we saw a political survey sent out by a senator to all of her constituents. Most of the questions asked respondents to rate certain proposals on a 5-point scale that consisted of 1 = *strongly disagree*, 2 = *disagree*, 3 = *neutral*, 4 = *agree*, and 5 = *strongly agree*. (This is called a *Likert scale*, which is a common way to solicit political opinions.) But it was the questions that were remarkable. Many were of the form "How do you feel about the federal government running up huge debts in order to . . . ?"[8] The problem should be obvious: The question is a *leading question* to which the only acceptable answer is disapproval of the federal government. Yet despite the poor methodology used, the senator will be completely within her rights to later state that some overwhelming percentage of her constituents disapprove of whatever the issue is. Although it is an all-too-common tactic in political and marketing research, creating the answers you want is not at all scientific.

As social scientists, we need to guard against this sort of data abuse in many ways, but two particularly apply. The first is that we have to be open about our methods. We have to describe in detail where and how we got our data, including making our questions public. The second significant protection against misleading data interpretations is to define and describe clear and consistent criteria for data evaluation before we even collect our data. These criteria have to follow from our research questions.

As social scientists, we also have to demonstrate the reliability and validity of our findings. We need to let our readers know, through a clear discussion of how we collected our data, just how sure we can be that our data accurately represent the population studied (*validity*) and whether or not we can expect that other researchers, using the same methods, would find similar results (*reliability*). And we have to be honest, analytical, and trustworthy in doing so! Although not every study has to be high in both reliability and validity (depending on the methodology used, sometimes that is impossible), we must clearly indicate just how valid and reliable our findings are. Unless we do so, those who read and rely on what we present will not be able to accurately judge the veracity of our findings.

Returning to the example of political policies, suppose we want to determine how popular or unpopular a group of policies is with voters. We would start by designing a set of procedures for measuring people's opinions. This might be in the form of a survey with a number of Likert-scale questions on it (though not the questions from the survey we have just seen). Recall that we had defined a 5-point scale, in which Answers 1 and 2 indicated disapproval, 3 was neutral, and 4 and 5 indicated approval. In this case, the analysis is easy. When all of the respondents' answers to the same question are averaged, the number can be interpreted on the same scale: Higher than 3 indicates approval. Of course, real studies often require much more complex criteria involving the interactions of many variables under different conditions. But the process always involves first laying out the criteria by which the data will be used to answer the question, then collecting the data, and only then drawing conclusions.

Where do clear and consistent criteria come from? How can we say that it is reasonable to expect a particular outcome or pattern of behavior and that it would be odd to find something else? The answer, of course, is that our research is driven by theory. Sociological theories offer explanations for group behavior. *Theories*—tested notions of how and why people do things—lead to testable propositions about how and why specific sets of people would do particular things. Conflict theory, for example, tells us that dominant groups will usually act in a great many consistent and predictable ways to maintain their dominance, including making claims about others' inherent inferiorities. Theories of gender and social roles in the United States tell us that men expect to have dominance in public roles, particularly those that involve the greatest amount of decision making and moneymaking—areas that preserve and reproduce this advantage. A gender role theorist might predict that men in leadership positions will routinely suggest that women are less capable of exercising leadership. *Do* they suggest that? That's a research question.

Sociologist in Action: Kevin Bales

Kevin Bales has used his sociological eye to expose present-day slavery. At first, Bales was dismissed when he told people that slavery is a major problem today. However, instead of giving up, Bales conducted research to prove that slavery is a major global problem. He threw off the veil over contemporary slavery with his book *Disposable People: New Slavery in the Global Economy*, first published in 1999. In *Disposable People*, Bales uses case studies and interviews to show that rapid population increase, the inequality of modern globalization, and fast-moving economic changes have led to conditions ripe for slavery. Moreover, modern slaves are cheap and easily replaced. The result is millions of "disposable people" trapped in incredibly harsh conditions of forced servitude, who can be cheaply and easily replaced with other slaves.

We now know, thanks largely to Bales, that 27 million people live in slavery today (Free the Slaves, 2012). Bales, however, has also helped us find ways to combat slavery. Putting his findings into action, Bales uses all his royalties from *Disposable People* to fund anti-slavery efforts. He cofounded the organization Free the Slaves in 2001. The goals of Free the Slaves include giving voice to those enslaved; encouraging businesses, consumers, and governments to combat slavery; and conducting research to determine what strategies are most effective to end slavery. Bales has won many awards for his efforts, including being named by *Utne Reader* as one of "50 Visionaries Who Are Changing Your World."

EXERCISE 3.1   Ethnography

1. Choose a public setting in which you can sit and take notes for at least an hour. The setting should be open to anyone and have lively social interaction. It must also be very unfamiliar to you, so that you can experience it as an "outsider." Begin your observations by writing out a general description of your setting. Who is there, and what are they doing? What sorts of activities go on in this place?

2. Describe how you fit into the setting. Are people noticing that you are observing them? How do you think these people view you?

3. For a 15-minute period, write down everything that you see happening. Try not to read anything into what you are observing. Observation notes might include things such as the following: "Two adults (1WM, 1WF [shorthand for 'one white male, one white female']) walk in pushing a stroller with a very young child in it. They talk. The man goes to the counter while the woman takes a table. The man orders and purchases two drinks and brings them to the table." Notes should not incorporate a lot of interpretation, the way this example does: "A couple with a child comes in. The husband asks his wife what she wants and then goes to get the drinks." You don't really know those things. You know that the two people are adults, but you don't know their relationship or the details of their conversation. Don't write down assumptions about what you see—just what you actually observe.

4. After your notes are complete, try to make sense of them. (a) What patterns of interactions did you see? (b) What do you think they reveal? (c) Why do you think that? (d) What other explanations can you come up with?(e) What would you need to observe or learn in order to know which explanation is the most likely?

5. What are the advantages and disadvantages of this type of data collection?

6. Would this be your preferred mode of data collection to understand what you observed? Why or why not?

EXERCISE 3.2   Gender and Leadership

1. Write a 10-question survey about the differences between men and women. Three of the questions should deal with issues of leadership and decision making. For each question, offer respondents the same three answers to choose from: Yes, No, or Not Sure. Make sure that your questions are worded in a way that is not leading.

(Continued)

(Continued)

2. Survey 10 people, and summarize the results. Describe what these results reveal.

3. Interview three people. Ask them the same questions about leadership, but for each answer they give, ask them why they think so. Do not lead them to answer in any particular way. Just ask them to explain themselves, and let them say whatever they want. Write down their answers in as much detail as you can.

4. For each of your interviews, analyze the reasons people give for their beliefs.

   a. How often do they express their answers in terms of personal beliefs or personal experiences?

   b. How often do they express their answers in terms of anecdotes—stories that they might have heard about people they do or do not know?

   c. How often do they refer to information they learned in one of their classes (if your respondents are students) or in news reports from reliable sources?

   d. How else do people explain their beliefs?

5. What do the answers to these four questions tell you about how most people in your sample form their beliefs about (a) gender and (b) how gender is related to leadership?

6. Compare your findings from your interviews and surveys. What kind of information did you get from each methodology? What benefits can be obtained by using both qualitative and quantitative data collection when you research a topic?

EXERCISE 3.3 Hate Crimes

Crimes that can be prosecuted by the federal government as hate crimes consist of criminal acts motivated by bias against members of a particular race, gender, religion, sexual orientation, or ethnicity, or those with a disability. Hate crimes may also be prosecuted at the state level, but what groups are protected under hate crime legislation varies among the states.

For this exercise, do the following:

1. Listen to the following three stories from National Public Radio: "Are Hate Crime Laws Necessary?" at http://www.npr.org/2012/04/10/150351860/are-hate-crime-laws-necessary, "DOJ Downplays Expectation

(Continued)

(Continued)

for Hate Crimes Law" at http://www.npr.org/search/index.php?search input=DOJ+Downplays+Expectation+for+Hate+Crimes+Law, and "Sikh Temple Shooting Stuns Congregation, Country" at http://www.npr .org/2012/08/06/158199106/sikh-temple-shooting-stuns-cong regation-country.

2. Research your college's policy on hate crimes. (This information will likely be in your student handbook or may be accessed by using the search engine on your college's website and typing in the keywords "hate crime policy.")

3. Interview five students to find out (a) what they know about hate crimes and, specifically, if they know the definition of a hate crime; (b) if they think that hate crimes legislation is necessary (and why); and, if so, (c) what groups should be covered (and why).

Your research will likely yield the most interesting results if some, but not all, of those you interview come from historical out-groups that have often been targeted by hate crimes (e.g., African American, Jewish, Muslim, gay or lesbian, immigrant, Latino).

4. Write a two-page paper analyzing your interviews in the context of the National Public Radio stories.

EXERCISE 3.4   The Pros and Cons of Different Methodologies

In this chapter, we've described a variety of methodologies (means of collecting data), including classic experiments, fieldwork, interviews, and surveys. Each has its own set of strengths and weaknesses.

In a one- to two-page paper, do the following:

a. Briefly describe each of the four methodologies (classic experiments, fieldwork, interviews, and surveys).

b. Describe the strengths and weaknesses of each methodology discussed in the chapter.

c. Discuss how you might use each methodology to examine the issue of academic cheating on your campus. What would be the advantages and disadvantages of each of these means of studying this issue?

DISCUSSION QUESTIONS

1. Think of a research question that explores the reasons behind a norm on your campus that most people do not question (e.g., If "hooking up" instead of dating is the norm on your campus, how might you research how that type of normative behavior is supported? Or if commuter students tend to be disengaged from campus activities, what social forces support that norm?).

2. Based on what you have read in this chapter, how will you determine if a politician is providing you with trustworthy or misleading information?

3. Think of something that you and members of your family have long believed to be true. How would you test this belief? If your research led you to change your mind, how could you convince others in your family to reconsider their own assumptions on the issue?

4. Which methodology covered in this chapter would you use to determine your classmates' attitudes toward global climate change? Why?

5. Kevin Bales exposed the plague of modern-day slavery through good, social scientific research. What social issue would you like to bring further attention to through social scientific research? Why?

6. If you were to conduct a study to determine if your campus has adequate supports for (a) students now in the armed forces and (b) veterans, how would you collect your data? Why?

7. Which methodologies covered in this chapter would typically be most useful for someone researching a topic from the perspective of (a) a conflict theorist, (b) a functionalist, and (c) a symbolic interactionist?

SUGGESTIONS FOR SPECIFIC ACTIONS

1. Find a website for an organization that advocates for or protests against something. Most such organizations have websites these days, so you can start by choosing an issue about which people fight (e.g., a flat tax, economic inequality, and genetically modified food); then, search out the groups that have positions on the issue. Select a website used by one of the groups. Identify two or three major claims that they offer on the website in support of their position. Do they present real evidence to back up these claims? How well do they document their sources? Try to verify the data on your own. Also, try to find contradictory information. Do you think they are being honest and factual or that they are not telling the full truth? What makes you think so? Create your own website (or alternate form of presentation, such as a fact sheet or PowerPoint presentation) that describes the same issue in a more balanced way.

2. Research a policy decision recently made by your college or university. Ascertain how the policy was designed. In particular, determine what research was undertaken to decide if the new policy was necessary. Was the research done in a social scientific manner? Based on the research undertaken, do you think the university policy was clearly needed and well formulated? Write a letter to the editor of your school paper that describes your examination of the policy and the research that culminated in it. Be sure to include your evaluation of the research in your letter.

Please go to this book's website at http://study.sagepub.com/korgen5e to find further civic engagement opportunities, resources, peer-reviewed articles, and updated web links related to this chapter.

NOTES

1. This dialogue is found in the Internet Movie Database (http://www.imdb.com).

2. However, it's important to remember that the passage of time does not always result in more rational thought among populations. Just three centuries ago, "witches" were being put to death in Salem, Massachusetts!

3. Similarly, "researching" what is the best car to buy by reading consumer guides like *Consumer Reports* is not conducting true social scientific research.

4. Sociology, like psychology, anthropology, and political science, is a social science. Physics, chemistry, and biology are natural sciences in that they study the physical world, or nature.

5. If you think you have an answer to that question, it's likely you are incorrect. Some people will exaggerate one way; others will exaggerate the other way. Many will guess, and almost none will really know. But there will always be a lot of different answers if you ask a lot of different people!

6. Please note that observational research, like all research dealing with human subjects, must be approved by your school's Institutional Review Board. In almost all cases, you will need to obtain written approval from the people you plan to observe, and you must provide assurances that no psychological or physical harm will come to them as a result of your research. See the book's website for more information about the ethics of social scientific research.

7. Many feminist researchers view traditional, social scientific, and quantitative research methods as constructed by men and influenced by a male-dominated view of society. Ethnography and other types of qualitative research, in contrast to quantitative work, tend to provide a more complete picture of, and a greater voice for, the individuals being observed.

8. This was not an actual question. We're exaggerating just a little to make the point.

REFERENCES

Bullard, R. D. (2000). *Dumping in Dixie: Race, class, and environmental quality* (3rd ed.). Boulder, CO: Westview Press.

Evans, M. D., Kelley, J., Sikora, J., & Treiman, D. J. (2010). Family scholarly culture and educational success: Evidence from 27 nations. *Research in Social Stratification and Mobility, 28*(2), 171–197.

Eves, H. (1976). *An introduction to the history of mathematics* (4th ed.). New York, NY: Holt, Rinehart & Winston.

Ewall, M. (2013). Legal tools for environmental equity vs. environmental justice. *Sustainable Development Law & Policy, 13*(1), 4–13.

Free the Slaves. (2012). *About slavery.* Retrieved from https://www.freetheslaves.net/SSLPage.aspx?pid=348

Garfinkel, H. (1967). *Studies in ethnomethodology.* Englewood Cliffs, NJ: Prentice Hall.

Liebow, E. (1967). *Tally's corner.* Boston, MA: Little, Brown.

Rainwater, L. (1968). Review of the book *Tally's corner: A study of Negro street-corner men* by Elliot Liebow. *Social Forces, 46*(3), 431–432.

Ribbons, J., & Edwards, R. (1997). *Feminist dilemmas in qualitative research: Public knowledge and private lives.* Thousand Oaks, CA: Sage.

Sax, L. (2002). How common is intersex? A response to Anne Fausto-Sterling. *Journal of Sex Research, 39*, 174–179.

4

Creating Civic Engagement Versus Creating Apathy

Culture

Have you seen the *SpongeBob SquarePants* episode where SpongeBob goes to Sandy's house for the first time? If you have seen the show, you know that SpongeBob is an underwater creature (a sponge), and Sandy is a squirrel (from Texas) who lives in an air-filled, underwater structure. SpongeBob did not appreciate the fact that he relied on water to survive until he stepped into Sandy's air-filled home, where he couldn't breathe, became brittle, and started to disintegrate. Similarly, most people do not recognize how much they rely on their culture until they find themselves immersed in somebody else's.

Whether we are aware of it or not, we rely on culture for almost everything we do. All our decisions—what clothes to wear, what to eat (and how to eat it), with whom to live, and what to do with our lives—are made based on our culture. Similarly, the languages we speak, the religions we follow, the sports teams we root for, and our goals for what will make our lives "successful" are all heavily influenced by our culture.

Generally, sociologists divide the study of culture into the following three categories: (1) values—what members of society deem important, (2) norms—the rules and expectations for behavior that guide people as to how to act in society, and (3) artifacts (material culture)—the tangible objects that people from a particular culture create and use. If values are what we believe in, what we want, and how we think our lives should be, norms are the set of rules we have established that govern how we can achieve those things we value. The values and norms that a society establishes will then influence which artifacts members of that society will develop and how they will make and use them.

Values and norms are *social constructions*, constantly created and re-created through interaction. That is, values and norms are produced and reproduced by social processes, often without plan, discussion, or decision. We just get used to doing things in a certain way that has been taught to us and modeled through our culture. These values change over time, and they differ from society to society. Although there are some values that are shared by many societies (e.g., most capitalist societies value hard work, money, and material possessions), values are not universal. For example, when a very trim and physically fit person we know spent a year in a poor South Asian nation as a member of the Peace Corps, the villagers with whom she lived were constantly encouraging her to eat and gain some weight. The people there associated her thin figure with poverty, a condition to be pitied. Meanwhile, back in the United States, she often experienced just the opposite reaction from the people around her. Many people envied her physique and wished that they could have a similar one! When one of us traveled to Lesotho, a small country in southern Africa, he was using a cane due to an injury. In Lesotho, he discovered that people who walk with canes are the most respected members of the society, those who have earned the cane through their wisdom. There is only a limited number of canes (and other supplies) in these communities, so they are given first to the elderly, those viewed to be the wisest members of the community. On his return to the United States, Jonathan was quickly reminded that having a cane in our country is a sign of injury and weakness—a stark contrast to the admiration and respect it brought him while in Lesotho.

Like values, social norms vary over time and from society to society. For example, in the contemporary United States, expected behaviors for men and women continue to change as new forms of interaction arise. Only a decade ago, it was commonly suggested that only desperate people might use the Internet to find a date, but "singles bars" were popular. Today, arranging dates through Internet services is much more socially acceptable or "normal." In fact, more than one third of couples who married between 2005 and 2012 had met online. Moreover, married couples who met online were more likely to stay together than those who met some other way (Cacioppo, Cacioppo, Gonzaga, Ogburn, & VanderWeele, 2013). Kathleen's brother met his wife online! Where people go on their dates also varies from culture to culture.

Kathleen remembers being rather startled as she took a stroll at dusk through a park in Cuernavaca, Mexico, to find *every* park bench filled with young couples. Most young people there lacked the money to gain access to the private (or at least indoor) places where people typically go on dates in the United States. Jonathan was surprised to find in his travels to the Maasai Mara region of Kenya that in some of the villages, uncles often arranged marriages between two young people, who never even had the opportunity to meet prior to their wedding ceremony. Girls and boys are also socialized differently in different cultures. For example, girls from one culture may be trained to hide their bodies, whereas those from another are taught to flaunt their physiques. While writing these words, one of us looked out the window of her New Jersey home and saw several women get out of their car to look at the house that was for sale next door. It was a hot August day, but the women were completely covered by dark robes. The driver wore black leather gloves that extended far up her arms, and only her eyes were uncovered. Although many other people had stopped to look at the house without drawing much attention from Kathleen, her focus was (momentarily) diverted to this group of prospective buyers because of the clothing the women wore. Their manner of dress indicated that they were members of a subculture, meaning that they are not only a part of the larger U.S. society but also part of a smaller group within it that has its own norms, values, and artifacts.

Subcultures

To varying degrees, subcultures exist within dominant cultures (the culture upheld by the group that has the most power in a society). A subculture is a group of people with cultural patterns (values, norms, and artifacts) that distinguish them from the dominant culture. College students, firefighters, stay-at-home parents, first-generation Jamaican Americans, environmental activists, Mormon Americans, paraplegic athletes, white antiracism activists, and working-class Americans are some of the many examples of subcultures in the United States. Chances are that *you* belong to one or more subcultures as well! Subcultures often arise around shared backgrounds. Italian Americans in an Italian enclave of a big city may form a subculture, whereas more "integrated" Italian Americans may not be a part of that group or may teeter between the subculture and the dominant culture. Subcultures also grow around shared activities. Surfers form one subculture, bikers another, and jugglers, perhaps, a third.

Yet sharing an activity is not enough to ensure the emergence of a subculture. There must be enough interaction for a common base of knowledge, habit, ritual, meaning, and values to develop. For example, college students, as a group, tend to share certain values, norms, and artifacts that differ from those of people not enrolled in college. They may value high grades instead of big paychecks (perhaps as a means to getting big paychecks in the future), tend not to sleep during the same times of day (or for the same number of hours) as most Americans, and research and write papers instead of handling or crafting material goods for purchase. Importantly, they also recognize each other as members of a common subculture.

Although they have some noticeably different ways of thinking and behaving, members of subcultures share the same *guiding* values, norms, and artifacts of the dominant culture. The things they do and think that distinguish them do not threaten or work against the dominant values, norms, and artifacts of their society. For example, your classmates on the football team and your classmates who are members of the College Republicans may learn to think and behave in some different ways. Through doing so, each group creates its own subculture. However, the majority of both college football players and College Republicans follow the dominant norms and share the dominant values of the school and the larger society. Likewise, first-generation immigrant Jamaican Americans may enjoy different types of food from the majority of Americans and may tend to be more family oriented than Americans socialized only under the dominant American culture. However, both groups (albeit to varying extents) share and follow most of the primary values of U.S. culture (e.g., material success, progress, freedom, and hard work).

Members of subcultures both influence and are influenced by the dominant culture. For example, second-generation Jamaican Americans will tend to hold and follow dominant American values and norms more than their parents did. At the same time, the larger culture changes somewhat as immigrant groups interact with other members of society. The increasing variety of ethnic foods becoming common fare for many Americans is a good example of how norms (in this case, what most Americans eat) change as the demographic makeup of the United States changes.

Countercultures

Groups of people who have cultural attributes that *oppose* those of the dominant culture are known as members of a counterculture. Such groups can be peace loving, like the "flower children" of the 1960s, or willing to use violence, such as the Ku Klux Klan and the neo-Nazis. Members of countercultures often find it difficult to avoid violent confrontations (and some incite them), simply because they stand in direct opposition to some of the core values, norms, and artifacts of the dominant culture. The violence that erupted during the American Indian movement (led by the group called AIM) of the early 1970s provides a good example of how the opposition of dominant and countercultural values and norms can lead to violent clashes. AIM is a countercultural group with views that directly challenge many of the dominant U.S. values and norms, such as individual ownership of property and faith in the integrity of the U.S. justice and political systems. AIM's goals include a review of more than 300 treaties signed between American Indian nations and the U.S. government (which the AIM leaders argued were broken by the U.S. government), autonomy for tribal governments, and a return to the traditional culture of the Native American nations.

Those who challenge dominant cultural rules, beliefs, and values can face dramatic and harsh reactions from those who adhere to the dominant culture. For example, when many of the dominant U.S. values and norms (individual ownership of property, faith in the U.S. justice and political systems) were directly challenged by AIM, the U.S. government responded to this threat with powerful efforts to stop AIM by jailing leaders and surrounding protest enclaves with heavy weaponry, which resulted in several shoot-outs. One member of AIM, the Native American political activist Leonard Peltier, was convicted and imprisoned for murder 30 years ago. However, he is widely believed to be innocent of the crime for which he was convicted and thus is thought to be a political prisoner.[1] Recently, members of the Taliban, an Islamic fundamentalist political movement, shot Malala Yousafzi, a Pakistani girl, in the head and left her for dead. The Taliban control areas of Pakistan where Malala and her family lived. They do not believe that girls should attend school, and they terrorized those who refused to obey their commands to stay at home. Malala was attacked for representing a countercultural group of girls advocating for their right to education. Malala fortunately survived and now stands as an even more powerful and well-known voice for girls' rights. She describes her decision to speak up, despite the danger she faced, this way: "I could either not speak and die, or speak and then die. I chose the second one" (Hamilton, 2014, para. 6).

Other countercultures include extreme religious organizations, cults, or other groups whose beliefs or goals place them in opposition to national laws. Such countercultural groups range from fundamentalist Mormons,[2] who believe in polygamy, to radical Islamic groups, such as Al Qaeda, and extreme right-wing Christian fundamentalists,[3] who use terrorism to promote their beliefs. All countercultural groups reject the dominant values, norms, and artifacts and seek out different ways of living. In some cases, they also try to impose their own culture against the will of the other members of society.

Recognizing Cultural Patterns

Now that we know what a culture consists of, we can begin to look for the patterns that help us recognize the dominant norms, values, and artifacts of different cultures, subcultures, and countercultures. Members of almost any group of people who gather together on a regular basis create their own *microculture*. Think of your own groups of friends. You probably have ways of speaking to one another, in-jokes, and perhaps even modes of dress that set you apart, somewhat, from the rest of society or at least the immediate dominant culture in which you live. The same is true for the group of people who constitute your school's student body. Every campus has its own microculture(s). You have probably heard people talking about the "campus culture." What they are referring to are the values, norms, and artifacts most people on their campus share, which are often different from those found on other campuses or in the town where their campus is located.

Every college or university has a reputation that is, in part, derived from the campus culture. For example, one of us received her undergraduate degree at a school known for its strong liberal arts education, Catholicism, heavy drinking among the student body, its commitment to social justice, and the ability to bring wealthy Catholics together to improve society and network effectively. As you can see, although we often speak of "the culture" of a community, it is clear that contradictory norms and values can exist within one culture.

The campus culture at Kathleen's alma mater included valuing sports, competition, academic achievement, and friendship; practicing the Catholic faith; working for social justice; and partying (not necessarily in that order). Some of the dominant norms were studying, playing sports, volunteering to help those in need, attending Mass, hanging out with friends, hooking up (rather than dating), drinking lots of beer, and wearing preppy clothing (not necessarily in that order). The artifacts of the campus included finely manicured lawns (award-winning, in fact); a well-financed and popular Campus Ministry office; beautifully maintained old buildings (including chapels) in which to study, learn, and pray; cramped on-campus housing; run-down off-campus apartments nearby to party in; and J. Crew clothing on almost every student on campus. These artifacts are more than just objects; they are manifestations of the values (some contradictory) of the college and the collective membership of the college community. The finely manicured lawns reflected a value of spending money on campus aesthetics rather than, for example, using some of that money to offer more scholarships to students from poor families. The Campus Ministry office, on the other hand, is indicative of the school's emphasis on Catholic social teaching and work for social justice.

Civic Engagement on Campus

Civic engagement appears to be on the rise on college campuses. Two thirds of all Americans between the ages of 18 and 24 used a social networking site (SNS) for political activity during 2012, and those with some college educa-tion were most likely to do so. The 2012 election saw a strong youth turn-out, and these young voters made a major impact in the ballot box. Voters between the ages of 18 and 29 favored President Obama by 24% and were a key factor in his victory (The Center for Information and Research on Civic Learning and Engagement, 2012).

Today, evidence of student interest in worker justice issues can also be found on campuses all over the United States. In 2008, the University of Wisconsin Oshkosh was the first institution of higher education certified as fair trade. By 2014, 109 colleges and universities in the United States sold certified fair trade products in their dining rooms and campus shops (Fair Trade Campaigns, 2014). As of 2014, there were 180 colleges and universi-ties affiliated with the Students Against Sweatshops–sponsored Worker Rights Consortium, an organization that monitors the enforcement of the Codes of Conduct signed by colleges and universities to ensure that clothing with their schools' logos is made in sweat-free factories. As discussed in Chapter 1, students at many schools (e.g., Wayne State University, Fairfield University, the University of Pennsylvania, the State Universities of New York, the University of Arizona, Boston College, Duke University, and California State College, San Bernadino) have convinced their university administrators to stop buying apparel made in sweatshops and to have the Worker Rights Consortium monitor the operation of the apparel factories they use (to prevent abuses of workers).

The Boot the Bell campaign, led by the Coalition of Immokalee Workers and supported by students across the nation, demanded that Taco Bell and its parent company, Yum, stop the practice of indentured servitude and increase the wages of tomato pickers. By the time it ended in victory in 2005, it had spread to more than 300 college and university campuses and 50 high schools (Student/Farmworker Alliance, n.d.). Since Yum Foods signed on in 2005, the following food companies have also pledged to participate in the Coalition of Immokalee Workers–initiated Fair Food Program and make sure the companies that provide them with tomatoes pay field workers an additional penny a pound and treat them fairly: Yum Brands (2005), McDonald's (2007), Burger King (2008), Subway (2008), Whole Foods Market (2008), Bon Appetit Management Company (2009), Compass Group (2009), Aramark (2010), Sodexo (2010), Trader Joe's (2012), Chipotle (2012), and Walmart (2014) (Greenhouse, 2014).

Students have also pushed colleges and universities to do their part to address global climate change. Among the college students surveyed by the Princeton Review (2014), well over half (62%) noted that "having information about a college's commitment to the environment would impact their decision to apply to or attend a school." Noting students' interest in this topic, the Princeton Review now publishes a guide on green colleges and provides similar information on its website, including an honor role of the "greenest" colleges and universities.

Many students across the country also made their campuses *divest* (withdraw all investments) from any corporations that were doing business with the genocidal regime in Darfur, Sudan, during the first decade of this century. As of 2012, there were more than 850 middle school, high school, and college chapters of the Students Taking Action Now: Darfur organization, which organized students to stand up against genocide in Sudan, Myanmar (former Burma), and the Democratic Republic of Congo, and throughout the world. Ultimately, this divestment movement played a significant role in ending, albeit tenuously, the genocide in Darfur.

University administrative leaders also realize the importance of teaching students how to fulfill their obligations as citizens effectively. Today, 250 state colleges and universities participate in the American Democracy Project, which focuses on providing service learning opportunities for students. In addition, almost 600 college and university presidents have signed the Campus Compact pledge to "educate citizens." Six hundred and seventy-nine U.S. institutions of higher education have signed on to the American College & University Presidents' Climate Commitment to reduce global warming and to "green" their campuses. Sociology students can use the tools of the discipline to be at the forefront of these efforts and to make sure they are carried out in effective and just ways.

Social Networking Sites and Civic Engagement

In recent years, civic engagement among the general public has also been spurred on by SNS. A recent Pew Research Center (2013) survey indicates that the percentage of Americans engaged in political activity on SNS jumped from 33% to 69% of the online population between 2008 and 2012. Two thirds of SNS users, or 39% of all adults, engage in political activities, such as posting political opinions or encouraging people to vote, on SNS. Approximately 60% of Americans now use SNS, such as Facebook and Twitter. Moreover, political activity online tends to lead to more political activity offline. For example, 43% of SNS users indicated that they were inspired to learn more about political topics and 18% reported that they were inspired to take action on a political topic because of what they had read online.

While some people have disparaged political activity online as "slacktivism," for its supposed lack of relation to offline political activism, the Pew study shows that this criticism cannot be supported. Online political activity has led many people to become more civically engaged. Forty-three percent of SNS users say that they decided to learn more about a political issue because of what they read on an SNS. Almost all those who are politically active online (83%) are active both on and offline (in the "real" world).

A Growing Ideological Divide Between Republicans and Democrats

Those who pay attention to politics and are engaged in the political process tend to be very ideologically divided (Abramowitz, 2010; Kohut, Doherty, Dimmock, & Keeter, 2011). The difference in values between Republicans and Democrats increased tremendously during the George W. Bush and Barack Obama presidencies and is now greater than those across gender, race, age, and class. Among Republicans, there are twice as many conservatives as moderates. While liberals do not dominate the Democratic Party (as conservatives dominate the Republican Party), the percentage of liberals in the party has grown and now equals that of moderates (Kohut, Doherty, Dimmock, & Keeter, 2012).

The greatest divide between Democrats and Republicans lies in how the members of each party view the role of government; and this divide has increased dramatically over the past quarter-century. For example, Republican support for the idea that government should aid the poor has dropped substantially over the past 25 years. In 1987, 79% of Democrats and 62% of Republicans believed that the "government should take care of people who can't take care of themselves," while in 2012, 75% of Democrats and just 40% of Republicans agreed with this statement (Kohut et al., 2012). These differing beliefs about government have contributed to a growing cultural divide between the two major political parties in the United States.

Sociologist in Action: Doug McAdam

Doug McAdam (1988), a professor of sociology at Stanford University, used sociological research to figure out what compelled so many (predominantly white and middle class) Northern college students to go to Mississippi to help register black voters during the famous Freedom Summer of 1964. Of the 961 who applied to work as part of the Student Nonviolent Coordinating Committee's drive to register black voters, McAdam found that the 720 who actually followed through and went to Mississippi (as compared with the 241 who did not) were much more likely to have had previous experience in civil rights activities and social activist organizations (many of them church related) as well as connections with other Freedom Summer participants. These results indicate that those who were willing to risk their lives, at that time, to register black voters were part of a subculture with norms that supported social activism and efforts to promote civil rights.

EXERCISE 4.1   Student Survival Guide

Pretend that one of your classmates is new to the United States (and from a very different culture).

1. Make a list of what he or she will need to know about the dominant culture in the United States. Make sure to include explanations about clothing, food, music, television, and everything that a non-American might need to know in order to "make it" in the United States.

2. Once your list is complete, make a list of the norms and values that the items on your list represent.

3. Look at the list of norms and values, and write a one-page essay analyzing what they tell us about American society.

4. Now, repeat this exercise, but pretend that you are writing it for a transfer student or an incoming first-year student to your campus who was born in the United States but who will need to adjust to the subculture on your campus.

EXERCISE 4.2   Campus Culture: Seeing What's Around Us

In an approximately three-page paper, answer the following questions:

1. Think about your own campus. List five of the dominant values on your campus. Now list five dominant norms and five artifacts that reflect those values or contradict them.

2. Do you think your campus culture is different from or typical of most college campus cultures? How do you know this, or why don't you know enough to answer this question?

3. Identify some of the visible subcultures on campus. What makes each a subculture rather than just a bunch of people who have something in common?

4. Do you feel as though you are part of the dominant culture on campus? A microculture? A subculture? A counterculture? Some of these? All of these? Explain.

5. Why is a campus culture important? How does it influence how you spend your time and energy in college?

6. Do you think your campus culture has encouraged you to become a more active citizen? Are you engaged with civic activities on campus? Off campus? Why or why not? If not, is there something in your campus culture that has discouraged your active citizenship? If there is, what is it, and what do you think might help change this type of culture?

EXERCISE 4.3   A Consumer Culture?

1. Write down an extensive list of what material goals you hope to achieve by the age of 30 (a car or cars, house, wardrobe, lifestyle, etc.). Or, if you are an older student, what do you hope to achieve by the next relevant decade?

2. Watch the video *What Would Jesus Buy?* at http://topdocumentaryfilms .com/what-would-jesus-buy/ and "The Story of Stuff" at http://www.storyof stuff.org.

3. Outline the major points made in each of the videos.

(Continued)

(Continued)

4. Now, analyze your own consumerist goals in light of the arguments made in the videos. Why do you think you have the consumerist goals that you have? What in American culture drives you in your quest for material success? Are there any downsides to having these consumerist goals? What do cultures that emphasize consumerism less than ours have that you find to be enviable, if anything?

5. How, if at all, has the economic recession that began in 2008 affected your material goals? Elaborate.

Extra credit: If you have concluded that Americans are too steeped in a consumerist culture, create a campaign to educate your campus about the issue. Produce a fact sheet to help argue your case with information you can find at http://www.newdream.org, http://www.adbusters.org, and the Small Planet Institute at http://smallplanet.org/, or from other readily available sources on the Internet.

EXERCISE 4.4	**Political Culture Data Collection for Dorm Dwellers**

Use participant observation to examine the political culture in your dorm.

1. Look at your dorm's list of organized events (social events, lectures, etc.), as well as unorganized, spontaneous events, and attend as many of them over the course of 1 month as possible.

2. Try to participate in as many informal discussions as possible with your dorm mates during the same month.

3. At each gathering, carefully note the following: (a) what type of gathering it is (friends studying together, watching a movie, gossiping about relationships) or, if it's a dorm event, the topic of the event, and so on; (b) how many times political topics were raised (if at all); (c) how many times political issues could have fit into the conversation but were not raised; (d) the reactions of others if and when political topics were raised (did the person who raised them receive positive or negative feedback or sanctions?); (e) (if political topics

(Continued)

(Continued)

were raised) whether someone mentioned participating in a political action to address the topic; and (f) the reaction to that suggestion.

4. What do your findings indicate about the political culture in your dorm?

Extra credit: Devise a plan to make your dorm a place that is more welcoming, and even encouraging, of political discussion. Be thoughtful, strategic, and specific.

EXERCISE 4.5   Participant Observation of a Political Protest or Other Political Event

Conduct a participant observation of a political event on campus.

1. Find out what student activist groups (officially recognized or ad hoc) exist on campus by talking to other students, professors, people in the campus activities office, and so forth.

2. Choose an organization whose goals you feel comfortable supporting. Do not "infiltrate" a group by misrepresenting your own views.

3. Participate in organizing and carrying out at least one campus event (protests count).

4. Throughout your time with the group, take note of how political issues are discussed. Do they represent dominant culture, subculture, or counterculture values and norms? Elaborate.

5. Which conversational topics are encouraged and which are discouraged (result in sanctions) in the group?

6. What are the reactions to the efforts of the group from fellow students, professors, professional staff, and administrators?

7. What do your answers to the questions above tell you about the norms and values of (a) the culture of the group in which you participated and (b) your campus culture?

EXERCISE 4.6   American Values and U.S. Policy

Do dominant American values match U.S. policy?

1. Go to the website http://www.publicagenda.org, and click on "Issue Guides."

2. Pick an issue under the Environment Issue Guides that you believe relates to a dominant value in U.S. culture.

3. Peruse the information available, and write a paper that answers the following questions:

   a. What was the issue you chose to study, and how does it relate to a dominant U.S. value?

   b. What were your own views on the issue before reading the information on the site, and how did you form your viewpoint on the issue (what aspects of your culture influenced your point of view)?

   c. Did your view on the issue change after reading the information on the site? Why or why not?

   d. Recommend several practical suggestions for working for change on the issue. Include a discussion of what can be done on your campus to work for change and what you can personally do.

Extra credit: Based on your suggestions in (d), organize a student group to begin working for these changes.

EXERCISE 4.7   Globalization: The Great Cultural Divider?

Go to David Brooks's column "All Cultures Are Not Equal" (2005) at http://www.nytimes.com/2005/08/10/opinion/11brooks.done.html?_r=0, and answer the following questions:

1. Do you agree with Brooks that U.S. citizens are increasingly separating into distinct and isolated subcultures? Do you think that this trend could lead (or has led) to more countercultures in the United States?

2. Write a one-page outline of how you would carry out research to test one (or more) of Brooks's statements in the above article.

DISCUSSION QUESTIONS

1. Describe a subculture to which you belong. What norms, values, and artifacts distinguish it from the dominant culture? How does belonging to this subculture influence your life?

2. Have you become more engaged in political issues through online sites? Why or why not? Why do you think so many young Americans take part in political activity both online and offline these days?

3. Can you recall a time when someone gave you discouraging feedback when you attempted to engage in a conversation about political issues? If so, why do you think the person discouraged you? How did it make you feel? How do you think you could have approached that conversation in a way that would have been better able to engage that person in a discussion about political issues?

4. Do you think political knowledge is valued on your campus? Provide examples to back up your answer. How often do you talk to others about political issues on campus? Why?

5. Think about the dominant culture in the United States. What are some of the dominant norms, values, and artifacts that (a) encourage or (b) discourage political participation by Americans?

6. Do you think recycling is a norm on your campus? What makes you think so? If it is a norm, what do you think brought about the addition of recycling to the campus culture norms? If recycling is not now a norm on your campus, why do you think that is? What could you do to help promote recycling on campus?

7. Why do you think Americans, in recent years, have become increasingly politically polarized? In general, how do you think such polarization influences nations with democratically elected governments? What do you think are some of the present and potential repercussions of political polarization on the well-being of the United States?

8. What methodology would you use if you wanted to determine the norms, values, and artifacts that represent your campus's microculture? Why? What theoretical perspective would you use to guide your research and make sense of your findings? Why?

SUGGESTIONS FOR SPECIFIC ACTIONS

1. Brainstorm with two or three of your classmates as to how you might promote civic engagement within the existing campus culture. If you do not think it is possible to do this within the existing culture of your campus, how might you change the campus culture to promote civic engagement on campus? Act on these ideas.

2. Organize a campus debate about a civic issue that affects the life chances (the chances one has to improve one's social class position and quality of life) of students on campus. Analyze the campus culture to figure out how to most effectively promote and advertise the event (and do so!).

3. Conduct three focus groups (after obtaining proper Institutional Review Board approval) that explore (a) how your fellow students define the ideal campus culture and (b) the actual dominant norms and values of the campus culture. Recruit interested members of the focus groups to come up with an action plan to disseminate and act on your findings.

Please go to this book's website at http://study.sagepub.com/korgen5e to find further civic engagement opportunities, resources, peer-reviewed articles, and updated web links related to this chapter.

NOTES

1. Two of the most well-known books that supply information about the Peltier case are Jim Messerschmidt's *The Trial of Leonard Peltier* (1983) and Peter Matthiessen's *In the Spirit of Crazy Horse* (1983/1992).

2. The Church of Jesus Christ of Latter-day Saints banned polygamy in 1890.

3. For example, Eric Robert Rudolph, a member of the white supremacist Christian identity movement, carried out the 1996 Centennial Olympic Park bombing and other bombings that targeted gay and lesbian Americans and abortion clinics.

REFERENCES

Abramowitz, A. I. (2010). *The disappearing center: Engaged citizens, polarization, and American democracy.* New Haven, CT: Yale University Press.

Brooks, D. (2005, August 11). All cultures are not equal. *The New York Times.* Retrieved from http://query.nytimes.com/gst/fullpage.html?res=990CE2DA143E F932A2575BC0A9639C8B63

Cacioppo, J. T., Cacioppo, S., Gonzaga, G. C., Ogburn, E. L., VanderWeele, T. J. (2013). Marital satisfaction and break-ups differ across on-line and off-line meeting venues. *Proceedings of the National Academy of Sciences, 110*(25), 10135–10140. Retrieved from http://www.pnas.org/content/110/25/10135.full.pdf+html? sid=a6de95b7–4f11–4d7d-b710–755efdc004da

The Center for Information and Research on Civic Learning and Engagement. (2012). *Youth turnout: At least 49%, 22–23 million under-30 voted.* Retrieved from http:// www.civicyouth.org/youth-turnout-at-least-49-22-23-million-under-30-voted

Fair Trade Campaigns. (2014). *Universities.* Retrieved from http://fairtradecampaigns .org/campaign-type/universities

Greenhouse, G. (2014, April 24). In Florida tomato fields, a penny buys progress. *The New York Times*. Retrieved from http://www.nytimes.com/2014/04/25/business/in-florida-tomato-fields-a-penny-buys-progress.html?_r=0

Hamilton, C. (2014, March 7). Malala Yousafzai: "I could either not speak and die, or speak and then die. I chose the second one." *The Independent*. Retrieved from http://www.independent.co.uk/news/uk/home-news/malala-yousafzai-shines-among-the-stars-as-she-inspires-thousands-of-schoolchildren-9177643.html

Kohut, A., Doherty, C., Dimmock, M., & Keeter, S. (2011, May 4). *Beyond red vs. blue: Political typology* (Pew Research Center for the People & the Press). Retrieved from http://www.people-press.org/files/legacy-pdf/Beyond-Red-vs-Blue-The-Political-Typology.pdf

Kohut, A., Doherty, C., Dimmock, M., & Keeter, S. (2012). *Trends in American values: 1987–2012: Partisan polarization surges in Bush, Obama years* (Pew Research Center for the People & the Press). Retrieved from http://www.people-press.org/files/legacy-pdf/06-04-12%20Values%20Release.pdf

Matthiessen, P. (1992). *In the spirit of Crazy Horse*. New York, NY: Viking Press. (Original work published 1983)

McAdams, D. (1988). *Freedom summer*. New York, NY: Oxford University Press.

Messerschmidt, J. (1983). *The trial of Leonard Peltier*. Boston, MA: South End Press.

Pew Research Center. (2013, April 25). *Civic engagement in the digital age*. Retrieved from http://www.pewinternet.org/~/media//Files/Reports/2013/PIP_CivicEngagementintheDigitalAge.pdf

The Princeton Review. (2014). *The Princeton Review gives 832 colleges green ratings*. Retrieved from http://www.princetonreview.com/green/press-release.aspx

Student/Farmworker Alliance. (n.d.). *Victory over Taco Bell*. Retrieved from http://www.sfalliance.org/tacobell.html

5

Learning How to Act in Society

Socialization

Would you like to make someone smile? Smile at the person! It's almost impossible not to smile back when someone is smiling at you. A smile is one of the first symbols we learn to use to communicate with others.

Babies learn to smile by interacting with their caregivers, who (often) smile at them as they play with, change, and feed them (see Lockhart, 2011; Messinger, 2005; Venezia, Messinger, Thorp, & Mundy, 2004). They quickly learn that smiling can make their parents happy (and, in particular, happy with them). The second daughter of one of us learned this trick, to great effect, when she was an infant. She could even get her exhausted parents to smile while changing her at 3:00 a.m. After fumbling their way to the changing table, they would look down to see her beaming at them with a big grin. Even those *very* sleep-deprived people couldn't resist the urge to smile back at the baby who had just awakened them from their slumber. How could they not? She looked so happy to see them!

On a more somber note about learned behavior, have you heard the tragic story of Isabelle, a girl who was kept locked in a closet until she was 6 years old (Davis, 1947)? When she was finally released, her behavior was like that of an untrained animal. She didn't know how to speak, eat with utensils, use a toilet, or even smile. Her lack of interaction with other humans had prevented her from going through a process of *socialization*, the way in which we learn how to interact effectively in society. Isabelle's experience (and that of other children deprived of social interaction) indicates that human contact and social interaction are crucial for proper human development.

The Looking-Glass Self

Everyone around us influences our self-perception and our behavior in some way. The early symbolic interactionist Charles Horton Cooley (1902) described how others affect our self-image with the term *looking-glass self.* By this, he meant that we perceive ourselves based on how we *think* others see us. For instance, as professors, we often find ourselves experiencing the looking-glass self when teaching a class. It is part of the job of a professor to continuously discern whether or not students understand a lecture and are engaged with the subject matter. Often, when we look at our students and see blank expressions, we assume that this means the class does not understand what we are saying. We may react to this by re-explaining the concept or trying to find a new way to present it. But what if the students are exhibiting the blank expressions because the concept is simple and the professor has already spent too much time on it? (Or what if they look that way because it's how they look when they are watching television, and they have blurred the difference between a recorded broadcast and a live interaction?) What Cooley's looking-glass self demonstrates is that our actions and behaviors are reactions to our *interpretations* of the people, objects, and situations we encounter.

What matters in the above scenario is *not* what the students are actually thinking but what the professors *think* they are thinking. This interpretation leads to subsequent behaviors, in this case reiterating a concept that the students have already understood! Or we may misinterpret someone's sarcastic comment "Nice outfit!" as a sincere compliment and keep wearing the outfit because we think that the person loved it. Cooley's theory can best be summed up this way: "I am not what I think I am, and I am not what you think I am. I am what I think you think I am."

The Generalized Other

George Herbert Mead established a theory of social behavior to show how individuals' personalities are developed through social experience. According to Mead (1913), we develop a *self* (the part of our personality that is a combination of self-image and self-awareness) by (a) interacting with others through the use of symbols and (b) being able to see ourselves through the perspective of others. "It is out of this conduct and this consciousness that human society grows" (Mead, 1918, p. 578).

Eventually, through social interaction, we complete our creation of the social self by developing a sense of how we might be seen through the eyes of any person (the *generalized other*) who espouses the prevailing norms and values of the society in which we live. We find ourselves watching and judging our own actions through the eyes of this generalized other, even when no other person is present. If you are reading this book alone, start singing the words you read. Now think about how doing so makes you feel. Do you feel embarrassed? If so, you have just experienced the influence of the generalized other. You have interacted with others enough to know how most people would react to hearing you sing the words in this text. Most likely, you've adjusted your behavior accordingly and stopped singing.

Ultimately, as Mead showed, we internalize the awareness of how our behaviors *seem* socially. Our personal identities, therefore, contain our sense of who we are in society and how others perceive us. No self can develop without social interaction.

The Id, the Superego, and the Ego

Sigmund Freud developed a theory of personality in the early 1900s that has influenced almost all studies of human personality since then. A crucial part of his work was to explore the role of the *unconscious* in human identity and behavior. He broke down the unconscious into three sections: the id, the superego, and the ego. According to Freud (Freud & Strachey, 1949/1989), the *id* consists of people's innate desires and urges (which are primarily centered on instant gratification, especially through sex and violence). The *superego* is the part of our unconscious that has internalized the dominant norms and mores of society (particularly what constitutes "right" and "wrong" behavior). It represents our awareness of others, especially their reactions to ourselves. The *ego* works to balance the desires of the id with the moral impulses of the superego. The ego is the part of the self with which we choose to act or not act on our desires. For Freud, the ego is constantly testing our sense of what we want against our sense of what is expected of us. Freud (2005) believed that "it is impossible to overlook the extent to which civilization is built up upon a renunciation of instinct" (p. 85). We learn about the dominant norms of society and how to balance them with our innate desires through socialization with other human beings.

Primary Socializing Agents

Of course, some people make more of an impact on us humans than others. These people tend to constitute or come from one or more of the primary socialization agents in our society. Today in the United States, there are five primary socializing agents: family, peers, education, the media, and religion.

Family

We cannot choose our parents, but they do have a tremendous influence over who we become. For most of us, from the moment we are born, our family members—particularly our parents—are those with whom we interact first and for the greatest amount of time. Whether a parent constantly tells us that we are mean and stupid or repeatedly praises us for being so caring and brilliant (or anything in between) can largely determine how we view ourselves (as dumb or smart) and how we behave (meanly or kindly). Similarly, being encouraged to be persistent and to keep working at difficult things until we succeed, or being scoffed at for failing to do things quickly, affects how we will deal with challenging situations in the future. These lessons of socialization can influence what we become. For example, we are much more likely to put time and energy into our work if we believe that we are smart and capable and that persistence pays off than if we think we are neither bright nor professionally competent if we don't get it "right" the first time.

Socialization also teaches us what we want (values) and helps to give us a road map to achieve these things (norms). We are not *born* as authors, Muslims, leaders, Republicans, or _____ (fill in the blank). We *become* these things because our families and other socializing agents have socialized us into becoming them. Parents from different families in our country, town, or neighborhood, with different values and norms, socialize their children in different ways and into different sets of norms and values. Likewise, parents from different societies (with different values and norms) socialize their children in different ways. For example, parents in the United States are likely to teach their children to desire different things from what parents in other societies, such as Afghanistan, El Salvador, or even Canada, would teach.

Families also influence how we behave as public citizens. For example, young adults are more likely to vote if they have parents who vote and discuss political issues with them (Cicognani, Zani, Fournier, Gavray, & Bom, 2012; McIntosh, Hart, & Youniss, 2007). Engaged parents often shape engaged young Americans. Youth activists and Free The Children, Me to We, and We Day founders Craig and Marc Kielburger discuss the ways in which their parents encouraged them to be global citizens from a young age, and they offer great insight into how to raise civically engaged young people in their book *The World Needs Your Kid: How to Raise Children Who Care and Contribute* (Kielburger, Kielburger, & Page, 2009).

Peers

Our peers also have a great effect on how we view ourselves, how we interact with others, and what we become. Who hasn't wanted to impress one's friends, and who hasn't at some point or the other taken on some of the values and norms of one's peer group, even if sometimes they have contradicted the values of one's family? As soon as we are able to interact with people outside our family, we begin to be influenced by peers (those similar to us in terms of age, social class, etc.).

The children you played with in your neighborhood, school, sports teams, and so forth constituted your peer group as you were growing up. To varying degrees, our peers influence our self-perception and behavior in the same way our family does. It is through our associations with others who are "like us," our *peer reference group*, that we learn what people like us are like.

One website for a summer camp included a quote from a camper saying, "At school I'm a nerd, but here I'm cool." You have probably heard other stories of people growing up with two different peer groups (e.g., one that consists of classmates during the school year and one of camp mates or children in the area where one vacations during the summer). While researching this book, we became aware of one young man who remembers being perceived (and thinking of himself) as a cool kid and a jock when around summer friends and as a lonely loser when among school peers. As a result, he found himself acting out the roles attributed to him by the different groups. He kept to himself and was rather shy and aloof with his classmates, but he found himself leading his summer friends on wild adventures he never would have dreamed of pursuing during the school year. His self-perception actually became a self-fulfilling prophecy. He changed his behavior from one environment to the other to become the person he thought his peers saw. This young man's story is a great illustration of the looking-glass self. Both his self-perception and his behavior were strongly influenced by how he imagined his peers viewed him.

For an earlier book project, when Korgen (1999) interviewed people who have a black and a white parent, she found that even people's racial identity could be influenced by how they think others view them. Phillip, a biracial young man whose physical features did not clearly indicate his racial background, adapted his racial identity to avoid getting beaten up in some of the rough neighborhoods in which he grew up. He described how his experience in a Puerto Rican and black inner-city neighborhood influenced his racial identity in the following way:

> I got beat up by [some] black kids for being half-white. I started saying, "No, no, no. I'm Puerto Rican. I'm Puerto Rican. I'm Puerto Rican." And then, next thing I know, it's all cool because of the fact that my uncle married a Puerto Rican woman. Another uncle of mine married a Puerto Rican. So that's two different sets of interbreeding and families, Puerto Rican, blacks, till it's all Puerto Rican. . . . . . . I'm Puerto Rican. (p. 73)

Not only did Phillip change his declaration of racial identity, but he actually began also to believe that he was Puerto Rican instead of black and white. Supported by his Puerto Rican relatives and his ambiguous racial features, Phillip became Puerto Rican.

Likewise our attitudes can also be influenced by those around us. For example, whether or not your roommate or partner is cheery or gloomy can influence your own outlook on life. A study at the university of Notre Dame indicated that some students who started college with a positive attitude but were assigned a roommate with a negative attitude were showing signs that they were at risk for depression 6 months later. On the other hand, others who began college with a gloomy perspective on life but were assigned cheerful and positive roommates had developed a more positive thinking style after 6 months (Haeffel & Hames, 2013). The key point is that attitudes can be altered through interaction (Vedantam, 2013).

Education

Institutions have multiple roles. Our educational experiences play a major, though often somewhat hidden, role in our socialization process. Schools serve the primary purposes of giving us the tools we will need to operate in society and socializing us to adapt to and follow the values that society has deemed most important. Another goal of schools, which sociologists can uncover using their sociological eye, is to teach Americans a "hidden curriculum": to respect the rules of how our society operates, to not challenge the status quo, and to act in nondisruptive ways (ways that will not disrupt the dominant norms of society). For example, among the first things you learn in school are how to raise your hand, wait your turn, sit quietly, and follow directions. Many of these habits are useful skills that kids need to learn to interact with other people. Yet these same practices also reveal that schools teach the values of conformity and obedience to authority through the hidden curriculum (Gracey, 1967). School also teaches the basic values and beliefs of our dominant culture (as outlined in Chapter 4). What we learn about different racial, ethnic, gender, and social class groups through our schools and textbooks (or what we *don't* learn because the information in school curricula and texts is limited and carefully selected) influences how we perceive and judge these groups throughout our lives. It also helps us understand our own social status and role in society.

Dominant (or popular) values and beliefs determine, to a great extent, what is taught in our schools at any given time. It is important to remember that history is taught through the perspective of the dominant groups in our society. An examination of how the portrayal of U.S. history has changed over the years (as different racial or ethnic groups have gained power in the United States) reveals this fact. Comparing U.S. textbooks with those recounting the same events in European textbooks or Russian textbooks will also reveal this fact.

Media

The *media* refers to any instrument or "medium" that disseminates information on a wide scale. Among the various media outlets, television is arguably the most important socializing agent today. The average American spends more time than ever watching television (Nielsen, 2012; Ravichandran & de Bravo, 2010). In fact, the average American child spends more than 35 hours each week watching television, a 2.2-hour increase since 2009 (Rothman, 2013). During those hours, children are exposed to shows created by corporations to draw viewers to the advertisements they use to market their products before, during, and after the programs. Children's perspective of the world, therefore, is influenced to a considerable extent by a carefully selected set of images (in both the television shows and the advertisements) that are used to promote business for advertisers. Accurate or not, television shows are one of the major windows many Americans have on the world around them.

In a nation increasingly segregated by race, ethnicity, and social class, television shows are also often the only way some Americans are exposed to other groups of Americans. Our perceptions of different age, gender, racial, ethnic, and other groups, and our images of ourselves (remember the looking-glass self), are influenced by the way these groups are portrayed in the media.

Religion

Americans are, overall, much more religious than citizens of other wealthy nations. According to a 2012 poll, 37% of Americans say that they attend religious services at least once a week (Pew Forum on Religion &

Public Life, 2012). Meanwhile, less than 10% of residents of France and Germany and between 10% and 15% of residents of Belgium, the Netherlands, Luxembourg, and the United Kingdom are weekly churchgoers (Manchin, 2004), and regular church attendance continues to decline throughout Europe ("Europe's Irreligious," 2010).

Those who attend religious services and read religious writings are exposed to teachings about certain ways to view and act in the world that influence how they view themselves and interact with others. For example, many of the student activists who participated in the Freedom Summer during the civil rights era did so because they were motivated by the Christian ethic of brotherly love, which they learned from attending religious services and participating in religious organizations (McAdam, 1988). Similarly, Andrew Goodman and Michael Schwermer, both of whom were murdered in the violence of the Freedom Summer, were driven toward creating social justice by the values they learned through their Jewish upbringing.

In terms of civic activism, what may be as important as the message people receive from their religious leaders is their interactions with others in their religious community. Belonging to a religious group increases the number of friends people have and their opportunities and inducements to join in civic activities. There is a unique moral pressure to join the efforts of those in your faith community. As Robert Putnam puts it, "Being asked to do something by a member of your congregation is different from being asked to do something by a member of your bowling league" (as quoted in Burke, 2009).

However, the number of Americans unaffiliated with a religious group has climbed rather dramatically over the past few years. Today, approximately 20% of Americans and 33% of 18- to 24-year-olds are religiously unaffiliated. Approximately two thirds of the unaffiliated say that they believe in God. "Overwhelmingly, they think that religious organizations are too concerned with money and power, too focused on rules and too involved in politics" (Pew Forum on Religion & Public Life, 2012, p. 10). One of the latent negative consequences of these trends is that not being affiliated with a religious organization, as Putnam points out, means that they are not exposed to the types of organized civic engagement opportunities that often come with being a member of an organized religious group (as cited in Burke, 2009). As religious affiliation among young people continues to decline, it has become more important than ever that schools and universities provide civic engagement opportunities for students. Sociology courses offer one of the best vehicles for participation in society, as seen in the Sociologists in Action box.

Sociologists in Action: Donna Yang, Christian Agurto, Michelle Benavides, Brianne Glogowski, Deziree Martinez, and Michele Van Hook

In the following paragraphs, students at William Paterson University describe how they used the sociological tools they gained in their Principles of Sociology course to educate their classmates about Kiva, a microfinance project designed to aid women and diminish poverty globally, and to participate in the organization's efforts.

After enrolling in an introductory sociology course at William Paterson University, we collaborated to complete a group assignment that was designed to utilize various sociological concepts developed within the classroom. We designed a project after learning about Kiva, an organization dedicated to helping ordinary citizens like us to become lenders to entrepreneurs throughout the poorer areas of the world who are seeking microfinance. We sought not only to raise money toward a Kiva loan, but—more important—to generate awareness about microfinance's ability to empower women and help fight poverty. The website, www.kiva.org, is designed to facilitate partnerships between everyday people with a passion to give and low-income entrepreneurs seeking financial services. Kiva partners with a microfinance institution to provide small loans, typically ranging from $25 to $3,000, that are temporarily financed by Kiva users who have browsed the profiles of potential entrepreneurs uploaded on the website.

Although gender inequality was central to our class project, there were many other key sociological issues that were incorporated within its framework. The purpose of the assignment was to promote the application of the two "core commitments" of sociology—using the sociological eye and promoting social activism. Utilizing our collective sociological eye, we were able to look beneath the surface of society and recognize patterns of inequality intersecting along both class and gender lines. We realized that social stratification has created hierarchies through which women are marginalized economically, politically, and socially. Microfinance programs such as Kiva seek to mitigate this unequal access to wealth by creating greater accessibility for low-income individuals to financial services. In this way, they help to redistribute the accessibility of wealth across a wider spectrum of social classes.

As a group, we felt passionate about Kiva because of its commitment to improve society by providing more equal lending opportunities. We raised more than $150 toward a group loan for the communal bank Mujeres Progresistas

(Continued)

(Continued)

(Progressive Women) in Cuenca, Ecuador. This bank is composed of 11 women working to improve their household economic situations through their jobs. Our specific loan was distributed to 2 women—both mothers of four—seeking loans to help finance their personal businesses in order to help support their families. Maria Huerta, who lives in the San Joaquin area, will use this loan to invest in buying chickens and chicken feed to begin running a chicken farm. Maria Suqui, who lives in the Feria Libre area, will be using the loan to help establish a snack shop, through which she hopes to earn enough money to eventually own a home.

In order to promote awareness about our project and Kiva's initiatives, we also created informational pamphlets and distributed them to students on our college campus. The pamphlets explained microfinance, how Kiva utilizes this process of lending to help low-income individuals around the globe, and how students can get involved. Additionally, a PowerPoint was presented to peers enrolled within the Principles of Sociology class in hopes of inspiring other peer members to join Kiva's efforts. This project helped us to realize the importance of sociology, its applicability within everyday life, and our obligation to act as socially conscious individuals in order to help promote greater social justice, including gender justice.

SOURCE: Courtesy of Donna Yang.

EXERCISE 5.1   Family Influence and Civic Engagement

Think about how your family has influenced your level of civic engagement.

1. Did your parents and other family members discuss political issues with each other when they were around you (at the dinner table, over coffee, etc.)?

2. Did your parents and other family members discuss political issues with you when you were growing up? Do you discuss political issues with them now? Why or why not?

3. If you answered yes to Question 2, have they asked you to participate in political activities with them? Have you? If so, in what ways? How did those experiences influence your own view of the importance of civic engagement?

(Continued)

(Continued)

4. If your parents and other family members are not active citizens, why do you think they are not? What do you think might encourage them to become active?

5. Overall, how do you think your parents' and other family members' level of civic engagement affected your own level of civic engagement?

6. After taking a moment to really evaluate the implications of this, describe how you feel about your own level of civic engagement.

7. How will you influence your own children's political participation (when or if you have kids)?

EXERCISE 5.2   Your Many Selves

Everyone acts (at least somewhat) differently among different groups of people. Write a one-page essay describing different situations in your life in which you act almost as though you are different people (different versions of yourself). Why do you act differently in these different situations? What role do you think the generalized other (Mead) and the looking-glass self (Cooley) play in socializing you into these different roles? Be sure to define these terms in your paper before you give examples of them and dig beneath the surface in your analysis.

EXERCISE 5.3   Peers and Civic Engagement

Think about how your peers have influenced your level of civic engagement.

1. Do your peers discuss political issues with each other when they are around you?

2. Did your peers discuss political issues with you when you were growing up? Do you discuss political issues with your peers now? Why or why not?

3. Do your peers vote? Have you ever gone to the polls with a peer? If so, what was that like?

(Continued)

(Continued)

4. Are your peers civically active? If yes, in what ways? Have they asked you to participate with them? Have you? If so, in what ways? How did those experiences influence your own view of the importance of civic engagement? If they have asked you to participate with them and you didn't, why didn't you? What do you think you might have lost out on by not participating? If your peers are not active citizens, why do you think they are not? What do you think might encourage them to become active?

5. Overall, how do you think your peers' level of civic engagement has affected your own activism?

Extra credit: Read "Young People Vote" at http://www.rockthevote.com/about/press-room/electronic-press-kit/youth-vote-stats.pdf. Having read this, does it change your perceptions about (a) the importance of voting, (b) whether you might vote in the upcoming elections, or (c) the ways you and your peers talk (or don't talk) about politics?

| EXERCISE 5.4 | The Hidden Curriculum: History, Values, and Socialization |

Find a U.S. history book currently used at a local public grammar, middle, or high school.

1. Note the title of the book. What image does the title convey? Is there a photograph or illustration on the cover of the book? If so, what message does it convey?

2. Look at the Table of Contents. What topics are covered? Think of five additional chapters you think could or should have been included in the book. Why do you think they could or should have been included? Why do you think they were not included? What does your study of this textbook tell you, sociologically, about the values that the school's curriculum indicates are most important? Besides the need to keep textbooks a certain length, why else do you think certain topics have not been included?

3. Compare how different racial, ethnic, gender, and social class groups are covered (or not covered) in the book.

(Continued)

(Continued)

4. Compare the Civil War chapter in the history book you obtained with Howard Zinn's chapter on the Civil War in his book *A People's History of the United States, 1492–Present* (2003). Your school library should have a copy, or you can find it online at http://libcom.org/a-peoples-history-of-the-united-states-howard-zinn/10-the-other-civil-war. What are the similarities? What are the differences? How do you think the differences relate to the "hidden curriculum" of the public school system in the United States?

5. How do you think members of different races and ethnicities, genders, and social classes would view their respective status positions and roles in society after reading each of the two chapters? What might they say is missing? What might they want to add?

EXERCISE 5.5   College and (Re)Socialization

Think back to when you were first accepted to college. As soon as you learned which college you would be attending, you most likely embarked on anticipatory socialization, during which you began to rehearse the new roles you would carry out as a college student. College is often a time for resocialization, when students learn to adapt to a different subculture and establish a new social identity. As noted in Chapter 4, college life in general, and each individual institution of higher learning in particular, has its own subculture or microculture. Each college has its unique set of norms, values, and artifacts, which students must become familiar with and adjust to in order to interact effectively on campus.

College, especially for students who attend a school with few, if any, people from their hometown, provides an opportunity to establish a new sense of self. For example, a shy, aloof high school student can become an outgoing, popular college student (or a popular high school student can become a shy college student) in the new setting of the college campus. Students have a chance to establish a new "self" when they are surrounded by people who have no preconceived view of them. Often, college can be like the summer camp experience of the boy, described above, who acted almost like a different person depending on whether he was with his school classmates or his summer friends.

The degree of resocialization needed in college depends on the student's particular environment. For example, a commuter student attending college for the first time will undergo less resocialization than a residential student

(Continued)

(Continued)

because he or she will be involved only in some aspects of the culture of the campus. Moreover, a young adult who is active in a civic organization 2 days a week, such as volunteering at a local nursing home or becoming an officer in a student group with a mission to create social change, will learn some new norms and values and become familiar with some new artifacts. This activity, though, will not necessarily completely change his or her sense of self. However, those who enter a total institution (a setting in which all parts of one's life are directed by the institution), such as the military or a prison, will undergo a more complete process of resocialization as they learn to adapt to a very different, all-encompassing environment. Their sense of who they are and how they are perceived by others changes radically as they adapt to this new environment.

1. Describe how you became resocialized when you began college. In doing so, be sure to answer the questions that follow.

2. What were some of the norms, values, and artifacts with which you had to become acquainted when you started college?

3. How do you think your status as a residential or commuter student affected your degree of resocialization?

4. How do you think your age, race, social class, and gender affected your degree of resocialization?

5. If you are in the military or are a veteran, describe how that has affected your degree of resocialization in college.

6. How did the college resocialization process influence your sense of self?

EXERCISE 5.6   **Coverage of Social Activism on Television News Programs**

For this assignment, you will be conducting a content analysis of 10 news programs. Your focus will be on how these news programs cover social activism. Make 10 copies of the Content Coding Sheet (Figure 5.1). You will fill these charts in as you view your news programs. As you fill out these charts, there are a few rules:

(Continued)

(Continued)

1. You must view news programs during the same time slots (e.g., early morning, midmorning, afternoon, prime time, late night) on one particular channel (e.g., ABC, NBC, CNBC, CNN, Fox News, CBS, PBS, BBC).

2. All 10 programs should be either local or national and international.

3. After having filled out your Content Coding Sheets, you will fill out your Data Summary Sheet (Figure 5.1). This will give you the overall numbers and percentages.

4. Once you have completed the data collection, join with three other members of your class to analyze your collective data (making sure that not all the members of your groups analyze the same news programs). What do your results tell you about how social activism is portrayed on the news programs you examined? What does this tell you about how we are socialized to view social activists and social activism? Why do you think the media portrays activism this way? What is missing from the portrayals of activists and activism? Is there a "hidden curriculum" in what we learn from the media?

Figure 5.1   Content Coding and Data Summary Sheet

Content Coding Sheet

Type of social activism: _____

Name of news program: _____

Station viewed on (provide channel and network): _____

Local or national/international: _____

Time of day (AM or PM): _____

Note the number of examples of social activism covered and note the type—for example, (a) violent or peaceful, (b) disruptive or nondisruptive—and how it is portrayed (positively or negatively) by checking under the appropriate columns.

(Continued)

Figure 5.1 (Continued)

Examples of Activism	Violent	Peaceful	Disruptive	Nondisruptive	Positively	Negatively
1.						
2.						
3.						
4.						
5.						

Data Summary Sheet

News program: _____

Station/network: _____

Local or national/international: _____

Time of day: _____

Type of Activism	Number Portrayed	
	Positively	Negatively
Violent		
Peaceful		
Disruptive		
Nondisruptive		
Total		

NOTE: Reproduction authorized only for students who purchase this book.

EXERCISE 5.7   Young Voters Matter

Listen to "Young Voters," an interview with Andy MacCracken, the executive director of the National Campus Leadership Council, at http://www.c-span video.org/program/311416-4, and then answer the following questions:

1. What were the main points discussed in this video? Were you aware of them before? Why or why not?

(Continued)

(Continued)

2. What questions from callers particularly interested you? Annoyed you? Why? How do they relate to the ideological divide in politics today?

3. Based on both your own experiences and what you learned in this video, if you were to advise a presidential candidate on how to turn out the college student vote, what would you suggest that he or she do?

DISCUSSION QUESTIONS

1. Think of the five primary socializing agents. Now rank order them from the one that influenced you the most (#1) to the one that influenced you the least (#5). Now, explain why you ranked them this way. How do you think you would be a different person if you had never interacted with #1?

2. Think about Cooley's concept of the looking-glass self. Do you see yourself as someone who can make a positive impact on society? Why or why not? In what ways has your own looking-glass self experience influenced this?

3. How do you think those with whom you interact the most affect your attitude? Do they make you more cheerful and positive or more gloomy and negative? Why? How do you think you affect their attitudes? How does this reflection help you to better understand how interactions can influence attitudes?

4. Which primary socializing agents could most effectively foster civic engagement across the United States? Why?

5. What worldwide socializing agents might effectively encourage civic engagement across the globe?

6. Which of the following sociological theories—conflict, functionalist, or symbolic interactionist—would you find most useful if you were to conduct a study on political participation in the United States? Why?

7. Have your values and norms about environmental issues, such as recycling or global warming (or the views of someone close to you), changed in recent years? If so, what were the social forces that led to this resocialization process?

8. Do you think you will go through a resocialization process after college? Why or why not?

9. When you became resocialized after starting college, did your political activism increase, decrease, or remain the same? Why? How does the culture of your college affect your response to this question?

10. How do you think we can create a society in which citizens are better socialized to become knowledgeable and effective participants and agents of social change?

SUGGESTIONS FOR SPECIFIC ACTIONS

1. Determine whether or not your college or university has committed itself to the educating citizens movement and whether it has taken steps to teach its students to become knowledgeable, effective citizens. One way to do this is to find out if your president or provost has signed the Campus Compact pledge (found at http://www .compact.org/resources-for-presidents/presidents-declaration-on-the-civic-responsi bility-of-higher-education), joined the American Democracy Project (http://www .aascu.org/programs/adp), or signed on to some other such initiative to promote civic engagement in higher education. If he or she has, then compare the goals of the initiative with the results you see on campus. Write a letter to your provost or president and your school newspaper that includes the results of your research. If your school has not embarked on such a mission, write a letter to your provost or president explaining what the educating citizens movement is about (after having looked at the Campus Compact and American Democracy Project websites) and asking what steps your school has taken to encourage well-informed and effective citizens.

2. Explore the institutional connections your college or university has established with the surrounding community (e.g., service-learning courses, school-sponsored community centers, school-sponsored tutorial programs, research partnerships between professors and community members, etc.), and write a letter to your local paper that summarizes your key findings (to help inform the campus and community about these matters).

3. Participate in one of the events your university uses to connect to the local community (sponsoring a community fair, volunteering to work in a soup kitchen or a local school, etc.). Use your sociological eye to examine the power dynamics behind how the event or program is coordinated through the school and community. For example, who designed the program (the school, community, or both)? Who coordinates the program? Who has authority over the program? Who funds the program? How do you think this type of coordination influences the overall program?

4. Set up an interview with the person who coordinates the orientation program for first-year students at your university. Inquire as to (a) how orientation socializes students into successfully learning and adopting the campus rules, norms, and values and (b) what mechanisms are used during the orientation process to socialize new students into the role of educated and engaged citizens. If no such mechanisms exist (or the ones that do exist are inadequate), offer some suggestions about what could be put into place to the person who coordinates the first-year orientation program.

   Please go to this book's website at http://study.sagepub.com/korgen5e to find further civic engagement opportunities, resources, peer-reviewed articles, and updated web links related to this chapter.

REFERENCES

Burke, D. (2009, May 14). Religious citizens more involved—and more scarce? *USA Today*. Retrieved http://usatoday30.usatoday.com/news/religion/2009-05-14-church-community_N.htm

Cicognani, E., Zani, B., Fournier, B., Gavray, C., & Bom, M. (2012). Gender differences in youths' political engagement and participation: The role of parents and of adolescents' social and civic participation. *Journal of Adolescence, 35*(3), 561–576.

Cooley, C. H. (1902). *Human nature and the social order*. New York, NY: Schocken Books.

Davis, K. (1947). Final note on a case of extreme isolation. *American Journal of Sociology, 52*(5), 432–437.

Europe's irreligious. (2010, August 9). *The Economist*. Retrieved from http://www .economist.com/blogs/dailychart/2010/08/religious_attendance

Freud, S. (2005). *Civilization and its discontents*. New York, NY: W. W. Norton.

Freud, S., & Strachey, J. (Eds.). (1989). *The ego and the id* (J. Riviere, Trans.). New York, NY: W. W. Norton. (Original work published 1949)

Gracey, H. L. (1967). Learning the student role: Kindergarten as academic boot camp. In D. Wrong & H. L. Gracey (Eds.), *Readings in introductory sociology* (3rd ed., pp. 215–226). New York, NY: Macmillan.

Haeffel, G. J., & Hames, J. L. (2013, April 16). Cognitive vulnerability to depression can be contagious [Online]. *Clinical Psychological Science*. doi:10.1177/2167702613 485075. Retrieved from http://cpx.sagepub.com/content/early/2013/04/15/2167702 613485075.full.pdf+html

Kielburger, C., Kielburger, M., & Page, S. (2009). *The world needs your kid: How to raise children who care and contribute*. Vancouver, BC, Canada: Greystone Books.

Korgen, K. O. (1999). *From black to biracial: Transforming racial identity among Americans*. Westport, CT: Praeger.

Lockhart, S. (2011). Active learning for infants and toddlers. *Resource, 30*(1), 5–10.

Manchin, R. (2004, September 21). *Religion in Europe: Trust not filling the pews* (Gallup.com). Retrieved from http://www.gallup.com/poll/13117/Religion-Europe-Trust-Filling-Pews.aspx

McAdam, D. (1988). *Freedom summer*. New York, NY: Oxford University Press.

McIntosh, H., Hart, D., & Youniss, J. (2007). The influence of family political discussion on youth civic development: Which parent qualities matter? *Political Science & Politics, 40*(3), 495–499.

Mead, G. H. (1913). The social self. *Journal of Philosophy, Psychology, and Scientific Methods, 10*, 374–380.

Mead, G. H. (1918). The psychology of punitive justice. *American Journal of Sociology, 23*, 577–602.

Messinger, D. (2005). A measure of early joy? Afterword to the republication of "All Smiles Are Positive, but Some Smiles Are More Positive Than Others." In P. Ekman & E. Rosenberg (Eds.), *What the face reveals: Studies of spontaneous facial expression using the Facial Action Coding System (FACS)* (2nd ed., pp. 350–353). New York, NY: Oxford University Press.

Nielsen. (2012). *Television measurement*. Retrieved from http://www.nielsen.com/us/en/measurement/television-measurement.html

Pew Forum on Religion & Public Life. (2012, October 9). *"Nones" on the rise: One-in-five adults have no religious affiliation*. Retrieved from http://www.pewforum.org/uploadedFiles/Topics/Religious_Affiliation/Unaffiliated/NonesOnTheRise-full.pdf

Ravichandran, P., & de Bravo, B. F. (2010, June). *Young children and screen time (television, DVDs, computer)* (National Research Center for Women and Families). Retrieved from http://www.center4research.org/2010/05/young-children-and-screen-time-television-dvds-computer

Rothman, L. (2013, November 20). FYI, parents: Your kids watch a full-time job's worth of TV each week. *Time*. Retrieved from http://entertainment.time.com/2013/11/20/fyi-parents-your-kids-watch-a-full-time-jobs-worth-of-tv-each-week/

Vedantam, S. (2013, June 24). *Gloomy thinking can be contagious*. Retrieved from http://www.npr.org/blogs/health/2013/06/24/193483931/Contagious-Thinking-Can-Be-Depressing

Venezia, M., Messinger, D. S., Thorp, D., & Mundy, P. (2004). The development of anticipatory smiling. *Infancy, 6*(3), 397–406.

Zinn, H. (2003). *A people's history of the United States, 1492–present*. New York, NY: HarperCollins.

6

Deviant Behavior and
Social Movements

What would be your reaction if you saw a man dressed in knee-length pants, wearing a wig, and snorting tobacco? Would you think his behavior is deviant? Probably! However, sniffing tobacco and wearing a wig and breeches were once considered normal for men. In fact, in colonial America, engaging in such behavior demonstrated high social status. Our understanding of what is deviant behavior is socially constructed and, therefore, changes over time and from society to society.

Although behaviors such as incest and killing innocent people are considered deviant in almost all societies, much else of what is considered deviant behavior varies across cultures and time periods. Notions of what constitutes deviant behavior can also be situational. There are circumstances in which acts that would normally be considered completely beyond the bounds of acceptable behavior, including many brutal acts of violence, can come to be seen as normal and appropriate. For example, soldiers' reports and memoirs frequently include accounts of acts that may seem unjustifiable once the fighting has ended but had seemed acceptable, even necessary, in the midst of it. This chapter will discuss (a) how deviance is defined, (b) how the three major theoretical perspectives and other theories view deviance, (c) why some social groups are labeled as deviant, and (d) how some social movements have changed society by "normalizing" behavior that had previously been thought of as deviant.

As you will recall from Chapter 4, cultural norms are socially constructed expectations for behavior. A society's norms include basic behaviors, manners and etiquette, and laws and legal code and follow the society's unique culture and ways of doing things. As members of a society, we learn which behaviors are appropriate through socialization. Our actions are guided by how we see others behave, what we are taught by our socializing agents, and the reactions of those with whom we interact.

Folkways are norms that are enforced through *informal rewards* and *sanctions* (e.g., approval or disapproval from others). For example, we follow folkways when we hold the door for someone behind us, let people we speak with finish their sentences without interruption, and make conversation with people we meet at parties. Violating these folkways might result in a dirty look or being considered rude, socially awkward, or strange. However, this type of deviant behavior hardly ever results in serious social consequences and never results in legal repercussions.

Mores, on the other hand, are those norms related to behaviors that reflect the values society holds most dear. Good sportsmanship, abiding by social and legal contracts, and adhering to certain sexual behaviors are all mores. Violating these norms results in much stronger reactions and, perhaps, criminal charges (many mores are supported by laws). For example, refusing to support a colleague in need, cheating on a girlfriend or boyfriend, or openly announcing you are bisexual often results in people expressing strong reactions that can have negative repercussions (e.g., being labeled as "not a team player" at work, being labeled as untrustworthy and selfish by friends, or being thought of as sexually abnormal by some).

Violations of our most powerful mores, those representing our deepest values (e.g., confining sexual relations to those not closely related, limiting our meat eating to animals rather than other humans), are called *taboos*. Incest—sexual relations between close family members—is a taboo in almost all societies. Cannibalism—the practice of eating humans—is also widely considered to be a taboo. Those who carry out such acts are regarded as socially repugnant and face widespread, if not universal, condemnation from the other members of their society.

Laws are norms that are formalized rules of behavior enacted by legislatures and enforced by formal sanctions carried out by the criminal and civil justice systems. Laws provide guidelines as to what people should do (e.g., drivers should stop at stop signs, citizens should pay taxes, parents should send their children to school) and what they should *not* do (e.g., commit rape, robbery, or insurance fraud, or possess or use certain drugs). Those who break laws are subject to fines, imprisonment, and possibly even capital punishment.

Functionalism and Deviance

Émile Durkheim (1895/1982) established the functionalist perspective on deviance. He maintained that deviant acts and those who commit them actually serve several useful and necessary purposes, or functions, for society. Deviants can help make the norms of society clearer to the majority population, unite the nondeviant members of society, and even promote social change.

Sometimes, it is difficult to know what the norms of society are until we see someone punished for violating one. When some members of society are punished for committing deviant acts, the rules of society are clarified and reinforced for everyone. For example, seeing someone pulled over for speeding usually makes other drivers slow down. Observing a classmate punished for plagiarism helps students recognize that stealing someone else's words or ideas is unacceptable behavior and that those who do so are liable to be punished. We already know that speeding and plagiarism are wrong, but seeing these mores violated reminds us of how important it is to abide by these rules and often (if only through fear of being punished) causes us to act as society wishes.

Bridging and Bonding Social Capital

According to Durkheim (1895/1982), deviants can also unify members of society. When people see deviant behavior as a threat, they come together to punish and root out the deviant members of society. United, they can create *social capital*, a network of interconnected people who can rely on one another and work together to accomplish a goal. For example, in the mid-1990s, the parishioners of St. Patrick's parish in Brockton, Massachusetts, became closely united when they organized to confront a prostitution and drug operation headquartered in abandoned buildings across the street from the church. The criminal activity centered in the abandoned buildings made the parishioners fearful when they came to church, and they were tired of being afraid. They knew that they really had to do something when the pastor was propositioned by a prostitute on the way to Mass! Working together, they compelled the city to take over the houses (in lieu of back taxes owed), raze them, and drive out those using them for deviant acts that made the parishioners fear going to church.

The experience of eliminating the deviants from their church neighborhood *bonded* the parishioners more closely as they learned that they could rely on one another and become a powerful force when united. The members of St. Patrick's parish were also able to make connections across the city of

Brockton and join with the members of different religious organizations to address safety issues, such as crime, that all Brocktonians faced. In doing so, they showed the power of what is known as *bridging* social capital. They were able to make connections (bridges) among different religious groups in Brockton that enabled them to begin to know and work with one another effectively (social capital).

Social capital is often a positive force. But when it works to bond members of a particular group to one another and isolate them from everyone else, rather than work as a bridge between groups, it can have negative effects. For example, crime rates in counties with greater percentages of residents affiliated with Evangelical Protestant churches are consistently higher than those in counties with relatively high numbers of mainline Protestants and Catholics. Evangelical churches tend to create *bonding* social networks that unite their members but isolate them from the larger society, whereas mainline Protestants and Catholics tend to promote bridging social networks that connect them to other groups in the larger community. These bridging networks allow members of different groups to unite and develop effective structures to combat and prevent criminal behavior (Beyerlein & Hipp, 2005).

Likewise, high levels of bonding capital among gang members can also lead to high crime rates in certain neighborhoods. Gang members bound to their fellow members can be a powerful force of negative deviant behavior (Choi & Sloane, 2012). Police officers know very well how difficult it is to combat gangs with high levels of bonding capital, which tie them to one another and isolate them from the larger society simultaneously.

Rational Choice Theory and Crime

According to *rational choice* theorists, people decide to either commit or not commit crimes based on the perceived costs and benefits of such behavior. If the punishment for crime is fairly certain and harsh and the rewards for good behavior are reliable and enticing enough, crime rates are generally relatively low. Some areas though, such as the city of New Orleans, have high crime rates. The violent crime rate in New Orleans in 2012 was more than twice the national average (City-Data.com, 2014). There are few rewards for good behavior in New Orleans. The former mayor Ray Nagin was recently convicted of taking bribes when in office. The poverty level in the city is more than double the national average. Meanwhile, many years of police corruption have left residents wary of trusting the police (Guarino, 2012). The present mayor, Mitch Landrieu, is aware of the problem and is trying to take steps to address it. He realizes the need for alternative opportunities for residents and for proper social controls on both the population and the police to bring down the high crime rates (Finn, 2012). Landrieu's office has established the NOLA for Life plan, with multifaceted goals such as the following:

1. Stop the shootings

2. Invest in prevention

3. Promote jobs and opportunity

4. Get involved and rebuild neighborhoods

5. Improve the New Orleans Police Department.

Mayor Landrieu credits the NOLA for Life plan with the 20% reduction in murders in 2013 (Harper, 2013; Martin, 2014).

Conflict Theory and Deviance

As you will recall from Chapter 2, Marxist and other conflict theorists maintain that society is made up of groups competing for power. In turn, they believe that norms and laws are largely created by and for the benefit of those who hold the most power in society. Marx argued that the members of the ruling class (the owners of the means of production) use every instrument at their disposal, including shaping norms and laws, to protect their interests. Therefore, the actions of the poor are more likely to be labeled as deviant and criminal than those of rich individuals or major corporations.

In *The Rich Get Richer and the Poor Get Prison*, Jeffrey Reiman uses the conflict perspective to argue that the criminal justice system is biased against poor people and is in favor of wealthy individuals and corporations (Reiman & Leighton, 2010). He maintains that corporations actually do much more harm to society by committing acts that are not officially labeled "criminal" than do individuals by committing acts that are considered crimes. For example, unsafe workplaces (e.g., leading to black lung disease, asbestos-based cancer, repetitive-motion injuries, or preventable deaths or injuries due to cave-ins in coal mines), unsafe medical practices (e.g., unnecessary surgeries, lack of proper medical care, prescribing combinations of drugs leading to drug interactions), environmental pollution (e.g., from cigarettes, from chemical and industrial factories), and lax oversight of consumer safety (e.g., defective tires, tainted meat) harm far more people than criminal acts carried out by individuals. However, they are relatively ignored by the judicial system, whereas the crimes of predominantly poor and minority citizens result in disproportionately severe punishments.

Symbolic Interactionism and Deviance

Symbolic interactionists maintain that people learn to conform to or deviate from the norms of society through their interactions with others. They stress that deviance is socially constructed and that deviant behavior is learned. Two of the most well-known theories on deviance that fall under the umbrella of the symbolic interactionist perspective are differential association theory and labeling theory.

Through his *differential association theory*, Edwin Sutherland (1947) maintained that people learn deviant behavior by associating with people who commit deviant acts. People tend to base their own behavior on the behavior of those with whom they interact. Therefore, those who are raised in families that violate social norms or spend much of their time with friends who break the norms of society will be more likely than others to act in deviant ways. For instance, Jonathan was involved in a mentoring program, Friends and Mentors for Change, for inner-city youth who are at high risk of not graduating from high school. His initial research results revealed that when these kids, who face negative situations at their schools or homes, are surrounded by external forces that may influence them in negative ways, they are much more likely to commit deviant acts than when they are spending time in the Friends and Mentors for Change program, surrounded by more positive role models.

Labeling theory, another symbolic interactionist perspective on deviance, focuses on the categorization of people as deviant. Howard Becker (1963), the founder of labeling theory, maintained that behaviors and individuals *become* deviant only when people with some social power *label* them as deviant. Once people so labeled accept this categorization, they begin to consider themselves deviant and act accordingly. For example, when a young woman becomes known to others as a drug addict, is ostracized by those who do not use illegal drugs, and is given the label "druggie," she begins to socialize more and more with fellow druggies and act like the druggie that people perceive her to be. We can see the effects of this on high school campuses when kids who have been given a label that makes them outcasts (e.g., "loser," "nerd," "burnout") begin to take on the qualities of that label, sometimes with violent results.

Labeling Some Social Groups as Deviant

As noted above, deviance is a *social construction*, which means that behaviors are not in themselves normal or deviant; they become deviant only when society defines them as such. Unfortunately, it is easy and common to define or perceive entire groups of people as deviant rather than merely defining specific behaviors as deviant acts. For instance, *racial profiling* is a controversial practice in law enforcement that involves subjecting people to greater scrutiny, or treating some people as potentially dangerous, based on stereotypes and prejudices associated with their perceived race.

The state of New Jersey became a focal point for a national debate on racial profiling in the 1990s. Black motorists complained, and an independent review confirmed, that they were being pulled over for routine traffic stops, and even searches, far more often than members of other racial and ethnic groups and often without cause (Lamberth, 1994). A whole new term has even entered our collective lexicon to describe this unfair treatment: *driving while black*. A series of reviews followed, including a number of hearings in the New Jersey State Senate, resulting in the establishment of guidelines for law enforcement officers that point out that "any officer can unwittingly or subconsciously fall prey to racial or ethnic stereotypes about who is more likely to be involved in criminal activity" (New Jersey Division of Criminal Justice, n.d., para. 5) and mandate that officers work to counter this fact by focusing on people's conduct rather than their racial or ethnic appearance (New Jersey Division of Criminal Justice, 2009). Police efforts still seem to disproportionately focus on racial minorities. For example, the New York City Police Department's "stop and frisk" policy seems to target racial minorities. In 2011, 87% of the 684,330 people stopped and questioned on the street by New York City police officers were either black or Hispanic. "Ten percent of the stops led to arrests or summonses and 1 percent to the recovery of a weapon" (Elignon, 2012, para. 15). In 2013, a judge declared the practice unconstitutional, saying that "the city adopted a policy of indirect racial profiling by targeting racially defined groups for stops based on local crime suspect data" (Goldstein, 2013).

Police and other law enforcement agencies have many forms of profiling at their disposal, most of which focus on behavior. A Rand Corporation commentary, "Racial Profiling: Lessons From the Drug War" (Riley, 2002), criticizes racial profiling as ineffective. The report advocates "tactical profiling," which would focus on behaviors rather than identities. Law enforcement personnel using tactical profiling would look for reasons *not* to suspect people when making otherwise random stops and searches, rather than focusing on reasons to target people.

Deviance and Organizing for Change

It is useful for the well-being and maintenance of society to construct norms and to recognize forms of deviance. Without these, people would need to navigate the basic rules of behavior in every situation they enter. How inefficient and chaotic that would be! However, social norms that reinforce the worldviews and interests of dominant groups (those in power) often act as repressive forces against the worldviews and interests of minority groups and all those who choose to deviate (even in harmless ways) from the dominant culture. Once a perspective takes on the veneer of "reality" or "truth" or "the right way," it is difficult to change. Usually, only concerted, organized effort can effectively counter such social forces. And the history of the United States is full of people doing just that—coming together to create the changes they desire for society.

In addition to noting how deviants can help bind the nondeviant members of society together, Durkheim (1895/1982) also maintained that deviants can promote social change. He believed that societies would stagnate if they did not change and that all social change begins with deviance. Laws that do more harm than good for society must be violated. Society needs people willing to break them. U.S. and world history is replete with examples of social deviants, such as women fighting for equal rights, American revolutionaries (before the war for independence was won), and civil rights leaders, who became heroes by protesting against and helping overturn unjust laws and governments. For example, Mildred Jeter, a black woman, and Richard Loving, a white man, were considered criminals when they married in 1958, in violation of the law in their state of Virginia that prohibited interracial marriage. However, their protest against this unjust law resulted in the 1967 Supreme Court decision (*Loving v. Virginia*) that declared such laws unconstitutional, leading to a tremendous increase in the number of interracial marriages in the United States.

The U.S. civil rights movement is probably the most famous example of people performing deviant acts to organize for social change. Before that movement, segregation laws in many areas of the country prohibited black Americans from using the same facilities or drinking from the same water fountains as white Americans. Under the "separate but equal" laws, blacks were relegated to inferior schools. During the 1876–1965 "Jim Crow" era in the South, local and state laws in that part of the country mandated racial segregation. Black people were harassed when attempting to vote during the period as well. Some were the victims of violence, and others were simply turned away without being allowed to cast their votes. Jim Crow laws also imposed a large variety of other restrictions on black people that limited their rights in areas such as the workplace, schools, housing, transportation systems, parks, public swimming pools, and various business establishments. Anyone breaking these laws was considered deviant and deserving of legal punishment. It took many decades of struggle, culminating in the civil rights movement of the 1950s and 1960s, to make opposing racism a socially approved, rather than a deviant, act.

Rosa Parks, famous for her refusal to give up her bus seat to a white person, was not the only black person arrested in 1955 for violating segregation laws, but hers was the perfect "test case" to take to the Supreme Court. She was poised, respectable, and fully prepared for the negative publicity. "People always say that I didn't give up my seat because I was tired, but that isn't true," Rosa Parks (1992) wrote. "No, the only tired I was, was tired of giving in" (p. 116). Parks, an elected officer of the local chapter of the National Association for the Advancement of Colored People, had been part of the group of activists who were strategizing the best way to challenge the segregation laws, not just in court but in public awareness too. She had not planned on getting arrested that day, but when she was told to move, she recognized the opportunity. By allowing herself to be taken off the bus by the police, she provided the spark for a campaign that had already started to challenge the laws that made black Americans second-class citizens.

Parks and other activists formed the Montgomery Improvement Association, a coalition of local groups, including several church organizations, whose purpose was to demand the desegregation of buses without appearing to be too radical or threatening. A young pastor with no known enemies or personal agenda, Dr. Martin Luther King Jr., was selected to head the campaign. Despite the hardships that poor people faced, getting to work each day without public transportation, threats from motorists as they walked along the roads, and warnings that they would lose their jobs if they could not get to work each day on time, the black citizens of Montgomery organized themselves effectively and boycotted the buses for more than a year. By the time they won their case in court, they had also fostered a national reexamination of the status of black people in America. Although African Americans still face routine de facto (meaning in practice, though not in law) segregation, discrimination, and racial insults, the Montgomery bus boycott helped mobilize the tremendous effort to tear down the laws that supported and "normalized" such actions.

Organizing for Environmental Change

Today, norms are being challenged to address global climate change (also known as global warming). In towns and on campuses across the United States, the norms of cranking up the heat or air conditioning and throwing away trash have been replaced with efforts to conserve energy and recycle all that citizens can. Though we have long been dependent on coal, our growing awareness of the devastating impact of coal by-products has made the "standard," black smoke–spewing coal plant a symbol of criminal negligence by corporations and the U.S. Environmental Protection Agency (EPA), which many people now view as having failed to use its full power to protect the environment. In 2008, frustrated at the inaction of the federal government, 12 states sued the EPA for violating the Clean Air Act by not setting standards to control greenhouse gas emissions in new vehicles.[1] The Supreme Court ruled that the EPA must regulate greenhouse gases. The EPA under the Obama administration has agreed to do so, declaring that such emissions "threaten the public health and welfare of current and future generations" (Woodside, 2009, para. 1).

The former U.S. vice president Al Gore and the United Nations' Intergovernmental Panel on Climate Change (IPCC) won the 2007 Nobel Peace Prize for their efforts to bring the impending environmental, social, and political catastrophes of global warming to the public's attention. The IPCC, a group of 1,300 independent scientific experts from nations all over the world, maintains that human actions are fostering climate change on Earth that will likely have a dramatic impact on the planet. While climate change has occurred throughout the history of the Earth, the Industrial Revolution sparked a dramatic increase in the production of heat-trapping gases, which if left unchecked will lead to drastic environmental and social upheaval (IPCC, 2007, 2012).

The fifth assessment report by the IPCC (2013) states,

Warming of the climate system is unequivocal, and since the 1950s, many of the observed changes are unprecedented over decades to millennia. The atmosphere and ocean have warmed, the amounts of snow and ice have diminished, sea level has risen, and the concentrations of greenhouse gases have increased. (p. 3)

The atmospheric concentrations of carbon dioxide (CO_2), methane, and nitrous oxide have increased to levels unprecedented in at least the last 800,000 years. CO_2 concentrations have increased by 40% since pre-industrial times, primarily from fossil fuel emissions and secondarily from net land use change emissions. The ocean has absorbed about 30% of the emitted anthropogenic carbon dioxide, causing ocean acidification. (p. 7)

Continued emissions of greenhouse gases will cause further warming and changes in all components of the climate system. Limiting climate change will require substantial and sustained reductions of greenhouse gas emissions. (p. 14)

Other studies indicate that warmer ocean temperatures will lead to higher levels of mercury in fish, as the metabolism of fish increases in warmer waters and they eat more. Mercury in humans has been connected to medical issues such as heart attacks, high blood pressure, and learning disabilities in children (Dijkstra et al., 2013; Fears, 2013).

Most nations have outlined plans and/or already taken clear steps to reduce greenhouse gas emissions; yet in the United States, fewer than half of all Americans believe that dealing with global climate change should be a high priority for the nation, and few political leaders discuss it (Knight, Robins, Clover, & Saravanan, 2011; Pew Research Center, 2011; Rosenthal, 2011). While 97% of peer-reviewed articles on the topic argue that global climate change is caused, at least in part, by humans, only 41% of Americans recognize that fact (Yale Project on Climate Change Communication, 2013). Just as there were once those who argued that tobacco was not harmful, some opponents of efforts to address global warming have tried to cast doubt on the veracity of the scientific evidence of climate change (Dash, 2011). As lethal storms and environmental disasters, like Hurricane Sandy in 2012, the typhoon in the Philippines in 2013, the massive tornadoes and flooding in parts of the United States in 2013 and 2014, and the flooding in Europe in 2013 and 2014 (to name just a few), accumulate, however, even many doubters are starting to realize the dangers of unchecked global warming. As the National Climate Assessment pointed out (U.S. Global Change Research Program, 2014), residents of the United States have already begun to experience its impact, and the impact will only become more severe as temperatures continue to rise.

Fortunately, efforts to address climate change exist on many fronts, including through higher education and through state, national, and global corporate initiatives. Young adults are those most likely to understand the threat of global climate change. In a 2013 survey, among voters 35 years and younger, 80% support efforts by President Obama to address climate change. Practically all those who view him favorably, and more than half (56%) of those who do not regard him favorably, support such efforts by the president (Levin & Strimple, 2013).

Businesses also understand that unchecked global climate change can have very damaging effects on their bottom lines. For example, Thailand faced the worst floods in half a century in 2011. Hundreds of Thai people were killed, about half a million had to flee their flooded homes, a large percentage of the agricultural land was flooded, thousands of places of work were closed, and hundreds of thousands of people could not work. The Thai economy suffered a steep decline, and the public was enraged at the government's inability to stem the flooding (Chachavalpongpun, 2011). Clearly, the Thai people suffered the most from the floods that hit their nation. However, the effects of the flooding in Thailand reached out across the globe. The supply chains of Toyota, Honda, Mitsubishi, Isuzu, Nissan, General Motors, Ford, and Mazda were disrupted. These companies had assembly and part-making plants in the areas of Thailand that were flooded, and the floods prevented the plants from operating.

So the floods in Thailand resulted in a lack of cars and parts for car factories in other areas of the world. These other factories, even though they were not flooded, were forced to remain idle (Vaidya & Rao, 2011). This negatively affected not just Thailand but also the global companies with factories in Thailand, the various national economies the companies support, and the individual workers who rely on salaries from those companies.

The Coca-Cola Company has also faced supply and distribution problems due to climate change and now recognizes "increased droughts, more unpredictable variability, [and] 100-year floods every two years" as economic threats to its global business. This perspective "reflects a growing view among American business leaders and mainstream economists who see global warming as a force that contributes to lower gross domestic products, higher food and commodity costs, broken supply chains and increased financial risk" (Davenport, 2014, paras. 3–4). Coke has embraced water-saving technologies and is encouraging nations where it does business to take steps to curb climate change (Davenport, 2014).

The World Bank has put climate change "at the center of the bank's mission" (Davenport, 2014, para. 10). In 2013, the president of the World Bank declared,

> No country—rich or poor—is immune from the impacts of climate-related disasters. . . .
>
> Damages and losses from natural disasters have more than tripled over the past 30 years. Years of development efforts are often wiped out in days or even minutes.
>
> While we've seen developed countries struggling to cope with blizzards and events like Hurricane Sandy, developing countries have even less resources to mitigate the economic and human costs of these disasters. At the World Bank Group we are stepping up our mitigation, adaptation and disaster risk management work. (Kim, 2013)

Many of the largest corporations in the United States, including Walmart and the five leading oil companies—ExxonMobil, ConocoPhillips, Chevron, BP, and Shell—"are planning their future growth on the expectation that the government will force them to pay a price for carbon pollution as a way to control global warming" (Davenport, 2013). They have accepted the fact that global climate change must be addressed and have made allowances for such efforts in their business plans. They understand that the negative repercussions of unchecked global warming will harm their businesses.

Fortunately, we know that organized efforts can have a dramatic impact on the threat of global climate change. They have already greatly reduced the threat from fluorinated gases, a type of greenhouse gas that once gravely threatened the ozone layer. These gases stem from human-made sources, such as refrigerants, fire extinguishers, and aerosol propellants (European Commission Climate Action, 2011). Thanks to the Montreal Protocol on Substances That Deplete the Ozone Layer, created in 1987, fluorinated gases have been reduced dramatically. All the nations in the United Nations signed the Montreal Protocol and agreed to reduce their use of products that emit these gases. This global effort has led to the survival of the ozone layer in our atmosphere and shows that global climate change can be addressed with a united global effort.

Other environmental success stories include the following:

- Since 1970, the Clean Air Act (substantially revised and expanded in 1990 and amended many times over the years) has led to a 72% decrease in levels of ozone, lead, carbon monoxide, nitrogen dioxide, and sulfur dioxide (EPA, 2014).
- In 2013, eight states—California, New York, Maryland, Oregon, Massachusetts, Connecticut, Rhode Island, and Vermont—promised to work together to substantially increase the number of zero-emission cars driven by ramping up the construction of charging stations. They want to make buying and charging such vehicles easy for consumers and to have 3.3 million battery-powered cars, plug-in hybrids, and other clean-burning vehicles on their roads by 2025 (Dearen, 2013).
- Thirty-eight states and the District of Columbia have Renewable Portfolio Standards that require energy providers to use renewable energy sources (e.g., solar, wind) as a portion of their energy supply (Leon, 2013).
- By 2011, the majority of nations (at least 119) had established some type of target for renewable energy or a renewable energy support policy (more than double the number that did so in 2005) (Sawin, 2011).
- Between 2005 and the end of 2009, Walmart reduced its global greenhouse gas emissions by almost 11%, and from 2010 to 2011, it reduced its plastic bag waste by 3.5 billion bags (Walmart, 2011).
- In 2007, Google became carbon neutral, and the company supports many "green" initiatives.
- In response to anticipated pressures from environmentalists and to help their own bottom line, "Western multinationals—and in some cases, their Asian suppliers—have in the last five years started to build more environmentally sound factories in developing countries, green-building experts say" (Ives, 2014, para. 5).

- In the United States and Canada, many hundreds of colleges and universities have made effective efforts to increase recycling efforts and reduce their greenhouse gas emissions and use of nonrenewable energy. In collaboration with the U.S. Green Building Council, the Princeton Review (2014) publishes *The Princeton Review's Guide to 322 Green Colleges*, which describes how these schools have displayed "a strong commitment to sustainability in their academic offerings, campus infrastructure, activities and career preparation."

These efforts show signs of some progress and the potential for more. However, for us to effectively mitigate and adapt to global climate change (it is too late to stop it), more people must become aware of its reality and potential impact. Without a more educated public, we cannot achieve the united global effort needed to deal with this serious global threat.

Sociologist in Action: Ellis Jones

On April 22, 1990, something changed for me. It was a Sunday. I was a student at the University of Southern California, and a friend invited me to walk down to a fair that was going on nearby. I didn't have any plans, so I decided to join him. Apparently, it was something called "Earth Day." There were tables and booths everywhere, and people were excitedly milling about from one to the next. Every booth I visited offered me a different way to make a positive environmental impact: recycling, composting, conserving water, reusing old clothes, . . . the list went on and on.

At the end of that day, I felt absolutely inspired to make the world a better place. In my mind, the environmental movement had experienced a stroke of true genius. They weren't asking people to join groups, attend meetings, or organize rallies. Instead, they had opened up a completely new realm of action for people—their own everyday lives. By engaging people in micro activism rather than asking them to commit to the much more intensive work undertaken by full-time activists, they were essentially democratizing access to social change. It was a way to expand the environmental movement to almost anyone despite their limits of time, money, skills, or circumstances.

As soon as I realized this, I imagined that thousands of others were having the same revelation at that same moment of history. The environmental movement was laying the foundation for all other social movements to do exactly the same thing! The human rights movement, the social justice movement, the animal rights movement, the feminist movement, the LGBT (lesbian, gay, bisexual, and transgender) movement, and all the rest would begin to adapt this new technique to engage people everywhere in actions they could take in their own lives to contribute to some much needed social change.

Granted, no particular action would add up to much in terms of impact, but if enough people were inspired to act, the collective impact of thousands or tens of thousands or perhaps even millions of people would redefine what kind of changes were possible around these issues. At the same time, all of these people would now feel more invested in the outcomes that they themselves had been working toward in their own way. Rather than relying solely on a relatively small group of activists to bear the weight of these daunting social and environmental problems, now everyone could take on a piece of that responsibility.

The more I thought about this potential, the more I became convinced that what people really needed (or at least what I really needed) was a book that would collect as many of these actions as possible into a single place. I was absolutely sure that someone would write it and I, in turn, would be first in line to buy it. Ten years later, I was a sociology graduate student at the University of Colorado, Boulder. I had waited, patiently, for the imaginary author of this hypothetical book to appear, and she or he had yet to step forward. In the meantime, I was teaching Social Problems, along with a number of other mainstay sociology courses, and found that my own students were constantly asking what they could actually do about all of these problems we were spending so much time reading about, discussing, and analyzing.

I had waited 10 years and decided that was long enough. So I roped in two of my closest friends (also fellow sociology grad students), and we spent the next year collecting all of the actions we could find, from every source we could get our hands on, and distilled the results into a single book. We added a section summarizing the latest data on some of the most significant social and environmental problems we seemed to be facing at the beginning of the 21st century, and the result was *The Better World Handbook: Small Changes That Make a Big Difference*. It has since sold 25,000 copies, been added to more than 300 college and university libraries worldwide, and been adopted in sociology classrooms across the country. But perhaps more important, it's even more widely used by people who've never taken a sociology class in their life.

The website (betterworldhandbook.com) has had more than 550,000 unique visitors since it was created. In a very practical sense, sociology provided the three of us with the tools we needed to uncover, understand, and translate our world's social and environmental problems into a form that allows each of us to personally contribute to their resolution.

SOURCE: Courtesy of Ellis Jones.

EXERCISE 6.1   Nonverbal Sanctions

Next time you see someone give a nonverbal, negative sanction (a look of disgust, a shake of the head, or some other nonverbal sign of disapproval), ask yourself the questions below.

As you answer these questions, be sure to define norms and socialization and distinguish between folkways and mores.

1. What norm was being broken (i.e., what was the act that led the person to give a nonverbal negative sanction)?

2. What was the reaction of the norm violator to the negative sanction?

3. What was your reaction to the interaction you witnessed between the norm violator and the person giving the negative sanction?

4. Why do you think you reacted this way? How did your own socialization process influence your reaction?

EXERCISE 6.2   Breaching Folkways

Often, we are so used to following the norms of society, we forget that we could behave differently. Harold Garfinkel (1967), a sociologist most famous for his "breaching" experiments, in which people would break folkways to expose them, had students do things such as act like boarders in their parents' home, offer to pay store clerks less or more money than the price indicated on an item, and question every statement a person made in a conversation. Through these experiments, his students challenged the norms of social interaction and, in the process, brought them to light.

Conduct your own breaching experiment on campus by carrying out the following steps:

1. The next time someone asks you how you are doing after saying hello, tell the person how you are really doing. In fact, take several minutes to thoroughly relate how you are feeling at that time.

2. Repeat Step 1 with four different people.

3. In a one- to two-page paper, describe (a) how the four people reacted to your experiment, (b) how you felt as you carried out the experiment, (c) how their and your reactions related to your relationship with them, and (d) what you learned about norms of interacting through carrying out this experiment.

EXERCISE 6.3   How Do You Explain Cheating?

1. Why do you, personally, think students cheat on your campus?

2. How would rational choice theory explain cheating on your campus? Do you think rational choice theory offers a good explanation? Why or why not? Be sure to first explain rational choice theory and then relate it to the example of cheating on your campus.

3. Are there one or more important factors that rational choice theory overlooks? If so, what are they? Why do you think these factors are overlooked?

4. Based on your answers to Questions 1 and 2, how would you propose to diminish cheating on your campus? Offer at least five practical suggestions.

EXERCISE 6.4   Global Climate Change and Pollution

One of the major social problems we all face today is global climate change. China recently overtook the United States as the leading producer of greenhouse gases (Oster, 2009). Read "The East Is Grey" at http://www .economist.com/news/briefing/21583245-china-worlds-worst-polluter-largest-investor-green-energy-its-rise-will-have. Then answer the following questions:

1. What are some of the social and economic forces behind the dramatic increase in pollution from China?

2. Why are some members of the Chinese leadership fearful of emphasizing environmental protection over economic growth?

3. What are some of the reasons why the Chinese government now feels some pressure to become more open about and to address pollution in China?

4. What has been the reaction of the United States up to now toward (a) global warming and (b) pollution from China?

5. If you were the president of the United States, what steps would you take to address pollution from China and global climate change in general?

EXERCISE 6.5   What's Your Ecological Footprint?

Go to the website http://www.myfootprint.org, and determine your ecological footprint and your own impact on global climate change.

1. Describe your ecological footprint.

2. Were you surprised by what you found? Why or why not?

3. Go to Earthwatch at www.earthwatch.org, click on your part of the world, and then click on "GET INVOLVED." How might you work with others to use social capital to connect (a) different groups on your campus, (b) different groups in your surrounding community, and (c) your campus and surrounding community to work together to address global climate change?

EXERCISE 6.6   Google and Duke University Team Up to Capture Methane and Show How It Can Be Done!

Learn about the Google and Duke University Partnership to Capture Methane at http://seedstock.com/?s=duke+and+google+hog+waste, and look through the video and article at http://googlegreenblog.blogspot.com/2011/09/sometimes-greening-google-means-getting.html. Then, write a two-page essay that describes what you learned from the video and the article and how they influenced your perspective on global climate change and how it should be tackled. Be sure to include a discussion of the roles of governments, corporations, and higher education in addressing climate change.

EXERCISE 6.7   Lunch Counter Sit-Ins and Other Nonviolent Protests

One of the more dramatic forms of protest during the civil rights movement was the "lunch counter sit-in." At these events, blacks took seats at lunch counters that served only whites and then refused to leave. During many of these sit-ins, white customers jeered, threw food at them, and threatened them, before the police came and dragged off the protesters.

Use your library's electronic databases (e.g., the JSTOR or Academic Search Premier database) to find three academic articles that focus on lunch counter

(Continued)

(Continued)

sit-ins during the civil rights movement. Also, watch the first segment of the *Eyes on the Prize* documentaries (your school library should have a copy), in which the sit-ins are covered. Then, write a two- to three-page paper that addresses the following questions:

1. Given the fact that the protesters knew that they were not going to be served, what did they hope to gain by doing this? Were they trying to change the law? Public opinion? The policies of the lunch counter establishments?

2. Do you think their strategy was successful? What are the benefits and positives of nonviolent protest? What are the negatives and limitations?

3. Considering public opinion toward black Americans today and given what you have learned about social movements, (a) what sorts of public actions could black Americans do today to bring attention to the kinds of discrimination they face and (b) what actions can you personally take that would help diminish racial discrimination? Hand in a complete bibliography of your sources along with your written answers.

EXERCISE 6.8 Studying a Social Movement

There have been numerous social movements (organized campaigns for social, cultural, or legal change) in the United States that have met with varying degrees of success over the past 50 years. The cultural period known as "the sixties" (roughly 1963–1973) saw the rise of the second wave of the women's movement, the American Indian movement, the Brown Power movement (Latinos), an antiwar movement (Vietnam), an international student and youth movement, and movements for poverty relief and fair housing practices, gay rights, environmental rights, and animal rights, among others.

Pick one of these movements. Use your library's databases to search for articles using key words and phrases such as "American Indian movement," "organization, successes, failures, media portrayal," and "goals." Then, answer the following questions:

1. What were or are the goals of the movement you have chosen?

2. How was or is the movement organized? How was or is it run? How was or is it viewed in the popular media? How do you think the movement was or is organized, and how has its portrayal in the media affected its ability to achieve its goals?

(Continued)

(Continued)

3. How successful or unsuccessful has the movement been in achieving its goals?

4. Imagine you were hired as a consultant to promote and advise the movement. What would you do or say to help it achieve its goals? Be specific and strategic, outlining plans to carry forth your proposal.

EXERCISE 6.9   Campus Activism: Then and Now

The 1960s were famous for student activism and student organizing. Who were these students, and for what were they advocating? How were they portrayed in the news media at the time? How are they being portrayed by the media and history textbooks today? How successful were they? Write a three- to four-page paper that answers these questions and describes your reaction to what you have read by carrying out the following steps:

1. Go to the newspaper archive in your library.

2. Choose one regional or national paper for which there are issues available from 1963 through 1973.

3. Scan through the issues published between 1963 and 1973 until you have located (and photocopied) at least 10 articles about on-campus student activism.

4. For each article, note the following: (a) Does the article tell you what the students wanted? (b) Does the article tell you why they had those goals? (c) Does the article appear to have a position in support of, neutral to, or opposed to the students? (d) For each case in which you have a clear sense of the students' goals, were they achieved? Did they change society?

5. Can you imagine 1960s-style student protests happening today on your campus? If yes, would the protesters have similar or different goals from those of the 1960s protesters you read about? If no, explain why you think they would not take place today. Have other styles of protest replaced them? Have students become less likely to protest and, if so, why?

EXERCISE 6.10   The Disability Rights Movement

Read "Welcoming Art Lovers With Disabilities" at http://www.american history.si.edu/disabilityrights/exhibit.html, and view, listen to, and read the Disability Rights Movement display at http://www.americanhistory.si.edu/disabilityrights/exhibit.html. Then, answer the following questions:

1. According to the Smithsonian's Disability Rights Movement display, what do those in the movement seek to gain? How have some of their tactics mirrored those of other social movements?

2. Have you ever acted to support the efforts of the Disability Rights Movement? Why or why not?

3. Describe how you could help achieve the goals of the Disability Rights Movement.

4. How would the success of the Disability Rights Movement benefit all members of society, whether or not they are disabled?

EXERCISE 6.11   Organizing to Address Hunger

1. Check out the videos and other sources of information on the Take Part website at http://www.takepart.com/place-at-the-table/videos and on the Feeding America website at http://feedingamerica.org/hunger-in-america.aspx to create a flyer about hunger that you can pass out in the cafeteria at your school.

2. Bring the flyers to your school cafeteria at a mealtime.

3. Sit down with different groups of students you do not know, give them your flyer, and engage them in a conversation about hunger in America. Then, ask them if they would like to work with you to find a way to assist the people in your area who are hungry. Be sure to put your contact information on the flyer and to have a sign-up sheet so that those who are interested can give you their names and contact information.

4. Set a meeting time, and send an e-mail out to announce the meeting. Then, meet with those interested, and during the meeting, formulate a

(Continued)

(Continued)

plan to help the hungry in your area. For tips on how to run a meeting, you can look at page 4 of this website: http://assets.filemobile.com/15/get-involved/resources/Campus%20in%20Action%20Toolkit.pdf.

5. Once you have formulated your plan, carry it out.

6. Report on (a) how you organized your group, (b) the results of your group's efforts, and (c) what students in general can do to help address the issue of hunger (based on what you learned on the hunger websites) in a letter to the editor or an article in your school's newspaper.

DISCUSSION QUESTIONS

1. What was the last norm that you broke? Think of the last folkway (rather than a more) that you violated. What was the reaction of those around you? How did it make you feel? Did the reaction affect your willingness to break the folkway in the future?

2. Imagine you own a global corporation. Why should you care about global climate change? What steps will you take to protect your business from its harmful impacts? How does your perspective on global climate change when you imagine you are an owner of a global corporation differ from the one you usually have? Why?

3. Have you ever broken a rule or law that you considered unjust? Why did you do so? Did you organize your "deviant" behavior with other people, or did you violate the norm on your own? What were the repercussions? Did your action result in any lasting social change? Why or why not?

4. What are the norms that guide your classroom behavior? What would you consider deviant classroom behavior by students? How did you learn these norms? What are the negative sanctions for those who violate classroom norms?

5. What do you think are the greatest criminal threats to U.S. society? Do you think the criminal justice system effectively addresses those threats? Why or why not?

6. Are there any laws that you find to be unfair or legal punishments for crimes committed that you think are too strong, harsh, or outdated? If not, why not? If so, what are they? Why do you think these laws and punishments exist even though they are unfair? What values (and whose values) do they reflect? What do these laws and punishments teach you about power relations in U.S. society?

7. What do you think life would be like without norms? Would it even be possible? Why or why not?

8. Think of some examples that support Durkheim's idea that deviance can serve positive functions for society. Now think of how deviance can have a negative influence on society. What are the situations in which deviance is most likely to have (a) a positive or (b) a negative effect on society?

9. Think about the social capital you have. Is it bonding or bridging—does it bond you to an isolated group in society, or does it work to connect you to other groups? Give some examples of groups on your campus that create (a) bonding or (b) bridging social capital. How do they affect the rest of the campus?

10. Do you conserve and recycle as much as you can? If so, why? If not, what would convince you to do so?

11. Review Durkheim's description of organic solidarity, and then describe why it is in the self-interest of most global business leaders to address global climate change. Why is it in your self-interest?

12. Recall what Cooley meant by the term looking-glass self. Do you think your college classmates see you as the type of person who would (a) participate in or (b) lead a protest on your college campus? Do you think your high school classmates would give the same answers? Why or why not?

SUGGESTIONS FOR SPECIFIC ACTIONS

1. Read "Can 'Global Warming's Six Americas' Become a Melting Pot for Meaningful Action?" at http://www.climatesciencewatch.org/2012/12/12/can-global-warmings-six-americas-become-a-melting-pot-for-meaningful-action/. Then, go to the Student Environmental Action Coalition website at http://seac.org/resources/. Use the guides there to organize a group action on your campus. Be sure to obtain your instructor's approval before beginning your project. Actions may be local or national, educational or political. Keep a journal of your project, its outcome, the feedback you get from others, and what you learned by doing it.

2. Identify a social issue that you support. (Consider movements to promote fair trade products, establish equal rights for gay Americans, create universal health care, etc.) Find a campus or local organization that works on this issue.

   a. Attend meetings, and participate in the activities of the organization.

   b. Write a letter to the campus newspaper explaining to your classmates what the issues are that the group is concerned with, how these issues affect students, how the group is trying to change people's opinions and feelings on this issue, and why they should join the organization too!

Please go to this book's website at http://study.sagepub.com/korgen5e to find further civic engagement opportunities, resources, peer-reviewed articles, and updated web links related to this chapter.

NOTE

1. You can read the states' petition at http://www.pewclimate.org/docUploads/Mass-v-EPA-Petition.pdf.

REFERENCES

Becker, H. (1963). *Outsiders: Studies in the sociology of deviance.* New York, NY: Free Press.

Beyerlein, K., & Hipp, J. R. (2005). Social capital: Too much of a good thing? *Social Forces, 84*(2), 993–1013.

Chachavalpongpun, P. (2011, October 24). Floods threaten global trade hub. *Yale Global.* Retrieved from http://yaleglobal.yale.edu/content/floods-threaten-global-trade-hub

Choi, H., & Sloane, D. (2012). Does working together prevent crime? Social capital, neighborhoods and crime. In N. Brooks, K. Donaghy, & G. J. Knaap (Eds.), *The Oxford handbook of urban economics and planning* (pp. 230–247). New York, NY: Oxford University Press.

City-Data.com. (2014). *New Orleans crime rate.* Retrieved from http://www.city-data.com/crime/crime-New-Orleans-Louisiana.html

Dash, J. (2011, December 6). *The Contrarians: Full essay with references.* Retrieved from http://climate.uu-uno.org/articles/view/148487/?topic=50699#Quacks

Davenport, C. (2013, December 5). Large companies prepare to pay price on carbon. *The New York Times.* Retrieved from http://www.nytimes.com/2013/12/05/business/energy-environment/large-companies-prepared-to-pay-price-on-carbon.html?hp&_r=0

Davenport, C. (2014, January 24). Industry awakens to threat of climate change. *The New York Times.* Retrieved from http://www.nytimes.com/2014/01/24/science/earth/threat-to-bottom-line-spurs-action-on-climate.html

Dearen, J. (2013, October 25). 8 states join to promote clean cars. *The Boston Globe.* Retrieved from http://www.bostonglobe.com/news/nation/2013/10/24/states-join-forces-promote-clean-cars/4aTkMlnkleI9rhYwGCMcGO/story.html?s_campaign=8315

Dijkstra, J. A., Buckman, K. L., Ward, D., Evans, D. W., Dionne, M., & Chen, C. Y. (2013, March 12). Experimental and natural warming elevates mercury concentrations in estuarine fish. *PLoS ONE.* Retrieved from http://www.plosone.org/article/info%3Adoi%2F10.1371%2Fjournal.pone.0058401

Durkheim, É. (1982). *The rules of the sociological method* (S. Lukes, Ed.; W. D. Halls, Trans.). New York, NY: Free Press. (Original work published 1895)

Elignon, J. (2012, March 22). Taking on police tactic, critics hit racial divide. *The New York Times*. Retrieved from http://www.nytimes.com/2012/03/23/nyregion/fighting-stop-and-frisk-tactic-but-hitting-racial-divide.html

Environmental Protection Agency. (2014). *Detailed summary: Clean Air Act results.* Retrieved from http://www.epa.gov/air/caa/progress.html#pollution

European Commission Climate Action. (2011, September 26). *Fluorinated greenhouse gases.* Retrieved from http://ec.europa.eu/clima/policies/f-gas/index_en.htm

Fears, D. (2013, October 13). Study links warmer water temperatures to greater levels of mercury in fish. *The Washington Post*. Retrieved from http://www.washingtonpost.com/national/health-science/study-links-warmer-water-temperatures-to-greater-levels-of-mercury-in-fish/2013/10/13/c86d43c6-3113-11e3-9c68-1cf643210300_story.html

Finn, K. (2012, May 22). *Mayor seeks more federal help to slash New Orleans murder rate* (Reuters). Retrieved from http://www.reuters.com/article/2012/05/23/us-usa-crime-neworleans-idUSBRE84M06Q20120523

Garfinkel, H. (1967). *Studies in ethnomethodology*. Englewood Cliffs, NJ: Prentice Hall.

Goldstein, J. (2013, August 14). Police dept's focus on race is at core of ruling against stop-and-frisk tactic. *The New York Times*. Retrieved from http://www.nytimes.com/2013/08/15/nyregion/racial-focus-by-police-is-at-core-of-judges-stop-and-frisk-ruling.html?hp

Guarino, M. (2012, January 19). *Rising murder rate may spoil Mardi Gras party* (Reuters). Retrieved from http://www.reuters.com/article/2012/01/19/us-crime-neworleans-idUSTRE80I1RQ20120119

Harper, J. (2013, August 16). New Orleans murder rate falls in first half of 2013, rape cases on the rise (NOPD reports). *The Times Picayune*. Retrieved from http://www.nola.com/crime/index.ssf/2013/08/new_orleans_murder_rate_falls.html

Intergovernmental Panel on Climate Change. (2007). *Climate change 2007: Synthesis report*. Retrieved from http://www.ipcc.ch/publications_and_data/ar4/syr/en/spm.html

Intergovernmental Panel on Climate Change. (2012). *Managing the risks of extreme events and disasters to advance climate change adaptation* (C. B. Field, V. Barros, T. F. Stocker, D. Qin, D. J. Dokken, K. L. Ebi, . . . P. M. Midgley, Eds.; A special report of Working Groups I and II of the Intergovernmental Panel on Climate Change). Cambridge, England: Cambridge University Press. Retrieved from http://www.ipcc.ch/pdf/special-reports/srex/SREX_Full_Report.pdf

Intergovernmental Panel on Climate Change. (2013, September 27). *Working Group I contribution to the IPCC fifth assessment report climate change 2013: The physical science basis summary for policymakers*. Retrieved from http://graphics8.nytimes.com/packages/pdf/science/27climate-ipcc-report-summary.pdf

Ives, M. (2014, January 7). Slowly, Asia's factories begin to turn green. *The New York Times*. Retrieved from http://www.nytimes.com/2014/01/08/business/international/asian-factories-see-sense-and-savings-in-environmental-certification.html

Kim, J. W. (2013, February 16). *World Bank president Jim Kim at G20 meeting: Climate change represents real, present danger.* Washington, DC: World Bank. Retrieved from http://www.worldbank.org/en/news/speech/2013/02/16/world-bank-president-jim-kim-at-g20-meeting-climate-change-represents-real-present-danger

Knight, Z., Robins, N., Clover, R., & Saravanan, D. (2011, January 13). *Climate investment update* (HSBC Global Research). Retrieved from http://www.research.hsbc.com/midas/Res/RDV?ao=20&key=68W7FaNQA0&n=288184.PDF

Lamberth, J. (1994). *Revised statistical analysis of the incidence of police stops and arrests of black drivers/travelers on the New Jersey Turnpike between Interchanges 1 and 3 from the years 1988 through 1991* (Unpublished manuscript). Department of Psychology, Temple University, Philadelphia, PA. Retrieved from http://www.mass.gov/eopss/docs/eops/faip/new-jersey-study-report.pdf

Leon, W. (2013, June). *The state of state renewable portfolio standards.* Retrieved from http://www.cleanenergystates.org/assets/2013-Files/RPS/State-of-State-RPSs-Report-Final-June-2013.pdf

Levin, A., & Strimple, G. (2013, July 24). *Recent polling on youth voters.* Retrieved from http://www.lcv.org/issues/polling/recent-polling-on-youth.pdf

Martin, N. (2014, January 2). New Orleans murders fall again in 2013 (NOLA.com). *The Times-Picayune.* Retrieved from http://www.nola.com/crime/index.ssf/2014/01/2013_new_orleans_murder_rate_d.html

New Jersey Division of Criminal Justice. (2009). *Eradicating racial profiling companion guide.* Retrieved from http://www.state.nj.us/lps/dcj/agguide/directives/racial-profiling/pdfs/ripcompanion-guide.pdf

New Jersey Division of Criminal Justice. (n.d.). *Overview of New Jersey's racial profiling policy.* Retrieved from http://www.state.nj.us/lps/dcj/agguide/directives/racial-profiling/pdfs/overview-racial-policy.pdf

Oster, S. (2009, April 21). Group urges Beijing to cut coal emissions. *The Wall Street Journal.* Retrieved from http://online.wsj.com/article/SB124021811385234435.html

Parks, R. (with Haskins, J.). (1992). *Rosa Parks: My story.* New York, NY: Dial Books.

Pew Research Center. (2011, June 10). *Views of Middle East unchanged by recent events* (Pew Research Center for the People & the Press). Retrieved from http://www.people-press.org/2011/06/10/views-of-middle-east-unchanged-by-recent-events

The Princeton Review. (2014). *The Princeton Review's guide to 322 green colleges.* Retrieved from http://www.princetonreview.com/green-guide.aspx

Reiman, J., & Leighton, P. (2010). *The rich get richer and the poor get prison: Ideology, class, and criminal justice* (9th ed.). Boston, MA: Allyn & Bacon.

Riley, K. J. (2002, Summer). Racial profiling: Lessons from the drug war. *Rand Review,* 26(2). Retrieved from http://www.rand.org/pubs/periodicals/rand-review/issues/rr-08-02/profiling.html

Rosenthal, E. (2011, October 15). Where did global warming go? *The New York Times*. Retrieved from http://www.nytimes.com/2011/10/16/sunday-review/whatever-happened-to-global-warming.html?pagewanted=all

Sawin, J. L. (2011). *Renewables 2011 global status report*. Retrieved from http://germanwatch.org/klima/gsr2011.pdf

Sutherland, E. H. (1947). *Principles of criminology* (4th ed.). Philadelphia, PA: J. B. Lippincott.

U.S. Global Change Research Program. (2014). *National Climate Assessment*. Retrieved from http://nca2014.globalchange.gov/

Vaidya, V., & Rao, V. (2011, December 8). Impact of Thailand floods on automotive industry and supply chain. *Logistics Digest*. Retrieved from http://www.logisticsdigest.com/inter-article/inter-logistics-insight/item/7429-impact-of-thailand-floods-on-automotive-industry-and-supply-chain.html

Walmart. (2011). *Building the next generation Walmart . . . responsibly: 2011 Global responsibility report*. Retrieved from http://walmartstores.com/sites/Responsibility Report/2011/WalmartGRR.pdf

Woodside, C. (2009, May 19). *Was an "historic" EPA ruling on GHGs reflected by historically good coverage?* (The Yale Forum on Climate Change and the Media). Retrieved from http://www.yaleclimatemediaforum.org/2009/05/epa-ruling-on-ghgs/

Yale Project on Climate Change Communication. (2013, June 3). *Scientific and public perspectives on climate change*. Retrieved from http://environment.yale.edu/climate-communication/files/ClimateNote_Consensus_Gap_May2013_FINAL6.pdf

7

Big Money Doesn't *Always* Win

Stratification and Social Class

Money, money, money . . . it's a rich man's world.[1]

—ABBA

D o you agree with the lyrics of this ABBA song? Do you think "it's a rich man's world"? In this chapter, we will discuss social stratification—how societies distribute the things of value to them and rank groups of people according to their access to what is valued. Although people may prize certain things more in some societies than in others (e.g., privacy, tea or coffee, certain spices, etc.), almost everyone everywhere places a high value on money.

In the United States, the desire for money, combined with a lack of government oversight of some banking practices, led to the Great Recession of 2008 to 2009, from which we have not yet fully recovered. The Glass-Steagall Act, passed in 1933 after the stock market crash of 1929, separated commercial banking (which accepts deposits and lends money) from investment banking (which issues securities and invests using credit). These changes were enacted to prevent banks from taking investment risks that could jeopardize their solvency. However, banks, desiring the ability to make more money, lobbied for the repeal of the act. Once the Glass-Steagall Act was repealed in 1999, commercial banks were once again able to invest their clients' deposited money and practice both investment and commercial banking within one company.

During the same time period, under a drive to give all Americans the opportunity to own their own homes, government mortgage providers Fannie Mae and Freddie Mac lowered their standards and began issuing mortgages to more people with below-average credit ratings and low incomes (Roberts, 2008). Meanwhile, as government regulators turned a blind eye, other mortgage lenders followed suit; housing prices rose dramatically as more and more people bought homes, and it became a seller's market. With no preventative government regulations, the mortgage lenders profited enormously by collecting fees to guide homeowners into taking on mortgages they could not afford. The lenders bundled toxic mortgages (whose owners were likely to default) into "collateralized debt obligations" (CDOs). They then divided the bundles into more CDOs and sold them to banks, which sold them to investors, which purchased insurance against possible losses on the bundled mortgages. The lack of government regulation and adequate oversight allowed the companies that insured the CDOs to fail to maintain the resources needed to pay possible insurance claims. Therefore, when the homeowners defaulted on loans they were never able to afford and investors filed claims to cover their losses on CDOs, the insurance companies were unable to cover the losses, and the entire system fell apart.

Credit rating agencies, whose job it is to grant credit scores that provide a rating of securities, also failed to do their jobs responsibly. These credit rating agencies (Moody's, Standard and Poor's, and Fitch), paid by the banks to which they issue credit scores, granted them high credit ratings, leading investors in these banks into thinking that their money was not at risk (Morgenson, 2008). When these CDOs started to fail, many investors lost money, and some banks, such as Bear Stearns and Lehman Brothers, went bankrupt, while others were saved through government bailouts to prevent further damage to the economy (The Financial Crisis Inquiry Commission, 2011).

As a result of the above events, the stock market suffered the worst decline since the Great Depression, and the housing market collapsed, as the worth of homes plummeted and toxic mortgages and high unemployment rates led to defaults on mortgages. Retirees lost money they counted on for living expenses. Institutions that relied on interest and dividends from investments (e.g., state pension funds, charities, colleges, art museums, and grant funders) faced drastic cuts in their income, and many had to stop providing services and lay off employees. The most vulnerable workers were hit the hardest by the recession. The working poor have faced the most job cuts and the greatest number of lost work hours. As Andrew M. Sum, director of the Center for Labor Market Studies at Northeastern University, states, "Low-income people are the big losers when the economy turns down" (quoted in Eckholm, 2008, para. 6).

A loss of a few hours of work each week, never mind a layoff, can be devastating for workers already trying to scrape by on low-wage work.

As we write these words, the efforts of the Obama administration and the leaders of other nations to stimulate the global economy seem to have had some positive impact. However, while the U.S. economy has begun to recover, its growth has been uneven, and inequality has increased. The economy has recovered for the very wealthy, as the stock market reached record highs in 2013. However, the average family income, when controlled for inflation, is actually lower today than it was 25 years ago (DeNavas-Walt, Proctor, & Smith, 2013; Irwin, 2013). Today, the richest 1% of U.S. households owns more wealth than *all* of the bottom 90% combined! Income and wealth inequality has not been so uneven since before the Great Depression hit in 1929. The share of income going to the very rich (the top 1%) has increased dramatically, from 8% in 1980 to 20.1% in 2010 (Fry & Taylor, 2013; Piketty & Saez, 2007; Prante, 2009; Saez, 2012). This trend is evident in the business world, as companies that cater to wealthy clientele, like Barneys stores and Capital Grille restaurants, have prospered and those that market to middle-class buyers, like Sears and Red Lobster, have struggled. Growth in General Electric sales of high-end appliances far outpaces the sales growth of more moderately priced appliances (Schwartz, 2014) (see Figure 7.1).

Theories of Social Stratification

Classical Theories

Of the three main theories we discuss in this book (functionalism, conflict theory, and symbolic interactionism), the consensus among sociologists is that conflict theory is the most useful when examining social stratification. The two founders of sociology who used the conflict perspective, Karl Marx and Max Weber, provided two of the most important classical theories of stratification. All of Marx's work, and much of Weber's, focused on examining and explaining inequality in society.

As you will recall from earlier chapters, Karl Marx spent his life examining how power is unequally distributed and how we might change society to make this distribution process fair. In most of his work, he maintained that there are only two classes in society: (1) those who own the means of production (the owners, or bourgeoisie) and (2) those who work for them (the workers, or proletariat). Marx believed that the workers would eventually develop a "class consciousness," realize that their interests are in opposition to those of the owners, and ultimately overthrow the bourgeoisie.

Weber, who lived a generation or so after Marx, expanded on Marx's ideas (see Weber, 1968). Whereas Marx maintained that power in society directly

Figure 7.1   An Uneven Recovery

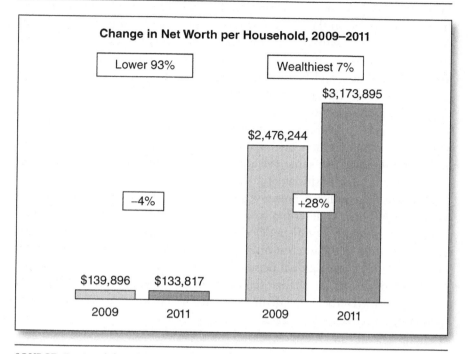

SOURCE: Retrieved from http://www.pewsocialtrends.org/2013/04/23/a-rise-in-wealth-for-the-wealthydeclines-for-the-lower-93/.

relates to ownership of the means of production (those who own industries), Weber recognized that nonowners who possess useful skills can also have some power. He added a third class to Marx's two-tiered class system. He divided the nonowners into a middle class (those who had skills based on knowledge) and a working class (those who did manual labor). Weber anticipated the fact that as societies became more complicated and technologically advanced, the skills of the middle class would become more in demand than those of the working class. The middle class would, therefore, be paid more and have greater access to the things valued in society (better schools, neighborhoods, housing, etc.) than the members of the working class. Unlike Marx, he didn't envision a class uprising that would result in the destruction of the owning class.

Contemporary Theories

Today, *power elite theories*, a modern offshoot of the classic conflict perspective, represent the dominant perspective in studies of economic and political power. These theories maintain that many people do not bother participating in the political process because they feel alienated from it.

Power elite theorists, such as C. W. Mills (1956/1970) and William Domhoff (1967/2005, 1983), note that a relatively small, organized group of people hold key positions in the major institutions of society and make continuous (and, overall, successful) efforts toward keeping themselves in power. Mills noted a connection among key players in the military, corporations (that supply the military and help finance campaigns for those seeking office in government), and the government (which chooses which corporations will supply the military). Domhoff (1967/2005) goes further, arguing that there is a "ruling class" composed of interrelated leaders in the corporate, political, and policy-planning network worlds. Members of this group grew up together, attending the same private schools, social clubs, and colleges. As adults, they occupy positions of power and "rule" America.

Bringing the conflict perspective to a global level, the sociologist Charles Derber (2000, 2003) describes a world in which corporations, rather than nations, increasingly dominate. Derber maintains that governments act disproportionately in the interest of global corporations rather than their own citizens. He calls for a global democratic grassroots movement, such as the Occupy movements, to change the mode of globalization and put "people before profit" (Derber, 2003). In doing so, he claims that we can reduce inequalities between social classes across the globe.

Social Class

What social class are you? Wait, we can guess (with at least 95% certainty) how you will answer! When asked on surveys, almost all Americans will say that they are middle class. Most, however, have no social scientific understanding of what "social class" actually means.

Neither do most Americans have any idea of the level of economic inequality in the United States. In one recent study, a representative sample of Americans were asked to look at three charts that represented different distributions of wealth and to guess which one indicated the wealth distribution in the United States. The chart selected by the majority of respondents actually showed the distribution of wealth in Sweden—the nation with the *greatest* economic equality! When they were asked which would be the most ideal degree of wealth distribution in a society, they selected the chart that indicated an even *more* equitable distribution of wealth than that found in Sweden. Few people were aware of the lopsided distribution of wealth in the United States and that the richest 20% of Americans actually own approximately 84% of the wealth, compared with 58% for the top 20% in Sweden and 32% for the wealthiest 20% in the "ideal" nation (Norton & Ariely, 2011).

We need to recognize economic inequality in order to understand the influence of social class on our society and on the lives of individual people. According to social scientists (those who measure class professionally), people in the same social class have relatively equal access to what is valued in their society (e.g., money, power, good schools, nice neighborhoods, etc.) and have similar lifestyles. Once people realize this, they can usually recognize the many differences concealed by the almost universal "middle class" label in the United States. For example, it quickly becomes clear that whereas both high-level managers and sales associates tend to refer to themselves as middle class, members of these respective occupations do not have similar lifestyles or access to what is valued in U.S. society. And all this doesn't even address the fact that your answer to the question "What social class are you?" was likely an answer about your perceived class *in the United States* and not about your perception of your class within the global economic system. In the global economic system, the majority of Americans would be considered upper class.

Because social scientists understand that almost all Americans will simply put down "middle class" if asked to specify their social class, most of them measure social class by looking at the income, education, and profession of the respondents. However, this still leaves some room for error.[2] In general, most truly middle-class people in the United States have some college education, have professions with salaries (rather than jobs where they are paid by the hour), and earn within a specified range around the median income. Sometimes, social scientists break down members of the middle class into two groups: middle class (white-collar workers) and working class (blue- or pink-collar workers[3]). Blue- and pink-collar jobs, which usually do not require as much education, tend to pay less than white-collar work.[4] White-collar work tends to require at least a bachelor's degree.

The importance of attaining a college degree cannot be overstated. Those who hope to attain a class ranking of at least middle class generally need to have one or more of the following: (a) a high level of education, (b) connections to those in power, and (c) a legacy of wealth passed down to them by their family. While one has to be born lucky to have the third requirement (passed-down wealth), the second (connections to those in power) also requires a certain degree of good fortune. You need to have access to people in power in order to establish connections with them. A high degree of education, while increasingly expensive and open only to those with a certain level of aptitude, remains the most readily available path to a middle-class life for most Americans. The gaps in income levels and employment rates between those with and without a college degree have never been greater. In 2013, the unemployment rate for those with a 4-year college degree was 2.8%, compared with 8.1% for those with a 2-year degree and 12.2% for those with only a high school diploma. Likewise, only 5.8% of those with 4-year college degrees were in poverty, compared with 14.7% of those with a 2-year degree and 21.8% of those with just a high school education (Pew Research Center, 2014).

Sex and race also relate to social class. In short, it helps to be male and white. Female heads of households are almost twice as likely as male heads of families and five times as likely as married couples to live below the poverty level. In 2012, an estimated 15% of Americans lived in poverty. The poverty rate also varies dramatically according to race. In 2012, 9.7% of non-Hispanic whites, 27.2% of blacks, 11.7% of Asians, and 25.6% of Hispanics lived in poverty (DeNavas-Walt et al., 2013). The recent subprime mortgage crisis has disproportionately affected minorities—those most likely to have such mortgages—and broadened the wealth divide between white males and Hispanic or Latino, black, and female Americans. We'll talk more about the connections between sex and race and social class in Chapters 8 and 9 of this book.

Social Class and Political Representation

Voter turnout is strongly related to social class. To put it simply, poor and working-class people are much less likely to vote than middle-class and wealthier Americans. Although always a feature of U.S. elections, the class gap has now become a chasm. Many poor Americans do not see the issues that they care about being addressed by politicians and, therefore, see no use in going through the hassles of registering to vote and voting. Some are also working so hard, piecing together two or three jobs, and so preoccupied with finding a way to pay the rent and buy food that they have little time or energy to keep up with current political issues and to vote. Homeless Americans, without proof of residence, face even more difficulty in exercising their right to vote.

The median household income in 2012 was approximately $50,000, meaning about half of American households made more and half made less than $50,000. In the presidential election of 2012, though, 59% of voters made $50,000 or more, while just 41% made less than $50,000 (Nonprofit VOTE, 2012). Therefore, middle- and high-income Americans hold more sway at the ballot box.

Education affects voter turnout as well. These days, candidates and political parties tend not to reach out to young people who do not attend college, and few of them tend to vote. In the 2012 election, 63% of young people with some college experience voted, compared with just 36% of those without any college experience (Nonprofit VOTE, 2012).

> The whole infrastructure of churches, grassroots political parties, local newspapers, and unions that once introduced working-class young people to politics is now shattered. And the sophisticated turnout operations of modern presidential campaigns focus on likely voters, meaning that college campuses get lots of attention but no one reaches young people who work in retail, service industries, and manufacturing. The hyper-efficient Obama campaign contacted just 5.8% of youth without college experience. (Nonprofit VOTE, 2012, p. 24.)

The decline of union power has particularly diminished the influence of working-class Americans on the electoral process. According to the Bureau of Labor Statistics (BLS, 2006, 2014a), union membership in 2013 had dropped to half of what it was in 1983, with a 35.3% membership rate for public sector workers and 6.7% for private sector workers. Wages of union workers remained much higher than those of nonunionized workers. In 2013, the median weekly salary of full-time union workers was $950, while the median weekly salary of full-time nonunion workers was $750 (BLS, 2014b). In addition to ensuring relatively good wages, unions have traditionally been a very powerful "get out the vote" force for (usually Democratic) candidates. However, as the power of unions has declined, so has the ability of the working class to have its economic interests addressed by politicians.

Even Americans who do vote realize that only a very small percentage of the population has the means to run for high political office. The amount of money people must be able to raise to establish a legitimate campaign prohibits the vast majority of people from running for such positions. For example, during the 2012 congressional elections, the average candidate running for a position in the House of Representatives or the Senate spent $526,818 and $2,318,358, respectively (OpenSecrets.org, 2012a). At the presidential level, the numbers are even more staggering: President Obama and Mitt Romney and their allies raised approximately a billion dollars each during the presidential election of 2012 (OpenSecrets.org, 2012b).

The overall result of the current electoral system[5] in the United States is that most poor and working-class Americans neither vote nor run for political office. In turn, they are largely ignored by political officeholders, who must respond to constituents who do vote and contributors who help them raise the vast sums of money needed to gain and maintain their positions.

The Power of Organized People

The information above may sound depressing to anyone committed to true democracy in the United States. However, it is only part of the picture. Although civic organizations may not exist in the size and number they once did (Skocpol, 2003), there are many grassroots political organizations successfully representing lower income Americans. While we usually do not hear about their efforts on the evening news, Barack Obama's experience as a community organizer has made more people aware of their existence. These organizations are accomplishing the vital task of giving voice to poor and working-class persons.

One vehicle for this is through broad-based organizing associations (organizations of organizations, including churches, synagogues, mosques, nonprofits, parents associations, and unions). These civic groups, in essence, teach people to use a "sociological eye" and a "sociological imagination" as they train them to become effective citizens. They train ordinary Americans to question the status quo, connect their personal problems to public issues, and hold politicians and business leaders accountable to the citizenry. While there are many of these organizations (the Industrial Areas Foundation [IAF], Pacific Institute for Community Organization National Network, Direct Action and Research Training, Organizing and Leadership Training Center, and Gamaliel are some), they all organize for power. Their ability to organize allows them to act as a kind of mediating institution for the poor, working, and middle classes and to negotiate effectively with those who have political and financial power.

The following description of the IAF, located on the organization's website (http://www.industrialareasfoundation.org/), provides an insight into the efforts of these types of organizations:

> The IAF is non-ideological and strictly non-partisan, but proudly, publicly, and persistently political. The IAF builds a political base within society's rich and complex third sector—the sector of voluntary institutions that includes religious congregations, labor locals, homeowner groups, recovery groups, parents associations, settlement houses, immigrant societies, schools, seminaries, orders of men and women religious, and others. And then the leaders use that base to compete at times, to confront at times, and to cooperate at times with leaders in the public and private sectors. (para. 1)

South Bronx Churches (SBC), an IAF affiliate composed of 8 Catholic and 17 Protestant churches, also provide a good example of the power of organized people. During the 1970s and early 1980s, the South Bronx community in New York City was burning. Largely abandoned by government and business leaders, drugs were everywhere, shootings were commonplace, and arson was incessant. A turning point came when SBC members began to talk to one another about their fears, frustrations, and hopes concerning their neighborhoods. They realized that alone, none of them could do much, but together they had the power to improve their community. Part of their multifaceted plan to revitalize the area was the "Nehemiah Homes" project, the creation of 1,000 houses for poor, working-class residents.[6] SBC's effort to save the South Bronx was a long struggle that included public confrontations with powerful mayors of New York City (David Dinkins, Ed Koch, and Rudolph Giuliani) and huge efforts to raise money from business leaders. In the end, the SBC won. The organization succeeded in raising millions of dollars and convincing the city of New York to donate land for the project. Today, 1,000 low-income, working New Yorkers own their homes where there were once just burned-out and decrepit buildings.

More important, this accomplishment inspired those who participated in the effort, and the many more who benefited from it, to become more active citizens. Felix Santiago, a key SBC member in the Nehemiah Homes project, described what the experience did for him.

> We own the community now! When we went around with the police in the van [identifying drug-dealing hotspots in the 1980s], we were kind of afraid. We thought that maybe the drug dealers were going to see us. But we were not afraid, together.
>
> Everywhere we go, from New York to Albany, from Albany back to Washington, we would carry our signatures with us and we would put them on the table and say, "These 100,000 people agree with our agenda for change." That made a big difference in our lives. We began to own more of the community. It's something you learn with South Bronx Churches. You don't fear anybody. You can stand in front of the President of the United States and you can talk to him like we are here. You have power. In 1986, I would have been afraid to sit down here and talk to you. I would say, no way, no way, you don't want to talk to me. But when you get picked to be a leader and own what you got, you have the right to represent the community. (Korgen, 2007, p. 120)

Felix Santiago does not just have a new home and a revitalized neighborhood; he has become an empowered, knowledgeable, and effective citizen. This kind of transformation is happening all over the United States.

As of 2014, the IAF has organizations in more than 65 cities across every region of the United States, Canada, England, Germany, and Australia.

They have helped pass living-wage bills (e.g., in Texas, Arizona, and New York City), funded thousands of new homes for low-income workers (in New York City, Philadelphia, Baltimore, and Washington, D.C.), established the successful Alliance School System (in areas throughout the West and Southwest), and convinced lawmakers to enact legislation to carry out large-scale blight removal and urban revitalization (New York City).[7] As noted above, the IAF is just one of the many community-based groups working to give power to organized people.

The National Employment Law Project (NELP) provides another example of a successful organizing effort. NELP has effectively brought together existing organizations throughout the United States to create fairer minimum-wage laws with their "Raise the Minimum Wage" campaign. As of April 2014, 24 states had raised their state minimum-wage levels above that of the federal $7.25 minimum, and several more were expected to do so soon. Two states (Connecticut and Maryland) have passed legislation to raise their rate to $10.10, as suggested by President Obama, and others have similar legislation pending. NELP helped establish a broad-based movement to harness the will of 69% of the U.S. public and a broad coalition community organizing groups in favor of raising the minimum wage and has effectively pushed for such legislation in states and many cities across the nation (Bloomberg, 2014).

Obama's experience as a community organizer in Chicago no doubt helped him during his campaigns for the presidency. He focused on building grassroots support, with advocates working in their local communities and encouraging neighbors to favor Obama and to make a plan to vote. The community-based Obama campaign organizations built during the 2008 election were strengthened for the 2012 campaign, particularly in swing states, and they played an important role in the president's reelection (Ball, 2012).

Obama's ability to organize and mobilize a largely ignored group of citizens deemed notoriously unreliable in elections—young people!—helped bring about his victory in the Iowa Democratic Caucus during the primary election in 2008. The participation of voters under the age of 25 in that state's 2008 caucus was 135% more than that in the 2004 election—and they responded enthusiastically to Senator Obama's calls for a "politics of hope and change." Young Iowa voters preferred Obama 4:1 over his competitors and gave him 20,000 of their votes. He beat Senator John Edwards by just 17,000 votes and gained the momentum needed for his later victories (Drehle, 2008). In 2012, the youth vote was as strong as it was in 2008 and proved decisive for President Obama's reelection (Nonprofit VOTE, 2012).

Sociologist in Action: Frances Fox Piven

Frances Fox Piven is a sociologist who never ceases to use her sociological research to influence society. When awarded the 2003 American Sociological Association's Award for the Public Understanding of Sociology, the Distinguished Professor of Political Science and Sociology at the Graduate School and University Center of the City University of New York was described as "a scholar who is equally at home in the university setting and the world of politics" ("ASA Award Recipients Honored in Atlanta," 2003, para. 25). The author or coauthor of renowned sociological texts on the disenfranchisement and political power of poor Americans (e.g., *Regulating the Poor*, 1972/1993; *Poor People's Movements*, 1977; *The New Class War*, 1982/1985; *Why Americans Don't Vote*, 1988; *Why Americans Still Don't Vote*, 2000), she puts her knowledge into action in the political arena. For example, in the 1960s, she used her research to expand welfare benefits. Her efforts to enfranchise the poor were instrumental in establishing the National Voter Registration Act of 1993 (popularly known as the Motor Voter Act).[8] She has fought an unrelenting battle against the "welfare reform" initiated in 1996 and has been a consistent proponent of the politics of disruption and mass protest.

In one article, Piven (2005) describes her advice for democratic reform movements today in the following way:

> Yes, we should work on our agenda of democratic reforms, including a national right to vote, a national voter registration system, the implementation of the National Voter Registration Act, Election Day a holiday, nonpartisan election officials, and so on. But we have to do more. . . . The time when mass protest is possible will come. We should be ready and receptive, obdurate and bold. The hip-hop voter registration campaign had a slogan, "Vote or die." They were on the right track. (para. 7)

Piven is one of the boldest living sociologists. Importantly, she is a dedicated social scientist as well as an activist. She conducts good social scientific research that can be examined and critiqued objectively.

Although not everyone, or even all sociologists, would agree with Piven's strategies for political action, many have been inspired by her efforts to make our society a democracy in which people of all classes are represented equally.

Sociologist in Action: Adrian Chevraux-Fitzhugh

Did you know that corporations have the legal right, under the First Amendment, as interpreted by the Supreme Court's decision in *Citizens United v. Federal Election Commission* (2010), to initiate and participate in political campaigns? Adrian Chevraux-Fitzhugh used the sociological tools he gained as a sociology master's student at Humboldt State University to examine people's knowledge about "corporate personhood" and their attitudes toward corporate involvement in political elections. He designed a county-wide telephone survey for Democracy Unlimited of Humboldt County (DUHC, 2005), which revealed that

> only 35% of respondents were familiar with the concept of "corporate personhood," which is the legal doctrine that allows corporations to claim the same constitutional rights of human beings. . . . [Moreover], a significant majority opposes allowing corporations to participate in local elections. (para. 4)

These results were utilized by DUHC in its ongoing efforts to educate citizens about the relationship between corporations and democracy in the United States. DUHC helped establish the organization Move to Amend, a coalition aiming to amend the Constitution to abolish corporate personhood (https://movetoamend.org). If you'd like to find out more about corporate personhood and determine whether you think it makes sense in a democracy, please go to www.pbs.org/now/politics/corprights.html.

EXERCISE 7.1   Pressures Facing the U.S. and World Economies Today

Go to *The New York Times'* "Economic Crisis and Market Upheavals" at http://topics.nytimes.com/top/reference/timestopics/subjects/c/credit_crisis/index.html?scp=1-spot&sq=credit%20crisis&st=cse.

Read three of the articles under "Latest Developments," and relate their contents to the information in this chapter. Be sure to describe how the information from the articles helped you better understand the economic pressures on the world and U.S. economies today.

| EXERCISE 7.2 | **How Unequal Is Wealth Distribution in the United States—and Why?** |

Look at the video on wealth inequality at http://mashable.com/2013/03/02/wealth-inequality/.

Now, write a one- to two-page essay that (a) describes your reaction to the video and (b) explains the information in it, using information from this chapter (and other parts of the book, if you like).

| EXERCISE 7.3 | **Social Class and You** |

At this point in the chapter, you are probably thinking about your own social class and how you became a member of it. Think about how the institutions of family, education, and occupation are related to one another, and answer the following questions:

1. What is the highest level of education completed by each of your parents?

2. Were you raised by two parents? If not, who raised you?

3. When you were growing up, what was the occupation of the head(s) of your household?

4. Have you been in different social classes at different times in your life? If so, why? If not, why not?

5. How do you think your answers to Questions 1 to 3 influenced your present social class?

| EXERCISE 7.4 | **Soup Kitchens and Hunger in America** |

Volunteer to serve a meal at an area soup kitchen. Your Campus Activities Office should be able to help you and even connect you with a group on campus that regularly volunteers at one.

1. Set up a time when the manager can give you some background on why the guests come to the soup kitchen. (In particular, ask what makes them need the services the soup kitchen offers.)

(Continued)

(Continued)

2. When you are there, be sure to pay attention to the people eating at the soup kitchen (while still taking time to interact with them, to serve them, and to enjoy your volunteer experience), and note the following: (a) Are they mostly families or individuals? (b) What is their racial and ethnic makeup? (c) What is the age range of those who have come to eat there? (d) Do most of them seem hopeful? Resigned? Angry? Happy? Depressed? (e) How do they react to your being there, and what are the ways they interact with you?

3. Next, write a two- to three-page paper that describes (a) the services the soup kitchen offers, (b) the demographics and attitudes of the people eating at the soup kitchen (based on the data you have gathered in Step 2), (c) why the people who eat there need to do so, (d) whether you could ever see yourself needing the services of a soup kitchen (and why or why not), and (e) how your experience at the soup kitchen made you feel.

Extra credit: Go to the website of Feeding America at http://feedingamerica .org, click on "Faces of Hunger," and then read the Hunger Fact Sheets under "Hunger 101." Incorporate the information from these fact sheets into the paper you just wrote.

EXERCISE 7.5   America: Who Votes?

1. Click on the latest edition of "America Goes to the Polls" at http://www .nonprofitvote.org/voter-turnout.html.

2. Compare voting rates by race, income, and educational attainment.

3. Based on the information in this chapter, why do you think the respective groups are more or less likely to vote than other Americans? What does this tell you about the connections (at least those that are perceived) between wealth and power?

4. What steps do you think should be taken toward engaging nonvoting Americans enough so that they will register and vote?

EXERCISE 7.6   The Influence of Money on State Politics

It's almost impossible not to be aware of the influence of money on presidential politics. However, money influences politics at the state level as well. Go to http://www.followthemoney.org, and submit your address. After looking through the findings for your area, answer the following questions:

1. What are three things you learned about the interaction between politics and money in your area from this website?

2. Were you surprised by any of your findings? Why or why not?

3. How have your findings influenced your opinion about how political campaigns should be financed? Why?

4. How can you use the information you found to influence campaign finance laws?

EXERCISE 7.7   Community Organizing

Find out what community-based organizing associations are operating in your area. You can do this by contacting your campus Community Center and asking for referrals to local community organizing groups or by checking out the websites of national organizations (IAF, Public Citizen, AFL-CIO, etc.) and finding the respective affiliates in your state.

Attend a meeting of a local community organization, and write a three-page paper that discusses (a) the issues on which the organization is currently focusing, (b) how it decided on those issues, and (c) the organization's strategy as it works on those issues. Discuss how these three items relate to (a) the sociological eye and (b) the sociological imagination and what suggestions you can make that might help the organization to be even more successful and powerful in accomplishing its mission. Finally, include a section analyzing how your university (or students from your university) could support the work of the organization.

EXERCISE 7.8   Fair Trade on Your Campus

1. Watch http://www.youtube.com/watch?v=NhQJrz-aDfI&feature=related; then, go to http://www.fairtradetownsusa.org, and find two other sources on your own that describe the Fair Trade movement.

2. Write a two-page paper in which you use the sources above to describe the Fair Trade movement today, and describe why your campus should or should not be a part of it (you can do this even if your campus is a Fair Trade Campus).

3. In addition, include a one-page strategy plan for working with your school cafeteria to provide fair trade coffee and other fair trade alternatives for students (or to expand these offerings if some are already available on your campus).

EXERCISE 7.9   Voting Rights

Go to "Voting Rights (Registration and Requirements)" at http://topics.ny-times.com/top/reference/timestopics/subjects/v/voter_registration_and_requirements/index.html.

Read three to five of the articles that focus on the efforts to promote either voter ID laws or the Voting Rights Act, and then, in two to three pages,

1. summarize the information in the articles and

2. explain whether or not you support (a) voter ID laws or (b) the Supreme Court decision to overturn key portions of the Voting Rights Act.

Be sure to back up your arguments with hard evidence (and cite your sources).

EXERCISE 7.10   Power and the Control of Seeds

Today, three corporations control more than half of all the commercial seed sold throughout the world (Center for Food Safety, 2013). Learn about how this trend relates to power elite theories on class conflict by completing the following exercises.

Watch "Seeds of Freedom" at http://topdocumentaryfilms.com/seeds-of-freedom, and then watch the brief video at the Navdanya website at http://www.navdanya.org.

(Continued)

(Continued)

Now read "Seeds and Genetic Diversity" at http://www.etcgroup.org/issues/seeds-genetic-diversity, and look up the information on the Just Label It website at http://justlabelit.org.

In one to two pages, answer the following question:

- Describe how a power elite theorist like Charles Derber might explain the centralization of food production under the control of huge companies like Monsanto.

DISCUSSION QUESTIONS

1. Before reading this chapter, did you know that corporations have the legal right to initiate and participate in political campaigns? Why or why not? How do you think this right, upheld by the Supreme Court decision in *Citizens United v. Federal Election Commission* (2010), affects elections and governance in the United States?

2. Why do you think so many people who are not part of the 1% are opposed to raising taxes on the wealthiest members of society? How would Marx explain their thinking (recall his concept of "false consciousness")? Do you agree with Marx? Why or why not?

3. Reread the discussion of Durkheim's ideas on external and internal inequality in Chapter 2 of this book. How might external inequality in the United States today influence who might be elected to public office?

4. Think of an issue you'd like to see addressed, and conduct a power analysis of who controls the decisions about that issue and how you might influence them. For example, say you want your school to serve fair trade coffee (if it does not already). Who decides what coffee the school purchases to sell on campus? How might you convince him or her to switch to fair trade coffee?

5. Have you ever worked (or are you now working) at a relatively low-wage hourly job? Why or why not?

6. What is your immediate reaction when you think about the fact that one in four households with children reports an inability to buy enough food? Why? How can more people become informed about this social problem and take action to alleviate it?

7. Do you think unions are needed for low-wage workers? Why or why not?

8. What do you think your life would be like if you worked at a low-wage hourly job for the rest of your life? How would it affect whom you may marry, what kind of family you will have, what kind of home you will live in, what you will do for entertainment, and so forth?

9. How, if at all, do you think the college degree you are planning to get will affect your social class? Why?

10. How did your social class influence your decision to (a) attend college and (b) attend the particular college in which you are enrolled?

11. Why might it make good economic sense for corporations to "go green"? If you were a CEO of a major corporation, what might prompt you to invest funds in reducing your company's "environmental footprint"? Do you think more companies will do so soon? If so, which ones (and where and why)?

SUGGESTIONS FOR SPECIFIC ACTIONS

1. Find a local community organizing association in your area. (You can do this by looking for affiliated organizations at the websites of the IAF, Public Citizen, AFL-CIO, and so forth.) Contact the lead organizer, and set up a meeting with him or her. Find out what issues the organization is working on at this time. Offer to use your skills as a college student to conduct some basic research for the group to help it learn about the issues.

2. Go to the Rock the Vote website at http://www.rockthevote.com/home.php, and follow the directions there on how to conduct a voter registration drive on your campus.

3. Go to United for a Fair Economy's website at http://www.faireconomy.org, and click on "Take Action." Look through the list of actions they are working on, and participate in one, or organize a teach-in at your home or school on a current issue related to social class, stratification, and the economic recession.

4. Read the story and watch the video "Uganda Fights Stigma and Poverty to Take on Breast Cancer" at http://www.nytimes.com/2013/10/16/health/uganda-fights-stigma-and-poverty-to-take-on-breast-cancer.html?ref=international-home&_r=0. Then, go to the Uganda Women's Cancer Support Organization at http://uwocaso.org.ug and http://www.uicc.org/membership/uganda-womens-cancer-support-organization-uwocaso. Contact the organization, and offer to organize a fund-raiser/awareness activity to benefit the organization. This would be a great activity for a sociology club or other campus organization.

Please go to the book's website at http://study.sagepub.com/korgen5e to find further civic engagement opportunities, resources, peer-reviewed articles, and updated web links related to this chapter.

NOTES

1. The lyrics of "Money, Money, Money" by ABBA were retrieved from http://www .metrolyrics.com/money-money-money-lyrics-abba.html.

2. For instance, this doesn't take into account student loans, whether one has a spouse who is working outside the home, whether one has children to support, and so forth.

3. White-collar workers are office workers, including managers, professionals, and other educated and salaried workers. Blue-collar work refers to manual unskilled or semiskilled labor, such as that carried out by mechanics, plumbers, and factory workers. Pink-collar work is unskilled or semiskilled work traditionally carried out by women, such as work done by waitresses, clerks, secretaries, and florists.

4. In general, skilled laborers earn higher wages than unskilled blue-collar workers. Some skilled blue-collar workers even earn higher salaries than some white-collar workers. For example, in 2004, the median salary of mental health workers (white collar) was $36,630, and the median salary for electricians (blue collar) was $45,200.

5. Actually, we do not have one unified electoral system. Elections are handled at the county and state level, with rules for registering voters, designing ballots, the type of voting machine, and so forth determined by local officials rather than by the federal government.

6. Anyone who knows anything about the tremendous need for affordable housing in New York City (and across the nation) will particularly appreciate this story.

7. See the IAF website at www.industrialareasfoundation.org/.

8. This act was a compromise that led to allowing those applying for a driver's license to register to vote. Poor people applying for government aid programs were also supposed to be encouraged to register. Unfortunately, although many, many Americans register to vote while acquiring their driver's license, relatively few government officials have followed through with the Motor Voter Act's requirement that they register poor people.

REFERENCES

ASA Award recipients honored in Atlanta. (2003, September/October). *Footnotes*. Retrieved from http://www.asanet.org/footnotes/septoct03/fn4.html

Ball, M. (2012, October 24). Obama's edge: The ground game that could put him over the top. *The Atlantic*. Retrieved from http://www.theatlantic.com/politics/ archive/2012/10/obamas-edge-the-ground-game-that-could-put-him-over-the-top/264031

Bloomberg. (2014). *U.S. issues*. Retrieved from http://www.bloomberg.com/info graphics/2014-03-12/national-poll.html#us-issues

Bureau of Labor Statistics, U.S. Department of Labor. (2006). *Working poor and education in 2004*. Retrieved from http://www.bls.gov/opub/ted/2006/jun/wk3/art03.htm

Bureau of Labor Statistics. (2014a, January 24). *Union members summary*. Retrieved from http://www.bls.gov/news.release/union2.nr0.htm

Bureau of Labor Statistics. (2014b, January 22). *Usual weekly earnings of wage and salarly workers fourth quarter 2013*. Retrieved from http://www.bls.gov/news.release/archives/wkyeng_01222014.pdf

Center for Food Safety. (2013, February 13). *Seed giants vs. U.S. farmers*. Retrieved from http://www.centerforfoodsafety.org/reports/1770/seed-giants-vs-us-farmers

Citizens United v. Federal Election Commission, 558 U.S. 310 (more) 130 S.Ct. 876 (2010).

Democracy Unlimited of Humboldt County. (2005, March 30). *Survey says: Yes to local democracy, no to corporate campaign contributions*. Retrieved from http://www.ufppc.org/us-a-world-news-mainmenu-35/2704-news-northern-california-county-survey-shows-only-35-have-heard-of-corporate-personhood.html

DeNavas-Walt, C., Proctor, B. D., & Smith, J. C. (2013, September). *Income, poverty, and health insurance coverage in 2012* (U.S. Census Bureau). Retrieved from http://www.census.gov/prod/2013pubs/p60-245.pdf

Derber, C. (2000). *Corporation nation: How corporations are taking over our lives—and what we can do about it*. New York, NY: St. Martin's Griffin.

Derber, C. (2003). *People before profit: The new globalization in an age of terror, big money, and economic crisis*. New York, NY: Macmillan.

Domhoff, G. W. (1983). *Who rules America now?* New York, NY: Simon & Schuster.

Domhoff, G. W. (2005). *Who rules America? Power, politics, and social change* (5th ed.). New York, NY: McGraw-Hill. (Original work published 1967)

Drehle, D. Von. (2008, January 4). Obama's youth vote triumph. *Time*. Retrieved from http://www.time.com/time/politics/article/0,8599,1700525,00.html

Eckholm, E. (2008). Working poor and young hit hard in downturn. *The New York Times*. Retrieved from http://www.nytimes.com/2008/11/09/us/09young.html?scp=1&sq=working%20poor%20and%20recession&st=cse

The Financial Crisis Inquiry Commission. (2011). *The financial crisis inquiry report*. Retrieved from http://www.gpo.gov/fdsys/pkg/GPO-FCIC/pdf/GPO-FCIC.pdf

Fry, R., & Taylor, P. (2013, April 23). *A rise in wealth for the wealthy; declines for the lower 93%* (Pew Research Center). Retrieved from http://www.pewsocialtrends.org/2013/04/23/a-rise-in-wealth-for-the-wealthydeclines-for-the-lower-93/

Irwin, N. (2013, September 17). The typical American family makes less than it did in 1989. *The Washington Post*. Retrieved from http://www.washingtonpost.com/blogs/wonkblog/wp/2013/09/17/the-typical-american-family-makes-less-than-it-did-in-1989/

Korgen, J. (2007). *My Lord and my God*. Mahwah, NJ: Paulist Press.

Mills, C. W. (1970). *The power elite.* New York, NY: Oxford University Press. (Original work published 1956)

Morgenson, G. (2008, October 22). Credit rating agency heads grilled by lawmakers. *The New York Times.* Retrieved from http://www.nytimes.com/2008/10/23/business/economy/23rating.html?_r=1

Nonprofit VOTE. (2012). *America goes to the polls 2012: A report on voter turnout in the 2012 election.* Retrieved from http://www.nonprofitvote.org/documents/2013/03/america-goes-to-the-polls-2012.pdf

Norton, M., & Ariely, D. (2011). Building a better America—one quintile at a time. *Perspectives on Psychological Science, 6*(1), 9–12.

OpenSecrets.org. (2012a). *2012 Overview: Stats at a glance.* Retrieved from http://www.opensecrets.org/overview/index.php?cycle=2012&type=A&display=A

OpenSecrets.org. (2012b). *2012 Presidential race.* Retrieved from http://www.opensecrets.org/pres12/#out

Patterson, T. E. (2004b). Where have all the voters gone? *History News Network.* Retrieved from http://hnn.us/articles/1104.html

Pew Research Center. (2014, February 11). *The rising cost of not going to college.* Retrieved from http://www.pewsocialtrends.org/2014/02/11/the-rising-cost-of-not-going-to-college/

Piketty, T., & Saez, E. (2007). Thomas Piketty and Emmanuel Saez respond to Alan Reynolds. *Economist's View.* Retrieved from http://economistsview.typepad.com/economistsview/2007/01/thomas_piketty_.html

Piven, F. F. (2005, Winter). Voting and voters. *Logos.* Retrieved from http://www.logosjournal.com/issue_4.1/piven.htm

Prante, F. (2009, July 30). *Income tax payment of top 1% of filers exceeds that of bottom 95%* (Tax Foundation). Retrieved from http://taxfoundation.org/article/income-tax-payment-top-1-filers-exceeds-bottom-95

Roberts, R. (2008, October 3). How government stoked the mania. *The Wall Street Journal.* Retrieved from http://online.wsj.com/article/SB122298982558700341.html

Saez, E. (2012, March 2). *Striking it richer: The evolution of top incomes in the United States* (updated with 2009 and 2010 estimates). Retrieved from http://elsa.berkeley.edu/~saez/saez-UStopincomes-2010.pdf

Schwartz, N. D. (2014, February 3). The middle class is steadily eroding: Just ask the business world. *The New York Times.* Retrieved from http://www.nytimes.com/2014/02/03/business/the-middle-class-is-steadily-eroding-just-ask-the-business-world.html?_r=0

Skocpol, T. (2003). *Diminished democracy: From membership to management in American civic life.* Norman: University of Oklahoma Press.

Teixeira, R., & Rogers, J. (2000). *Why the white working class still matters.* New York, NY: Basic Books.

Weber, M. (1968). *Economy and society.* Totowa, NJ: Bedminster Press.

8

What Does a "Typical American" Look Like Today?

Race and Ethnicity

Does race matter? How you answer that question has a lot to do with your own experiences and your knowledge about society. Your answer also depends on your understanding of how racial groups have been treated throughout the history of the United States. In this chapter, we will examine the relationships among immigration and race and ethnicity,[1] the social construction of race, and the persistence of racism in the "color-blind" era.

Immigration and Race/Ethnicity

Emblazoned on the Statue of Liberty is a poem by Emma Lazarus (1883/2009) representing the statue as the "mother of exiles" as it proclaims "worldwide welcome" to those spurned by other nations. The mother of exiles tells the other nations to

> Give me your tired, your poor,
>
> Your huddled masses yearning to breathe free,
>
> The wretched refuse of your teeming shore.
>
> Send these, the homeless, tempest-tost to me.

Ironically, this poem was written a year after the enactment of the first law to restrict immigration in the United States, the Chinese Exclusion Act of 1882.

Whereas earlier immigrants came primarily from northern and Western Europe, the late 1800s saw southern and eastern Europeans seeking refuge from persecution or economic opportunity. On the West Coast of the United States, Chinese and Japanese immigrants also began to arrive, looking for jobs. Pseudoscience that "proved" that Western Europeans were a race superior to eastern Europeans, southern Europeans, and all people of color spurred negative racial *prejudice* (irrational feelings about a racial group) and racial *discrimination* (actions for or against people based on their race) against the groups deemed to be inferior. This racism, coupled with periodic economic downturns that led to increased competition for work, resulted in restrictive, race-based immigration policies that remained in place until 1965.

After the Chinese Exclusion Acts of 1882 and 1892, and the Gentlemen's Agreement of 1907, which largely curtailed Japanese immigration, a further series of laws prohibited or limited immigration of non-Western Europeans. These restrictions on immigration culminated in the National Origins Acts of 1921 and 1924, which established quotas (by nation of origin) and allowed only a trickle of immigration to continue. The 1924 Immigration Act enacted 2% immigration quotas per nation, based on the 1890 U.S. Census.[2] So, for example, Italy could send only 2% of the number of Italian people residing in the United States in 1890. A provision to the 1924 act limited immigration to those eligible for citizenship. Because only those of white and African American descent could become citizens, this, in effect, prohibited all further Asian immigration.

These restrictions remained in effect until the Immigration Act of 1965 was passed at the height of the civil rights movement and amid worldwide pressure to overturn legalized racial discrimination in the United States. It abolished national quotas (replacing them with quotas for the Eastern and Western Hemispheres) and did much to increase immigration and alter the racial makeup of the United States. The foreign-born population rose from 4.7% in 1970 (Gibson & Lennon, 1999) to 13% in 2010 (U.S. Bureau of the Census, 2012a). Among those U.S. residents in 2010 who had been born outside the United States, 53% were from Latin America and the Caribbean, 28% from Asia, 12% from Europe, 4% from Africa, 2% from North America, and less than 1% from Oceania (U.S. Bureau of the Census, 2012a).

It is important to understand that people do not generally leave their homes and families unless they have very strong reasons to do so. Immigrants move to new nations due to a variety of "push" and "pull" factors. Push factors can include lack of economic opportunity in their home countries, war, famine, genocide, political persecution, and so on. Pull factors from the receiving nation can include economic expansion and better opportunities for jobs, peace, and family or friends who have already emigrated. If you look at the history of immigration to the United States, you can see the impact of these factors on immigration policies (relatively open when we are in peaceful, economic boom times and much more restrictive when we are at war and/or in economic downturns).

A change in push and pull factors has resulted in the recent downturn in immigration to the United States from Mexico (Cave, 2011). Anti-immigration measures have increased in the United States amid persistently high unemployment since the Great Recession of 2008 to 2009. Meanwhile, Mexico has become more prosperous, its people more educated, and its families smaller in size. The result is that the large flow of immigration from Mexico to the United States has started to decline. In fact, in 2012, the numbers of Mexicans moving back to Mexico from the United States were greater than those of Mexicans moving to the United States, and the largest numbers of new immigrants were Asian rather than Hispanic (Passel, Cohn, & Gonzalez-Barrera, 2012; Pew Research Center, 2012).

The status of the various immigrant groups in the United States reflects the global status of their nations of origin and their levels of education. Some Southeast Asian immigrants (such as war refugees from Vietnam, Cambodia, and Laos) came to the United States with little money or education. Today, other vulnerable Asians (such as young women from poor areas) are brought over illegally to work as indentured servants in sweatshops in the Chinatowns of major cities. The vast majority of Asians immigrating to the United States today, however, are educated people with some money who immigrate legally to find greater economic opportunity than exists in their nation of origin. On the other hand, Latin American immigrants are better able to enter the United States in relatively large numbers without either education or money due to their closer proximity. One result of the disparity in education levels of the various entering immigrant groups is the difference in the positions they achieve in the U.S. workforce and in their subsequent socio-economic status. For example, among foreign-born workers in 2012, 43.6% of Hispanics had less than a high school diploma and only 12.6% had a college degree. On the other hand, 58.1% of Asian foreign-born workers were college graduates. This relates to their income, with foreign-born Asian workers making almost double what Hispanic foreign workers make per week (Mosisa, 2013).

The Social Construction of Race

How do people racially identify you? It depends on where you live, as well as what you look like and the racial identity of your ancestors. Race is a social construction, meaning that it is defined differently from society to society and sometimes, over time, even within the same society. For example, the same person could be seen as a member of one racial group in Brazil and another in the United States.

In the United States, some groups have been placed in different racial categories over time. For example, in the 1930 U.S. Census, Mexican Americans were included under the category "Mexican." However, in 1940, they were placed under "white," "unless they appeared to census interviewers to be 'definitely Indian or of other Nonwhite races' (U.S. Bureau of the Census, 1943:3)" (Rodriguez, 2000, p. 84). Today, they are asked to choose a racial category listed on the census and indicate that they are ethnically Hispanic-Latino/Mexican. In many ways, Hispanics-Latinos are treated as a distinct racial group because of their appearance and language or accent (all of which vary and largely determine the extent to which they face racial discrimination; Rodriguez, 2000).

Hispanics-Latinos are not the first ethnic group to be racialized and seen as inferior, however. Many young Italian and Irish Americans may be surprised to learn that most Americans considered members of these ethnic groups to be "less than" white until decades after they arrived in the United States in large numbers.[3] Today, sociologists define a race as a group of people *perceived* to be distinct on the basis of physical appearance, not genetic makeup[4] (Rosenfeld, 2007). Ethnicity refers to cultural rather than physical differences. All this gets even more complicated when dealing with Hispanic-Latino Americans, who, as noted above, are a distinct ethnic umbrella group but can be of any race.

Today, as Table 8.1 indicates, the racial and ethnic makeup of the United States is still mostly white. However, the percentages of Hispanics-Latinos and Asian Americans are rapidly increasing. Table 8.1 indicates the racial demographics of the United States based on 2012 Census figures. A "biracial baby boom" over the three decades since the Supreme Court struck down laws against interracial marriage in 1967 has added to the diversity. Between 1970 and 2010, the racial intermarriage rate (which includes Hispanics as a racial category) grew from less than 1% to 7% of all marriages (Lee & Edmonston, 2005; Pew Research Center, 2013a). By 2010, 8.4% of all marriages and 15.1% of new marriages were interracial (Pew Research Center, 2013a). In 2010, more than 25% of Asian and Hispanic American newlyweds married someone of a different race, while 17% of black and 8% of

Table 8.1   U.S. Racial Demographics (as of 2012)

Race	Percentage
White, alone	77.9
White (not Hispanic-Latino)	63
Hispanic-Latino	16.9
Black or African American, alone	13.1
Asian, alone	5.1
American Indian or Alaska Native, alone	1.12
Native Hawaiian and Other Pacific Islander, alone	0.2
Two or more races	2.4

SOURCE: U.S. Bureau of the Census (2014).

NOTE: Based on how people racially identify themselves (total percentages do not equal 100).

white newlyweds did so. More than one out of every three Americans (35%) has an immediate family member or a close relative now married to someone of a different race (Wang, 2012).

Some sociologists who research racial issues maintain that the racial classification system in the United States is changing. George Yancey (2003) and others maintain that Asians and Hispanics-Latinos will eventually "become White." Other scholars, such as Eduardo Bonilla-Silva (2009; Bonilla-Silva & Embrick, 2005), say that the United States is beginning to establish a three-tiered racial hierarchy with "*Whites* ('traditional' whites, new 'white' immigrants; and, in the near future, assimilated Latinos, some multiracials [light-skinned ones], and individual members of other groups [some Asian Americans, etc.])" at the top (Bonilla-Silva & Embrick, 2005, p. 33). Next will come a middle group composed of "*honorary Whites*" (most light-skinned Latino Americans, "Japanese Americans, Korean Americans, Asian Indians, Chinese Americans, the bulk of multiracials . . . and most Middle Eastern Americans"—Bonilla-Silva & Embrick, 2005, p. 34). The bottom group, the "*collective Black*," will consist of black Americans, dark-skinned Latino Americans, Vietnamese Americans, Cambodian Americans, Laotian Americans, "reservation bound" Native Americans, and "maybe Filipino Americans."[5] No matter what the *future* racial hierarchy will look like, racial inequity continues to exist in the present-day United States.

W. E. B. Du Bois (1903/1989) wrote that "the problem of the twentieth century is the problem of the color-line" (p. 35). Unfortunately, the "color-line" (though it is shifting) is still very much a problem today. In fact, some current scholars maintain that "racism is an integral, permanent, and indestructible component of this society" (Bell, 1992, p. ix).

In an increasingly diverse society, race-centered theorists seek to understand how the racial hierarchy adjusts to changing racial and ethnic demographics. Sociologists who use a race-centered theoretical perspective today look at society, as Du Bois did, through the prism of racial inequality. Moreover, they see race as "an independent and irreducible social force in the United States, a distinct aspect of social organization and a unique lens onto the whole of social life" (Hartmann, 1999, p. 23). Unlike Marx, they maintain that divisions in society are based on race rather than class.

Race-centered theorists focus on how and why racial hierarchies are actively maintained by those who benefit from them. They point out the glaring gaps in wealth, income, education, incarceration rates, and so forth among white, black, Hispanic, and Native Americans as some of the many indications of the still high levels of racial inequality in the United States. Moreover, they examine the racial ideologies, identities, and other aspects of social cultures that help perpetuate racial divisions and inequality.

Critical race theorists, like Patricia Hill Collins, use a race-centered interdisciplinary perspective to both examine issues of racial inequality and advocate for racial justice. Like many other sociologists today, critical race theorists are keenly aware of intersecting types of oppression. For example, a black woman must deal with both gender and racial inequality at the same time. Collins (1990) uses the term *intersectionality* to describe the experience of facing multiple sources of oppression.

Certainly, race remains a social construction with very real consequences. Civil rights laws and affirmative action programs abolished *de jure* (by law) discrimination and provided some opportunities for well-educated minorities to rise in socioeconomic status. *De facto* (by practice) racial discrimination persists, however.

Black and Hispanic Americans still lag behind most other racial groups of Americans in terms of income, wealth, education, and employment. According to the U.S. Bureau of the Census (DeNavas-Walt, Proctor, & Smith, 2013), the median household income in 2012 for Asian Americans was $68,636, and for white, non-Hispanic Americans it was $57,009, but it was just $33,321 for black and $39,005 for Hispanic Americans. Wealth, which requires time to accumulate, reveals even starker disparities between whites and black and Hispanic Americans. The average white American has 20 times the wealth of the average black American and 18 times that of the average Hispanic American (Kochhar, Fry, & Taylor, 2011). While 52.4% of Asian Americans and 30.3% of white Americans are college graduates, only 19.8% of black and 13.0% of Hispanic Americans have college degrees (U.S. Bureau of the Census, 2012b). In March 2014, the unemployment rate was 5.4% for Asian Americans, 5.8% for white Americans, 7.9% for Hispanic-Latino Americans, and 12.4% for black Americans (Bureau of Labor Statistics, 2014).

Is this news to you? If you are white, it may well be. The research of many sociologists reveals that "white people are more likely [than black people] to believe that the socioeconomic status of black people is better than it actually is . . . [and that] the playing field is level (Grant-Thomas, as quoted in Valbrun, 2013, para. 16). This ignorance, reflecting a gap between what white Americans *think* is real and what the data show, is partially due to the way race has been depicted in the mass media since the mid-1990s.

The media has a powerful effect on how whites perceive racial minorities, particularly black Americans, because media outlets are the only places where most whites see and "get to know" people of color.[6] Relatively few whites (24%) live in racially integrated neighborhoods (Ellen, Horn, & O'Regan, 2012). So many tend to formulate their opinions about the socioeconomic status of persons of color (and everything else about racial minorities) from what they see in the media or hear from other secondary sources.

Unfortunately, the media sends a conflicting message. On the one hand, some rappers and sports figures glorify the lives of "gangbangers," connecting blackness with street life and violence (Bowser, 2012; Oliver, 2006). On the other hand, the media also sends messages that race-based disparities no longer exist. In magazines, movies, television, and so forth, U.S. society is often portrayed as if race no longer matters. Interracial couples and integrated friendship groups are depicted in advertisements for everything from restaurants to sneakers; popular television shows such as *Grey's Anatomy*, *Psych*, and *Scandal* have interracial casts that never speak about race; and rarely do news programs or public officials devote time to exposing and analyzing the great racial disparities that continue to persist in the United States today.

Therefore, few white Americans realize that they benefit from *white privilege*. The concept of white privilege refers to the fact that almost every aspect of life (e.g., finding a mate, buying a car, securing a mortgage, shopping for clothes, attaining employment, driving) is measurably easier for white Americans than for Americans of color. This privilege can be "invisible" to white Americans if they have never faced racial discrimination themselves and are disconnected from those who do experience race-based discrimination on a regular basis.[7]

The Color-Blind Ideology

Obama's 2008 speech on race during the Democratic presidential primary will be long remembered because he addressed and contextualized the race-based resentments of both black and white Americans in a straightforward (and eloquent) manner. His doing so was unprecedented and downright remarkable for a public figure seeking the highest political office in the United States. When Obama won the presidency a few short months later, many commentators declared that his election signaled that we are now in a "postracial" era. However, that is, of course, not the case. His election did not change the fact that racial inequality still exists in the United States. Although the election of an African American president certainly marks a moment of great progress, the points Obama made during his March 2008 speech on race were true in November 2008 and still ring true today.

Many Americans today do not want to hear about the realities of racial inequality. Echoing the media portrayal of race described above, a popular view among many Americans—particularly white Americans—is that race no longer matters. A racial ideology that grew out of conservative arguments against affirmative action programs in the 1980s, the *color-blind ideology* is now the dominant racial ideology in the United States (Bonilla-Silva, 2009; Brunsma, 2006; Korgen & Brunsma, 2012). Promoters of the color-blind ideology maintain that we should all act as though we are "color-blind" when it comes to race. Many even go so far as to say that people who talk about and notice racial differences are actually causing racial friction that would otherwise not exist. However, as President Obama pointed out, this is far from true. Racial tensions and racial inequalities have existed in the United States for centuries and continue to the present day. Trying to avoid noticing them will not alleviate them.

It is also important to recognize that people's racial experiences influence how they view issues of race. This was painfully apparent after George Zimmerman, a neighborhood watch coordinator in Sanford, Florida, was declared not guilty of shooting and killing Trayvon Martin, an unarmed black teenager walking back to his father's condominium. Patrolling the area for the neighborhood watch organization he led, Zimmerman spotted Martin, made the (racially informed) assumption that he was up to no good, followed him, got out of his car to pursue him on foot, became involved in a fistfight with Martin, and then pulled out his gun and shot him during the fight.

The vast majority of black Americans were outraged when Zimmerman was found not guilty of second-degree murder and manslaughter, but many white Americans were not. According to a Pew Research Center (2013b) poll taken shortly after the trial, 86% of black but just 30% of white respondents were dissatisfied with the verdict (21% of whites and 9% of blacks declared that they "didn't know" if they were satisfied or dissatisfied).

In a press conference a few days after the verdict, President Obama explained why the black reaction was understandable given their experience in the United States.

> I think it's important to recognize that the African-American community is looking at this issue through a set of experiences and a history that doesn't go away. . . .
>
> There are very few African-American men in this country who haven't had the experience of being followed when they were shopping in a department store. That includes me. . . .
>
> And I don't want to exaggerate this, but those sets of experiences inform how the African-American community interprets what happened one night in Florida. And it's inescapable for people to bring those experiences to bear. (Quote found in Resnick, 2013, paras. 3–6)

As Obama's remarks and our everyday experiences indicate, people notice the racial appearance of those around them almost instantly (Apfelbaum, 2012). However, the influence of the color-blind ideology has led most people to feel uncomfortable talking about race, particularly with members of another race (those most likely to provide us with a different perspective). One of us found through her research (Korgen, 2002) that even blacks and whites who are close friends tend to avoid talking about racial issues. While all Americans are affected (at least somewhat) by the color-blind ideology (Bonilla-Silva, 2009), white Americans, who do not tend to be confronted by racism in their day-to-day lives, are particularly susceptible to its influence.

The negative repercussions of acting as if we do not notice race are many. For example, trying to ignore race in the workplace can result in less productive management styles and a lack of trust among coworkers (Apfelbaum, 2012). Not acknowledging the race of your friends can prevent you from understanding how race affects their lives, their perceptions of themselves, and the society in which you all live. This avoidance is problematic for anyone interested in promoting racial justice. If we want to end racial discrimination, we first have to acknowledge that it exists.

Effective efforts to fight racial discrimination can come only after we uncover and confront patterns of racial discrimination. Likewise, we must make the "invisible privileges" (Rothenberg, 2004) of whiteness visible. To do so, we need to notice and keep track of how different racial groups are treated. For example, if we did not do so, we would not know that in Milwaukee, Wisconsin, and New York City, among equally qualified white and black job applicants, whites were more than twice as likely to be offered a second interview. Even criminal records did not erase the advantage white applicants had over black applicants. Whites with criminal records were just as likely as, if not more likely than, black applicants *without* a criminal record to get a second interview (Pager, 2008).

Nor would social scientists (and, in turn, the general public) be able to learn that New York City had a "pattern, practice and policy of intentional discrimination against black applicants" to the fire department (Baker, 2010, para. 2). Nor would we know that black and Hispanic emergency room patients are less likely to receive medicine to reduce pain than white patients (Heins et al., 2006; O'Leary, 2013; Terrell et al., 2010) or that Asian, Hispanic, and black customers were charged more than whites for auto insurance (Consumer Financial Protection Bureau, 2013).

If we did not keep track of racial patterns, we, likewise, would be unaware of environmental racism. Robert D. Bullard, known as the "Father of Environmental Justice," has conducted sociological research since the late 1970s to uncover and lead campaigns against environmental racism. His work has helped bring to public attention the fact that people of color suffer disproportionately from environmental hazards and that governmental responses to emergencies differ based on the race of the citizens affected (Bullard, 2008). Bullard's award-winning book, *Dumping in Dixie* (2000), remains essential reading for all those interested in learning about environmental racism and working for environmental justice. A member of the National Environmental Justice Advisory Council, Bullard participated in drafting President Clinton's Executive Order 12898, which ordered every federal agency to make environmental justice a part of its mission, and has been an indefatigable advocate for environmental justice. Bullard's work and the studies mentioned above (and the myriad more that exist) illustrate conclusively that race *does* matter and that we cannot be color-blind when it comes to creating and implementing policy in the United States.

The color-blind perspective on race also runs counter to the discipline of sociology. It undermines two of the most powerful goals of sociology: (1) to observe how society really works and (2) to give voice to the marginalized and minority groups within it. It is our obligation as sociologists to expose the negative repercussions of the color-blind ideology and to support efforts to promote racial justice.

Racism Is a Global Issue

Racism is not just an American problem. The concepts of race and ethnicity have been used to separate and distinguish groups of people from all over the globe. Wherever you go in the world, you will find, to varying degrees, some racial and ethnic tension. Western Europe provides a good example of past and present racial tensions. Historically, the peoples of Western Europe have suffered many wars among their nations that were, at least in part, due to racism and *ethnocentrism* (the belief that one's ethnic or racial group is superior to all others). In fact, the leaders of Nazi Germany deemed the Aryan race to be the ideal race and Jewish people to make up a race that must be eradicated. They succeeded in killing 6 million Jews in history's largest genocide and made Western Europe a place where few Jewish people remain.

Over the past 2 decades, Western Europe has become more racially and ethnically diverse due to the arrival of increasing numbers of Asian, Middle Eastern, and African immigrants searching for work. With this diversity have come new types of racial and ethnic tension. When plenty of jobs exist and immigrants are needed to take the ones that the citizens of those nations do not want, immigrants tend to be more welcome. However, when jobs become scarce and citizens feel that they must compete with others for them, immigrants can become easy targets. The different races and religions of many of the immigrants in European nations have helped spark anger toward, and sometimes violence against, nonwhite and non-Christian immigrants.

Even prominent members of European society have faced the wrath of racists. For example, Cécile Kyenge, the Italian minister for integration, the first black minister in Italy, has faced a torrent of racist insults. One member of parliament—a deputy speaker for the Northern League party in Italy—said she had "the features of an orangutan," a deputy mayor likened her to a prostitute, and bananas were thrown at her while she was giving a speech (Kington, 2013). In France, the justice minister, a black woman, has faced an onslaught of racism, with crowds and far-right politicians comparing her to a monkey (Beardsley, 2013).

Evidence of racism and ethnocentrism also abounds in soccer stadiums across Europe. Today, "almost every country in Europe has racist signs, chants and even violence at soccer stadiums, particularly from rightist groups that single out blacks, Jews, Muslims or other ethnic groups" (Vecsey, 2003, Section 8, p. 1). Indeed, racism has been described as the "scourge" of soccer stadiums in Europe (Bohlen, 2013; Pugmire, 2009). A 2012 BBC documentary included footage of fans in Ukraine and Poland "giving the Nazi salute, making monkey chants, and displaying anti-Semitic behavior" and other fans viciously attacking students from Asia attending a match in a Ukrainian soccer stadium (Longman, 2012). The following Sociologist in Action section describes one college student's encounter with racism in Italy.

Sociologist in Action: Anna Misleh

Anna Misleh is a student at St. John's University in Queens, New York, studying sociology with minors in social justice, Spanish, and theology. She is a leader in the Ozanam Scholars social justice scholarship program at St. John's.

In the spring of 2013, a group of students from St. John's University in Queens, New York, were involved in a "study abroad" program in Rome, Italy, and performed weekly service work in a Roma (gypsy) population to better understand an ethnic group that experienced discrimination. In the process we, as college students, learned we could raise awareness of the discrimination of the Roma and its impact. We worked one-on-one with Roma children living in Monachina, a settlement camp of Roma that is not officially recognized, but is tolerated, by the Italian government. Through our work at the camp, interviews with Italians knowledgeable about the Roma, and interacting closely with one of the families at Monachina, my peers and I were able to better understand the Roma lifestyle and the discrimination they face in Rome, Italy.

To deepen our understanding of the Roma population in Rome, we interviewed two Italian women involved in a *doposcuola* (after school) program at Monachina. These women had been visiting Monachina for several years and understood the culture at the camp and the views of Italians towards the Roma. We also read and researched all we could about the Roma to supplement the information given to us by the women involved in the doposcuola program. The Roma who reside in Rome, and other European cities, have come from dozens of different countries. Most have fled political unrest in their home countries. The Roma at the Monachina camp, for example, migrated to Rome in the early 1990s when the country of Yugoslavia dissolved and ethnic wars broke out across the area.

Italians were not pleased by the arrival of the Roma. Generally, Italians stereotype them as an inferior ethnic group that is lazy, dirty, uncooperative, and unwilling to assimilate into Italian culture. This has led to a self-fulfilling prophecy. The discrimination the Roma face prevents them from obtaining reputable jobs, owning property, receiving a good education, and generally integrating into Italian society.

Our response to this discrimination of the Roma, which we saw evidenced in the Monachina community, was to raise awareness. We invited students from several U.S. universities to visit Monachina with us and meet the Roma. Through this experience, they gained a deeper understanding of the Roma and how they are an oppressed minority group in Italian society. They were able to

(Continued)

(Continued)

see that the stereotype of all Roma being lazy pickpockets was far from the truth. We also took time to discuss with them how this discrimination negatively impacts Italian society as well as all other European countries that host these Roma populations and see them through the eyes of negative stereotypes. Being seen only as a societal nuisance hurts both the life chances of the Roma and their ability to fully contribute to the societies in which they live.

After experiencing the plight of the Roma population firsthand, my peers and I were able to use our sociological imagination to relate what we saw to the social issue of racial and ethnic discrimination. Sociology has taught me that a well-functioning society has institutions that support and respect the rights and dignity of all its members. Seeing the discrimination against the Roma at the Monachina camp in Rome, Italy, has brought this truth home to me in a very real way and made me more committed than ever to teach others that racial and ethnic discrimination hurts everyone in a society—not just those who are its direct victims.

SOURCE: Courtesy of Anna Misleh.

EXERCISE 8.1　Immigration and Demographics

Read "Better Lives for Mexicans Cuts Allure of Going North" at http://www.nytimes.com/interactive/2011/07/06/world/americas/immigration.html.

Then, write a two- to three-page essay that describes how social scientific research can be used to influence our understanding of immigration from Mexico and immigration policies in general.

EXERCISE 8.2　Africa and the Legacy of Colonialism

At the same time the civil rights movement was under way in the United States, a global movement for black rights was taking place. One of the results of this global movement was the end of colonial rule in Africa. (All of Africa, except Liberia and Ethiopia, had been colonized by European nations.)

1. Go to the Library of Congress's Country Studies website at http://lcweb2.loc.gov/frd/cs.

(Continued)

(Continued)

2. Select an African nation (other than Liberia or Ethiopia), and write a background paper that includes information about (a) when it was colonized, (b) what nation colonized it, (c) what conditions were like under the rule of the colonizers, (d) when it became a free nation, (e) how its borders were established, (f) how the establishment of its borders affects the nation today, and (g) the overall legacy of colonialism in the nation today.

Extra credit: Analyze the current social, political, and economic well-being of the country you have chosen. How has globalization helped or hindered the nation's growth and the overall quality of life of the citizens? You may want to look at the website http://www.hrw.org/en/africa or http://www.amnesty.org/en/human-rights/human-rights-by-country for more information and insight.

EXERCISE 8.3   **Affirmative Action, Diversity, and Productivity**

1. In two or three paragraphs, describe your opinion about affirmative action programs and how your socialization process influenced your opinion.

2. After carrying out Step 1, read "In Professor's Model, Diversity = Productivity" at http://www.nytimes.com/2008/01/08/science/08conv.html.

3. Describe the key points you learned from the article and how they influenced your understanding of and opinion about affirmative action programs.

EXERCISE 8.4   **Survey on Race in the United States**

Conduct a survey of the members of one of your classes. On the survey, ask respondents to respond to the following statements and questions:

(Provide them with the following options for Statements 1 to 3, and ask them to circle one to indicate their level of agreement: Strongly Agree, Somewhat Agree, Not Sure, Somewhat Disagree, Strongly Disagree.)

1. The socioeconomic status of whites and people from other races in the United States is relatively equal.

2. Racism is often exaggerated by members of minority groups.

(Continued)

(Continued)

3. People of all races have relatively equal chances to become successful in the United States today.

4. What, if any, college courses have you taken that deal with racial and ethnic relations?

5. What is your race and ethnicity?

Compare the answers of (a) respondents from different racial and ethnic groups and (b) those who have and those who have not taken any courses that deal with racial and ethnic relations. Analyze your results.

EXERCISE 8.5 **Racism in Sports**

Go to "Beautiful Game Turned Ugly: Racism in Europe's Soccer Arenas" at http://www.youtube.com/watch?v=W-iRLmaZf4A and "Sol Campbell Warns Fans to Stay Away From Euro 2012" at http://www.bbc.co.uk/news/uk-18240143. Based on the information in the videos and what you have read in this chapter, answer the following questions:

1. Were you surprised by the information in the videos? Why or why not?

2. If you were the commissioner of FIFA (the international football [soccer] federation), what would you do to curb the racist behavior at the stadiums? What makes you think your efforts would succeed (or not)?

3. How might addressing racial inequality in European nations be more or less difficult than addressing it in the United States?

EXERCISE 8.6 **Has Martin Luther King Jr.'s Dream Been Realized?**

1. Go to the website http://www.holidays.net/mlk/speech.htm.

2. Read and watch Dr. Martin Luther King Jr.'s "I Have a Dream" speech.

3. List the points King makes about when he will be "satisfied" with the situation for black people in America.

(Continued)

(Continued)

4. Check off those goals that have now been achieved. Provide evidence for your decisions to check off or not check off each point. Some of these may be partially achieved, whereas others may have been fully achieved or not at all.

5. Listen to "Racial Profiling" at http://www.npr.org/news/specials/america transformed/essays/010925.robertfranklincommentary.html and "The Legacy of the 'Little Rock Nine'" at http://www.npr.org/templates/story/story.php?storyId=14692397.

6. Based on all of the above, do you think Martin Luther King Jr. would be satisfied with the status of racial and ethnic minorities today? Why or why not? If not, how do you suggest that we move toward a fuller realization of his dream? What specific policy recommendations would you make?

EXERCISE 8.7 White Privilege

Peggy McIntosh did much to bring white privilege to public recognition with her essay "White Privilege: Unpacking the Invisible Knapsack" (1989), in which she listed some of the "daily effects of White privilege" on her life.

If you are white, come up with a list of approximately 10 privileges that you (personally) enjoy for being white. (Do not, for example, state that you would have an easier time getting a mortgage unless you actually have a mortgage and you had an easy time getting it.) If you are a person of color, come up with a list of approximately 10 privileges that you think a white person receives for being white that you do not have.

Compare your answers with those of other members of the class.

1. What are the most significant differences among the lists?

2. Who do you think had the most difficult time coming up with the 10 privileges? Who had the easiest time? Why?

EXERCISE 8.8 Your Family and Issues of Race

Write a one- to two-page paper that answers the following questions:

1. When you were growing up, what did you hear about racial issues from your family? (For example, were racial issues ever seriously discussed? If so, why and

(Continued)

(Continued)

how often was race a topic of serious discussion? Did your family tend to bring up race only when making jokes or insulting comments about members of other races? Did they speak from a viewpoint of color-blindness and thus discourage any discussion of the real, pressing issues associated with race and racism?)

2. How do you think the racial makeup of your family influenced how race was discussed (or not discussed) in your family?

3. How do your answers to the first two questions relate to what you have learned in this chapter? How does the information in this chapter help you, if at all, to reevaluate your views on race, immigration, and racism?

EXERCISE 8.9   "A More Perfect Union"

Go to http://www.youtube.com/watch?v=pWe7wTVbLUU, and watch Barack Obama deliver his "A More Perfect Union" speech.

Write a two- to three-page paper that describes (a) the major points Obama makes in the speech, (b) how they relate to what you learned in this chapter (making sure to address how this speech challenges the color-blind ideology), and (c) your reaction to the speech. (If you heard the speech when it was first given on March 18, 2008, compare your reaction to it then and your reaction to it now, after reading this chapter.)

EXERCISE 8.10   The Negative Impact of the Color-Blind Ideology

Read "Opinion: The Risks of Ignoring Race in the Workplace" at http://www.cnn.com/2012/01/31/opinion/apfelbaum-colorblind/index.html. Then, write a two-page paper that incorporates information from the article and this chapter and answers the following questions:

1. How have most Americans been socialized to deal with racial differences since the color-blind ideology became the dominant racial ideology?

2. Why is it important to "acknowledge the (racial) elephant in the room" (a) at the workplace and (b) in the rest of society?

(Continued)

(Continued)

3. How have you been socialized to handle matters of race? Why? How has your own racial background influenced how you deal with racial issues?

4. What can you do to help overcome the impact of the color-blind ideology in (a) your own life, (b) your campus, and (c) the larger society?

EXERCISE 8.11 Environmental Racism

Environmental racism refers to a type of environmental inequality that negatively affects people of color. An examination of environmental inequality in the United States reveals evidence of environmental racism. For example, Americans of color are more likely than white Americans to be exposed to a variety of pollutants and poisons in their homes, neighborhoods, and workplaces.

Read "11 Facts About Environmental Racism" at https://www.dosomething.org/tipsandtools/11-facts-about-environmental-racism, "Silent Discrimination: Issues of Environmental Justice" at http://www.mindthe sciencegap.org/2012/01/16/silent-discrimination-issues-of-environmental-justice, and "Pollution, Poverty, People of Color: The Factory on the Hill" at http://www.environmentalhealthnews.org/ehs/news/2012/pollution-poverty-and-people-of-color-richmond-day-1, and then answer the following questions in a two- to three-page paper:

1. What is environmental racism? Had you heard much about it before? If not, why not? If so, what had you heard, and what have you learned from these readings?

2. Why are Americans of color more likely than white Americans to be exposed to pollutants?

3. How do you think your own racial and class background influence your reaction to the information in these articles?

4. How might you devise a plan to use the information in these articles and the rest of the chapter to mobilize students on your campus to organize against environmental racism in your area?

DISCUSSION QUESTIONS

1. Close your eyes, and picture an American citizen. What does the person you pictured look like? Why do you think you imagined the race and ethnicity of the person in the way you did? (It might be interesting to ask people who are not in this course the same question after you have answered for yourself. If you ask them only to "describe" the person, note whether they mention the race.)

2. Do you have a good friend who is of a different race from yourself? If so, how did you meet? Do you ever talk seriously about racial issues? Why or why not? Do you think you understand the impact of race on your friend(s)? Why or why not? If you do not have a good friend of another race, why do you think that is?

3. How can sociology be used to (a) recognize, (b) publicize, and (c) combat racial discrimination? Be specific, and clearly explain your answers.

4. Why do you think so many people want to believe that "race doesn't matter anymore"? What do you think would happen if we no longer kept track of different racial groups in our society? What might be the beneficial effects? What might be the negative consequences?

5. What do you think your parents would say if you told them you were going to marry someone of a different race? Why? Would it depend on what race? Why?

6. If you were in charge of U.S. immigration policy, how would you determine who should be allowed to enter the United States? What do you think the nation needs from immigrants? What types of immigrants do we want to "pull" here? Why? How should we deal with those people who feel "pushed" to come here? Why? How closely do your proposed policies relate to the message emblazoned on the Statue of Liberty?

7. Which groups of prospective students (other than racial groups) do you think have an easier time gaining admittance to and paying for a college education than other groups of prospective students? Why do you think people have a harder time accepting race-based affirmative action programs than the preferential treatment given to other, non–race-based groups?

8. Do you think multiracial Americans should be given a separate "multiracial" box to check on the U.S. Census? What do you think would be some outcomes of the establishment of such a category?

9. What do you think Marx would say is the root cause of racial discrimination? Do you agree? Why or why not?

10. How might community-organizing groups make people of all races and ethnicities realize their common self-interests? Can you think of an issue that would unite students of all races and ethnicities at your school? What is it? What could you do to organize all racial groups on campus around that issue?

SUGGESTIONS FOR SPECIFIC ACTIONS

1. Conduct interviews with top administrators at your school to find out (a) what they think is the obligation of an institution of higher education regarding combating racism in society and (b) what specific things your school is doing to combat racism. If you think the school should be doing more, organize a group of like-minded students, faculty, and staff to create more antiracism efforts on campus.

2. Go to the NAACP website at www.naacp.org/home/index.htm. Look over the volunteer opportunities listed there, and find one you are interested in pursuing. Find the number of your local NAACP chapter (by calling 877-NAACP-98), and offer your services.

   Or join or volunteer with another race and/or ethnicity-based organization (e.g., MANA at http://www.hermana.org/homfrm.htm, League of United Latin American Citizens at http://lulac.org, CAPAL [Conference on Asian Pacific American Leadership] at http://www.capal.org/ee/pages, or the American Indian Movement at http://www.aimovement.org).

   Please go to this book's website at http://study.sagepub.com/korgen5e to find further civic engagement opportunities, resources, peer-reviewed articles, and updated web links related to this chapter.

NOTES

1. Although we have noted that ethnicity and race are two distinct concepts, we group them together in several places in this chapter. We typically do so when we are including Hispanics-Latinos in the discussion, because they are an *ethnic* group that tends to be viewed—both by its own members and by other Americans—as a distinct *racial* group.

2. The quotas were based on the U.S. population back in 1890, when the numbers of darker-skinned Europeans (e.g., Italians) were lower than they were in 1924.

3. In the middle decades of the 1800s, Irish Americans were commonly portrayed in newspaper and magazine cartoons as apes.

4. Thanks to the Human Genome Project, we now know that physical differences vary more within than among races (Jorde & Wooding, 2004).

5. Bonilla-Silva and Embrick (2005) acknowledge that some individual members of these groups may fall outside the designated tier.

6. Black Americans are more isolated than either Hispanic or Asian Americans (see Charles, 2003).

7. For a great discussion of "invisible privileges," see Paula Rothenberg's (2004) *Invisible Privilege: A Memoir About Race, Class, and Gender.*

REFERENCES

Apfelbaum, E. P. (2012, January 31). *Opinion: The risks of ignoring race in the workplace* (CNN.com). Retrieved from http://edition.cnn.com/2012/01/31/opinion/apfelbaum-colorblind/

Baker, A. (2010, January 13). Judge cites discrimination in N.Y. fire dept. *The New York Times*. Retrieved from http://www.nytimes.com/2010/01/14/nyregion/14fire.html

Beardsley, E. (2013, November 15). In France, some ask if racism is on the rise. *NPR*. Retrieved from http://www.npr.org/blogs/parallels/2013/11/15/245295614/in-france-some-ask-if-racism-is-on-the-rise

Bell, D. (1992). *Faces at the bottom of the well*. New York, NY: Basic Books.

Bohlen, C. (2013, January 3). A struggle with identity and racism. *The New York Times*. Retrieved from http://www.nytimes.com/2013/01/05/world/europe/05iht-letter05.html?_r=0

Bonilla-Silva, E. (2009). *Racism without racists: Color-blind racism and the persistence of racial inequality in America* (3rd ed.). Lanham, MD: Rowman & Littlefield.

Bonilla-Silva, E., & Embrick, D. G. (2005). Black, honorary white, white: The future of race in the United States. In D. Brunsma (Ed.), *Mixed messages: Multiracial identities in the color-blind era* (pp. 33–48). Boulder, CO: Lynne Rienner.

Bowser, B. P. (2012). *Gangster rap and its social cost: Exploiting hip hop and using racial stereotypes to entertain America*. London, England: Cambria Press.

Brunsma, D. (2006). *Mixed messages: Doing race in the color-blind era*. Boulder, CO: Lynne Rienner.

Bullard, R. D. (2000). *Dumping in Dixie: Race, class and environmental quality* (3rd ed.). Boulder, CO: Westview Press.

Bullard, R. D. (2008). Differential vulnerabilities: Environmental and economic inequality and government response to unnatural disasters. *Social Research, 75*(3), 753–784.

Bureau of Labor Statistics, U.S. Department of Labor. (2014). *The employment situation: March 2014*. Retrieved from http://www.bls.gov/news.release/empsit.nr0.htm

Cave, D. (2011, July 6). Better lives for Mexicans cut allure of going north. *The New York Times*. Retrieved from http://www.nytimes.com/interactive/2011/07/06/world/americas/immigration.html

Charles, C. Z. (2003). The dynamics of racial residential segregation. *Annual Review of Sociology, 29*(1), 167–207.

Collins, P. H. (1990). *Black feminist thought: Knowledge, consciousness, and the politics of empowerment*. New York, NY: Routledge.

Consumer Financial Protection Bureau. (2013, December 20). *CFPB and DOJ order Ally to pay $80 million to consumers harmed by discriminatory auto loan pricing*. Retrieved from http://www.consumerfinance.gov/newsroom/cfpb-and-doj-order-ally-to-pay-80-million-to-consumers-harmed-by-discriminatory-auto-loan-pricing/

DeNavas-Walt, C., Proctor, B. D., & Smith, J. C. (2013, September). *Income, poverty, and health insurance coverage in the United States: 2012.* Retrieved from https://www.census.gov/prod/2013pubs/p60-245.pdf

Du Bois, W. E. B. (1989). *The souls of black folk.* New York, NY: Penguin Books. (Original work published 1903)

Ellen, I. G., Horn, K., & O'Regan, K. (2012, May). *Pathways to integration: Examining changes in the prevalence of racially integrated neighborhoods.* Retrieved from http://furmancenter.org/files/publications/Pathways_to_Integration_May_2012_2.pdf

Gibson, C. J., & Lennon, E. (1999). *Historical census statistics on the foreign-born population of the United States: 1850 to 1990* (Working Paper No. 29; U.S. Bureau of the Census, Population Division). Retrieved from http://www.census.gov/population/www/documentation/twps0029/twps0029.html

Hartmann, D. (1999). Toward a race-critical sociology (University of California, San Diego Critical Monograph Series). *Critica: A Journal of Critical Studies,* 21–32.

Heins, J. K., Heins, A., Grammas, M., Costello, M., Huang, K., & Mishra, S. (2006, June). Disparities in analgesia and opioid prescribing practices for patients with musculoskeletal pain in the emergency department. *Journal of Emergency Nursing, 32*(3), 219–224.

Jorde, L. B., & Wooding, S. P. (2004). Genetic variation, classification, and "race." *Nature Genetics, 36,* S28–S33. Retrieved from http://www.nature.com/ng/journal/v36/n11s/full/ng1435.html

Kington, T. (2013, September 7). Italy's first black minister: I had bananas thrown at me but I'm here to stay. *The Guardian.* Retrieved from http://www.theguardian.com/world/2013/sep/08/cecile-kyenge-quest-for-tolerance

Kochhar, R., Fry, R., & Taylor, P. (2011). *Wealth gaps rise to record highs between whites, blacks, and Hispanic* (Pew Research Center). Retrieved from http://www.pewsocialtrends.org/2011/07/26/wealth-gaps-rise-to-record-highs-between-whites-blacks-hispanics/

Korgen, K. O. (2002). *Crossing the racial divide: Close friendships between black and white Americans.* Westport, CT: Praeger.

Korgen, K. O., & Brunsma, D. (2012). Avoiding race or following the racial scripts? Obama and race in the recessionary part of the colorblind era. In A. Jolivette (Ed.), *Obama and the biracial factor: The battle for a new American majority* (pp. 191–204). Bristol, England: Policy Press.

Lazarus, E. (2009). *The new colossus* (Academy of American Poets). Retrieved from http://www.poets.org/viewmedia.php/prmMID/16111. (Original work published 1883)

Lee, S. M., & Edmonston, B. (2005, June). New marriages, new families: U.S. racial and Hispanic intermarriage. *Population Bulletin, 60*(2). Retrieved from http://www.prb.org/pdf05/60.2NewMarriages.pdf

Longman, J. (2012, May 30). Racism and soccer are in play at a big event in east Europe. *The New York Times.* Retrieved from http://www.nytimes.com/2012/05/31/sports/soccer/concerns-of-racism-precede-european-soccer-championships.html?pagewanted=all

McIntosh, P. (1989, July). *White privilege: Unpacking the invisible knapsack.* Retrieved from http://www.isr.umich.edu/home/diversity/resources/white-privi lege.pdf

Mosisa, A. T. (2013, July). *Foreign-born workers in the U.S. labor force* (U.S. Bureau of Labor Statistics). Retrieved from http://www.bls.gov/spotlight/2013/foreign-born/pdf/foreign-born.pdf

O'Leary, L. (2013, September 13). How race can impact your health care. *Marketplace Money.* Retrieved from http://www.marketplace.org/topics/your-money/health-care/how-race-can-impact-your-health-care

Oliver, W. (2006). "The Streets": An alternative black male socialization institution. *Journal of Black Studies, 36*(6), 918–937.

Pager, D. (2008, August 9). *Study: Black man and white felon—same chances for hire* (CNN.com). Retrieved from http://ac360.blogs.cnn.com/2008/08/09/study-black-man-and-white-felon-same-chances-for-hire

Passel, J., Cohn, D., & Gonzalez-Barrera, A. (2012, June 1). *Net migration from Mexico falls to zero—and perhaps less* (Pew Hispanic Center). Retrieved from http://www.pewhispanic.org/2012/04/23/net-migration-from-mexico-falls-to-zero-and-perhaps-less

Pew Research Center. (2012, June 19). *The rise of Asian Americans.* Retrieved from http://www.pewsocialtrends.org/files/2012/06/SDT-The-Rise-of-Asian-Americans-Full-Report.pdf

Pew Research Center. (2013a, January). *Intermarriage on the rise in the U.S.* Retrieved from http://www.pewresearch.org/daily-number/intermarriage-on-the-rise-in-the-u-s/

Pew Research Center. (2013b, July 22). *Big racial divide over the Zimmerman verdict.* Retrieved from http://www.people-press.org/files/legacy-pdf/7-22-13%20 Zimmerman%20Trial%20Release.pdf

Pugmire, J. (2009, February 2). Little done to stop racism in European soccer. *USA Today.* Retrieved http://www.usatoday.com/sports/soccer/2009-02-07-1089560368_x .htm

Resnick, B. (2013, July 22). President Obama was right: For black Americans, racial context of Travyon Martin is "inescapable." *National Journal.* Retrieved from http://www.nationaljournal.com/whitehouse/president-obama-was-right-for-black-americans-racial-context-of-travyon-martin-is-inescapable-20130722

Rodriguez, C. E. (2000). *Changing race: Latinos, the census, and the history of ethnicity in the United States.* New York, NY: New York University Press.

Rosenfeld, M. J. (2007). *Age of independence: Interracial unions, same-sex unions, and the changing American family.* Cambridge, MA: Harvard University Press.

Rothenberg, P. (2004). *Invisible privilege: A memoir about race, class, and gender.* Lawrence: University Press of Kansas.

Terrell, K. M., Hui, S. L., Castelluccio, P., Kroenke, K., McGrath, R. B., & Miller, D. K. (2010, July). Analgesic prescribing for patients who are discharged from an emergency department. *Pain Medicine, 11*(7), 1072–1077.

U.S. Bureau of the Census. (2012a, May 10). *Census Bureau reports foreign-born households are larger, include more children and grandparents.* Retrieved from http://www.census.gov/newsroom/releases/archives/foreignborn_population/cb12-79.html

U.S. Bureau of the Census. (2012b). Table 229: Educational attainment by race and Hispanic origin 1970 to 2010. In *Statistical abstract of the United States: 2012.* Retrieved from http://www.census.gov/compendia/statab/2012/tables/12s0229.pdf

U.S. Bureau of the Census (2014, March 27). *Quickfacts.* Retrieved from http://quickfacts.census.gov/qfd/states/00000.html

Valbrun, M. (2013, August 19). Widespread bias continues in America despite claims of post-racial society. *America's Wire* (Maynard Center on Structural Inequity). Retrieved from http://americaswire.org/drupal7/?q=content/widespread-bias-continues-america-despite-claims-post-racial-society

Vecsey, G. (2003, February 2). SOCCER: England battles the racism infesting soccer. *The New York Times,* Section 8, p. 1. Retrieved from http://www.nytimes.com/2003/02/02/sports/soccer-england-battles-the-racism-infesting-soccer.html?pagewanted=all&src=pm

Wang, W. (2012, February 16). *The rise of intermarriage rates: Rates, characteristics vary by race and gender* (Pew Research Center). Retrieved from http://www.pewsocialtrends.org/2012/02/16/the-rise-of-intermarriage/2/#chapter-1-overview

Yancey, G. (2003). *Who is white? Latinos, Asians, and the new black/nonblack divide.* Boulder, CO: Lynne Rienner.

9

Sex, Gender, and Power

I magine you have just found out that you are going to be a parent. What are your hopes and dreams for your child? What games will you play with your little one? Can you picture yourself as the coach of one of your child's sports teams? Can you imagine you and your child baking cookies together? Now, think about some of your child's characteristics. Is your child going to be tough? Sensitive? A leader? A follower? More than likely, these questions are difficult for you to answer without first picturing whether your child will be a boy or a girl.

Although the physical characteristics and genetic makeup of girls and boys play a major role in the adults they will become, so do the gender roles assigned to them. All parents see their children through glasses tinted by gender socialization. Through gender socialization, we learn to consciously and subconsciously apply dissimilar social roles to boys and girls. The result is that we treat boys and girls differently, and they, in turn, learn to act in "masculine" or "feminine" ways. In this chapter, we examine how gender is socially constructed, how gender construction relates to the distribution of power in society, the status of women as a minority group in the United States (minority or majority status is based on power not on percentage of population), and how we might address the inequality of power between men and women.

The Social Construction of Gender

A person's sex is determined by the physical characteristics that distinguish males and females,[1] whereas gender is determined by the social roles assigned to males and females in society. As such, gender is socially constructed. Sex differences remain constant (almost always[2]), while gender differs over time and from society to society. For example, in the mid-1900s, there were more male than female doctors in the United States, but women dominated the medical field in the Soviet Union. Today, voting and driving a vehicle are both perceived as inappropriate (and, in fact, illegal) behaviors for women in Saudi Arabia, whereas they seem natural and appropriate for women in much of the rest of the world.

Here in the United States, until recently, it was seen as inappropriate for girls to play ice hockey because it was thought to be too physical a game for them and was considered unfeminine. However, over the past 15 years, as women's roles and the idea of femininity have been reconstructed, the number of girls and women who have registered with USA Hockey has jumped from 10,000 in 1992–1993 to 65,500 in 2012 (Francisco, 2012).

Although people's personalities, talents, and outlooks on life are based on a combination of genetic (nature) and social (nurture) factors, sociologists focus on the social factors. In the case of gender and sexuality, we study the social roles applied to men and women through gender socialization. While doing so, it is important to remember that gender socialization intersects with how people deal with race, ethnicity, age, sexual orientation, and so forth. So when we discuss how gender socialization affects men and women, also keep in mind that racism, ethnocentrism, ageism, and homophobia exist alongside socialized gender roles and sexism. These are the intersectionalities we discussed in the previous chapter, and unfortunately, many people face multiple forms of discrimination.

Sometimes, gender socialization can have life-or-death consequences for babies. For example, in many nations, more boy than girl babies are carried to term and born. In South and East Asian nations like China, Vietnam, and India, but also in other areas of the world, such as the Caucasus and Southeast Europe, the sex ratio of births is more than 110 males for every 100 females (UNFPA, 2012). Recent headlines in the United Kingdom reveal that "sex-selective" abortions occur in highly developed nations, as well (Watt & Newell, 2013). One societal consequence of this female infanticide is that there is now a shortage of women for men to marry in these nations. On an even deeper level, infanticide reveals that males are more valued than females.

As males and females move from birth to childhood to adulthood, they learn that they are expected to conform to the gender roles society has assigned to them. This process involves learning what toys to play with, how to speak (what tone, how often, to whom, etc.), how to present oneself in public, what sports to play (if any), what jobs or professions to consider, and so on. One of the authors of this book is the proud uncle of 16-year-old triplets (among a total of 13 nieces and nephews). Two of the triplets are boys and one a girl. It has been telling for him to watch the various gender socialization messages his niece has received, mostly from her peers and other socializing agents outside the family, and imagine how this might negatively affect her life chances and opportunities.

Gender socialization affects how men and women view the world as well as each other. For example, the political issues people deem most important tend to vary by gender. There is much evidence that women today, as a group, have different political opinions from men. There has been a "gender gap" in every U.S. presidential election since 1980. The gender gap refers to the percentage difference in men's and women's choice for president. For example, in 2012, 55% of women but only 44% of men voted to reelect Barack Obama to the office of U.S. president (*The Washington Post*, 2012).

Gender Socialization and Sex Roles

Gender socialization also includes learning sex roles (how to act in dating situations and sexually). As they grow older, boys and girls learn different lessons about with whom it is appropriate for them to act in a sexual manner, when it is permissible to have sex, and how they should have sexual relations. Although some societies are more open than others, and many are becoming much more accepting of same-sex romantic relationships, the majority of people in almost all modern societies view heterosexual behavior (sex between men and women) as more appropriate and socially desirable than homosexual or bisexual behavior. This, of course, has negative ramifications for those who, despite gender socialization, are sexually attracted to people of the same sex or members of both sexes.

As noted above, though, there are many indications that norms around sexual orientation are beginning to shift and that increasing numbers of people support same-sex romantic relationships. Television shows with gay characters, such as *Modern Family* and *Glee*, have brought gay people into the living rooms of millions of Americans and helped change many people's attitudes about gay men, women, and youth. The music industry has also begun to recognize and support more gay artists. One notable recent example of these changes comes from the world of hip-hop. Frank Ocean, a well-known rhythm and blues and hip-hop artist, came out as gay in 2012 and was immediately supported by renowned figures in the field such as Russell Simmons and Jay Z. Even Tyler, the Creator, who has penned many antigay lyrics, has publicly supported Ocean, with whom he has collaborated in the group Odd Future (McKinley, 2012). In 2013, Macklemore hit the top of the charts with his song "Same Love," painting gay marriage as a human rights issue and scolding those in the hip-hop community for their homophobia. Madonna joined him when he performed his song at the Grammy Awards. Immediately after the song, Queen Latifah conducted a live marriage cere-mony for thirty-three couples, including many same-sex couples. Other examples are two National Football League players, Brendon Ayanbadejo and Chris Kluwe, who have publicly proclaimed their support for gay mar-riage (Himmelsbach, 2012); Michael Sam, a new pro football player, who has announced that he is gay; and Jason Collins, the first openly gay player in the National Basketball Association (NBA). As an indication of the chang-ing support for gay athletes, Collins's NBA shirt has become one of the most in demand in the whole league, despite the fact that he is not one of the game's superstars (Net Income, 2014).

Legal support for same-sex marriage is also growing across many areas of the globe. Since The Netherlands recognized same-sex marriages in 2000, other nations such as Belgium, Canada, Spain, South Africa, Norway, Sweden, Portugal, Iceland, Argentina, Denmark, Uruguay, New Zealand, France, Brazil, and Britain have also officially accepted such marriages. On the flip side, Uganda has cracked down legally on homosexuality, and those who are identified as gay are often met with deep discrimination and violence.

Many think it is just a matter of time before same-sex marriage becomes legal throughout the United States, as increasing numbers of people favor its legalization. Today, more Americans support (51%) than oppose (42%) the legalization of gay marriage, and the percentages of those who *strongly* support the legalization of gay marriages has grown to equal the percentage of Americans who strongly oppose it. This is a rapid change from just a decade ago. In 2004, just 31% of the American population supported and 60% opposed gay marriage. American adults under 30 are those most likely to favor gay marriage, and they do so by a more than 2:1 ratio (65% in favor, with only 30% opposing). Even more Americans—71% of those of all ages—believe that the legalization of same-sex marriage is inevitable (Pew Research Center, 2012; Pew Research Center for the People & the Press, 2013).

In the United States, same-sex marriage is now legal in the states of New Jersey, Delaware, Minnesota, Massachusetts, Iowa, Vermont, New Hampshire, New York, Maine, Maryland, Washington, Rhode Island, and Connecticut and the District of Columbia (and likely even more states by the time you read these words). Also, the federal government now recognizes gay marriages and awards married same-sex couples the federal benefits accorded all married people in the United States.

The battle to end discrimination against lesbian, gay, bisexual, or trans-gendered (LGBT) people in the United States is far from over, however. The majority of states still do not protect gay workers from discrimination. As of May 2014, it was still legal in 29 states to fire someone because of his or her sexual orientation (Confessore & Peters, 2014). Moreover, hate crimes continue to be committed against those perceived to be outside the heterosexual norm. In 2009, almost 9 out of 10 middle and high school LGBT students faced harassment because of their sexual orientation (Kosciw, Greytak, Diaz, & Bartkiewicz, 2010). This has led to LGBT teens being much more likely to attempt suicide than their heterosexual peers (Hatzenbuehler, 2011).

Gender Roles

Gender roles basically confine members of both sexes to certain types of behavior and limit their freedom to act otherwise without fear of social disapproval. Those who vary from their gender-based roles face negative sanctions. For example, husbands who choose to stay at home and take care of their children while their wives work outside the home may still be looked upon as not "true" men. Several years ago, the neighbor of one of us was called a "girly-man" because he took time off from full-time employment to be at home with his young children while his wife worked.[3] However, his wife faced no such negative sanctions when she stayed home with their children for the preceding 3 years!

Today, though, gender roles for mothers and fathers have started to shift. Due to the growing need for two incomes to support a family, there are fewer stay-at-home mothers. Among couples who decide that one parent should stay at home, it is no longer an automatic choice for the stay-at-home parent to be the mother. While in 1975, only 47.4% of mothers with children under 18 worked outside the home, 70.5% of such mothers did so in 2012 (Bureau of Labor Statistics, 2011, 2013c). Most couples decide that if they can afford to keep one parent at home, it should be the parent who would make the least money—and in four out of five households with preschool children, the mother is the primary caregiver (U.S. Bureau of the Census, 2011). In most states, even basic day care at a child care center costs more than tuition at a public university. The burden can be overwhelming for parents from the lower to upper middle classes. For example, "day care costs for middle-class New Yorkers can easily equal $25,000 to $30,000 per child. In New York, child care is the single greatest expense among low-income families in the city, surpassing both food and housing" (Quart, 2013). Some women decide that the cost is too much and drop out of the workforce to care for their child. Many of those who do so tend to have trouble reentering the workforce and attaining a job with similar status and pay.

Fathers who stay in the paid workforce also face the strain of dealing with changing gender roles. According to a 2011 study (National Study of the Changing Workforce), men now feel that they must be both providers and active parents and partners. Today, men believe that an "ideal" man "is not only a good employee, working long hours to be a successful breadwinner, but also an involved and nurturing husband/partner, father and son" (Aumann, Galinsky, & Matos, 2011, p. 3). Just as working mothers have faced the strain of trying to "do it all," working fathers are now feeling the pressure to meet expectations from both their family and their employer (and their own perceptions of an "ideal" man).

Gender Roles and Power

All in all, though, despite the recent changes in gender roles that have accompanied women's increased role in the economic sphere, the behaviors we assign to masculine and feminine roles still provide men with more social, political, and economic power than women. In general, although the norms for gender roles are constantly evolving, boys are still more often trained to be tough, competitive, and self-promoting,[4] whereas girls still tend to be socialized to be sensitive, cooperative, caring, and self-deprecating. These respective gender roles clearly give men an advantage in both private and public arenas (Commuri & Gentry, 2005; Slaughter, 2012).

Even in societies where there is *de jure* (legal) equality for women, gender socialization can promote *de facto* (in fact) inequality between the sexes. For example, in the United States, there are more women than men. However, women have less power than men and are, therefore, considered to be a minority group by sociologists and others who study power. Below, we outline some of the social, political, and economic inequalities between men and women in the United States. As you will see, these different aspects of power relations are interrelated, and they feed off one another.

Social Inequalities

Through gender socialization, both sexes are more likely to view men rather than women as experts and in possession of the tools of legitimate power. The different ways men and women communicate, with men more likely to interrupt and speak over others, influence the power dynamics between the sexes (Tannen, 2001; Wood, 2009). The fact that most people in leadership positions are men reinforces the perception that men have more leadership abilities and should be paid attention to more than women (Ely, Ibarra, & Kolb, 2011). This pattern appears throughout society. The traditionally male-dominated Harvard Business School and Fortune 500 Companies (of which only 21 have female CEOs) are two notable examples (Kantor, 2013). This attitude often manifests itself in everyday interactions when men and women enter a public event, meeting, or place of business together. Men tend to be greeted and attended to first.

The tasks that men and women are socialized to do in their own households also benefit men over women. As the number of dual-income households has increased, in the majority of households, women are still expected to come home from work and shoulder the majority of the burden of domestic chores, including cooking, cleaning, and especially child care. Arlie Hochschild (2003) has famously called this social phenomenon "the second shift."

Today, working women who are married spend less time on housework than women used to in earlier decades, when they tended not to work outside the home (University of Michigan Institute for Social Research, 2007). However, one out of two women but only one out of five men do household chores, such as laundry and cleaning, on a typical day. Many more men have started to cook or clean up after meals, but women are more likely to do these chores as well (42% of men compared with 68% of women; Bureau of Labor Statistics, 2013a). These figures make it clear that women still bear the brunt of the second shift.

In addition to giving up more of their time for housework, women are also more likely than men to give up their own spending money for the good of the family. Men are more likely to spend money on themselves (Commuri & Gentry, 2005; Zeliker, 2011). These findings have made lenders and policy-makers realize that families—and whole societies—tend to benefit more when women have control over the family finances (Zeliker, 2011). Internationally, this social fact is the main reason why most microcredit and microfinancing loans are granted to women, as they are much more likely to use the money responsibly for the advancement of their families.

Political Inequalities

Although the first wave of the women's movement led to the passage in 1920 of the Nineteenth Amendment, which gave women the right to vote, women are still far from attaining equal representation in politics. Today, more women vote than men. However, as of 2013, women number only 5 out of 50 state governors, and only 77 out of 435 representatives and 20 out of 100 senators in the U.S. Congress (Pesta, 2012). Globally, only 17 out of 143 current heads of state or government are female (Sedghi, 2012).[5]

Women who run for political office (or any position of power) must, in some ways, resocialize themselves. They have to learn to be self-promoters rather than self-deprecators, to be tough as well as sensitive, and to speak up rather than defer to others. At the same time, they must trust that voters will be more impressed with their leadership credentials than turned off by their stepping out of the traditional "feminine" gender role. As anyone who followed the Democratic presidential primary race in 2008 knows, this juggling act proved difficult for Hillary Clinton (as it would for any woman running for president). For example, while many Americans were thrilled to vote for a woman for president, others frowned on Clinton's stepping outside the gender norm. Many will long remember how she was taunted while campaigning by a man who screamed at her to "iron my shirt" (Associated Press, 2008). When asked to explain his actions, the heckler said, "I just don't think a woman should be president" (Joyner, 2008).

While the United States has not yet elected a female president or even a female vice president, women have achieved greater political gains lower down the political ladder. For example, in 2012, 23.7% of state legislators were women, representing, according to CAWP (2012), a quintuple increase since 1971. Although the gain in the percentage of female state legislators has slowed in recent years, the increase in female representation that has occurred at the local and state levels is very important because many officials in higher office start their political careers in these types of political positions. Still, women remain disproportionately underrepresented even at the local level, considering that women currently constitute 51% of the total U.S. population.

Economic Inequalities

Women have made tremendous progress in the economic sphere over the past five decades. The civil rights movement and the second wave of the women's movement brought about the passage of the Equal Pay Act in 1963 and the Civil Rights Act in 1964, Title IX's prohibition of sex discrimination in schools (and in funding for school sports), acknowledgment of sexual harassment as a social issue, and the inclusion of women in affirmative action programs. These legislative acts, inflation, and the decline in the number of jobs paying enough for one earner to support a family all contributed to women making up 47% of the workforce in 2011 (Bureau of Labor Statistics, 2012). However, in 2011, women held only 14.1% of executive officer positions and just 7.5% of top-earner positions at Fortune 500 companies (Soares et al., 2011).

While there are fewer women than men on the top of the economic ladder, women make up a disproportionate percentage of those clinging to the bottom of the ladder. Women who are heads of households, and their children, are particularly likely to live in poverty. In 2010, an estimated 31.6% of female-headed households lived in poverty, compared with 15.8% of male-headed households (DeNavas-Walt, Proctor, & Smith, 2011). Many children bear the brunt of this *feminization of poverty*. While 11.6% of children residing in married-couple families are in poverty, four times that number (46.9%) of those living with just a female head of house (with no husband present) are in poverty (DeNavas-Walt et al., 2011). Overall, more than one in five (21.5%) children lives in poverty.

Although more and more women of all races and economic classes are giving birth outside marriage (40.1% in 2010), female heads of households are disproportionately poor women (and disproportionately poor women of color [Hamilton, Martin, & Ventura, 2011]). In 2011, just 33% of black and 60% of Hispanic children lived with both parents, compared with 75% of white and 85% of Asian children (Child Trends, 2012). To put it bluntly, it is more difficult for poor women—particularly poor women of color—to find "marriageable" partners (men who have a job, who are not in prison, etc.) than for middle-class and wealthy women (Edin & Kefalas, 2005). As noted in earlier chapters, the unemployment rates for black and Hispanic Americans are dramatically higher than for white Americans, and whereas 1 in 87 working-age white men are incarcerated, 1 in 36 Hispanic men and 1 in 12 black men are in jail or prison (Pew Charitable Trusts, 2010).

Education also plays a role in who marries and the resulting inequalities. Twelve percent of mothers in their twenties with a college degree give birth outside marriage, compared with 59% of mothers with a high school degree or less (Child Trends, 2014). The divorce rate for more educated parents is also lower than for those with less education (Heller, 2012). The result is a growing gap in income and other parenting resources between married parents and single parents. This gap, in turn, creates a disparity in life chances between the children of these different types of parents. This inequality tends to be passed down further and leads to a cycle of poverty, as those with less educated and single parents are more likely to leave school earlier and have their own children outside marriage (DeParle, 2012).

The Wage Gap

Despite all the progress that the women's movement has made, women today still make only 81 cents for every dollar made by men (averaging full-time work across all occupations) (Bureau of Labor Statistics, 2013b) and still face a "glass ceiling" when trying to advance into higher levels of management, for a variety of reasons including the following:

- Gender socialization influences (a) what subjects girls study and are encouraged to study in school (e.g., girls are still heavily underrepresented among math and science majors in college), (b) what career paths they are directed toward and choose, and (c) their ability to think of themselves, present themselves, and be perceived by others as capable professionals and leaders.
- Only women can become pregnant and give birth to children. If women want to have children, they must take at least some time off work to give birth, recover from childbirth, and care for their newborn. Women end up doing most of the child care and housework even when working outside the home (Bureau of Labor Statistics, 2013a; Hochschild, 2003). This affects their ability to spend extra hours at their paid job and advance in their career. Ironically, this factor further fuels the stereotype that women are less capable than men and less hard-working, when in fact they are juggling more and working longer hours than men (when housework and child care and professional work are combined).
- Sex discrimination and sexual harassment still exist and work to hamper the economic progress of women, as the following examples show:
  - A 2012 Yale study revealed that both female and male scientists ranked identically qualified candidates for a lab manager position differently based on their gender. The male candidates were perceived as more competent and deserving of higher salaries than the female applicants (Moss-Racusin, Dovidio, Brescoll, Graham, & Handelsman, 2012).
  - New York City settled a gender bias lawsuit against the Emergency Medical Service of the New York City Fire Department for more than $1.25 million dollars. The plaintiffs maintained that it was much harder for women than men to earn promotions above the rank of lieutenant (promotions to lieutenant were based on Civil Service exam results) (Goldstein, 2013).
  - Bank of America paid $39 million dollars in a settlement decision for discriminating against women in its Merrill Lynch brokerage operation (McGeehan, 2013).
  - The U.S. Equal Employment Opportunity Commission forced FedEx Freight to pay $115,000 for choosing an unqualified man for a position over three qualified women, Amtrak to pay $171,483 to compensate a female worker for wage discrimination and then retaliating against her for complaining, and the Big Vanilla Athletic Club to pay $161,000 for sexually harassing female employees and then firing them when they complained (Equal Employment Opportunity Commission, 2009, 2011, 2012).

Clearly, challenges still exist for women in the social, political, and economic spheres. However, progress toward equality has been made through effective, organized efforts. Our culture and gender roles are continually changing and adjusting to the social and structural forces at work in our society. Legislation like the Nineteenth Amendment, the Equal Pay Act of 1963, and the Civil Rights Act of 1964, which prohibited employment discrimination on the basis of sex (as well as race, color, religion, and national origin), did much to change the actions and, gradually, gender socialization of Americans. Sociological tools have been, and will continue to be, effective means for uncovering and addressing gender inequality in U.S. society and across the world. The Sociologist in Action section below is a good example of how sociology can be effectively used in this endeavor.

Sociologist in Action: Melissa Sheridan Embser-Herbert

During the summer of 2011, I had the opportunity to make my first visit to Rwanda, explore the culture, plan a course bringing students to Rwanda, and learn, more directly than books allow, about the 1994 genocide. Yes, I saw the mountain gorillas—up close and personal—and I bought too many hand-woven baskets, but I also saw—and smelled—stacks of bones and piles of bloodied clothing at genocide memorials. In 2012, with a colleague and 12 students, I returned to Rwanda to study restorative justice and reconciliation in postgenocide Rwanda.

It's one thing to watch a video or read a book about genocide. It's another to visit the country where it happened and see the mass graves, the number of people missing limbs, and—as my colleague experienced—talk with someone who says, "I killed seven people. I've made peace with six families. I hope to with family seven." While our central aim was to learn about restorative justice and reconciliation, we also considered other issues that impact postgenocide Rwandan society. One key issue is the role of women in Rwandan society.

While we were in Rwanda, we visited the market in Musanze. In Rwanda, most women are employed in agriculture, with "off-farm" opportunities being quite limited. Women are far less likely to have access to financial services, including microcredit, often required for starting their own businesses. If the independent participation of women in the nonagricultural labor market is to increase, more support must be found for women who have the skills and initiative to become entrepreneurs. Via our interpreter, one student, Angela, started talking with one of the women at the market who sewed, wanting to know about her life. On the class blog, Angela wrote, "Mama Joyce went on to tell me that she makes 30,000 RWF (Rwandan francs), or about 50 USD [US dollars], per month, and from that she pays 20,000 RWF, or 33 USD, in rent for her sewing machine.... Her income supports the majority of her family's basic needs and definitely doesn't allow for anything extra. They net only 17 USD a month. I was astounded to learn that the cost to purchase her own machine would be about 70,000 RWF, or 115 USD. Cripes! I spend approximately that much on my cell phone bill each month." Angela decided to make a personal donation so that Mama Joyce could purchase a sewing machine. But she had also received $100 from her department in case she had the opportunity to conduct interviews while in Rwanda. Angela was told that should that not be possible, she could donate the money as she wished. She decided to give Mama Joyce that money for the purchase of a second sewing machine. The idea was that the women who sewed together might start a cooperative, a business that they would run together, sharing in its profits. But she didn't stop there. Upon her return to the United States, Angela started exploring how to establish her own nonprofit to help other women in Musanze, Rwanda. *Begin* was begun.

Still a fledgling nonprofit, Begin aims to raise funds to allow more women in Musanze to purchase their own sewing machines. Referring to the money that would no longer be spent renting machines, Angela writes, "This is money that she [Mama Joyce] could be using to buy food and clothes for her children... or money she could be using to reinvest in her community.... By building a park, for example. Or maybe a kindergarten." Mama Joyce is the primary wage earner for her family. Her husband, having left military service, has been unable to find permanent, full-time work. This shift in responsibility is not unique to Mama Joyce, or to Rwanda. Women across the globe share these experiences. Angela recognized this need and then took steps to address it.

My students and I used our sociological imaginations to recognize patterns of systemic inequality in the institutions of Rwanda, including the economy. Our commitment to using that knowledge to make a positive impact on society led some to take action. While these steps are relatively small, we know that there are many other sociologists in action—some reading this piece right now—taking steps of their own. Together, we can change the world for the better.

SOURCE: Courtesy of Melissa Sheridan Embser-Herbert.

EXERCISE 9.1   It Gets Better

1. Read at least one of the research reports at the Gay, Lesbian, and Straight Education Network (n.d.) at http://www.glsen.org/cgi-bin/iowa/all/research/index.html.

2. Go to the It Gets Better Project website at http://www.youtube.com/user/itgetsbetterproject, and watch at least two of the It Gets Better videos. Then, go to http://www.youtube.com/watch?v=TdkNn3Ei-Lg, and watch Jonah Mowry's "Whats Goin On."

3. Write a two- to three-page reflection paper that describes

    a. some of the findings from the research report(s),

    b. how those findings relate to the videos you watched,

    c. how your own sexual orientation (and related experiences) influence your reaction to the videos and report(s), and

    d. what steps you can take to make society a safer place for gays and lesbians.

EXERCISE 9.2   Gender, Relationships, and Socialization

1. Make a list of the 10 characteristics you are most looking for in a boyfriend or girlfriend.

2. On a separate piece of paper, make a list of the 10 characteristics that you think a man or woman is most looking for in you.

3. Have your professor collect these and tally up the results, following the instructions we have provided on our website (http://study.sagepub.com/korgen5e).

4. Analyze the results. What are men most looking for? What are women most looking for? What are the differences between these? What are the causes of these differences? What are the social effects of these differences—that is, how do they affect the gender roles and the social power of men and women?

5. For further analysis, explore the following: What did women think that potential partners were looking for in them? What did men think that potential partners were looking for in them? Compare these results with those found in the responses to Question 4.

(Continued)

(Continued)

6. Were women or men more accurate in guessing what their potential partners were looking for? Why? How does gender socialization help explain this?

7. How does gender socialization promote heterosexuality at the expense of other sexual orientations?

EXERCISE 9.3   Discrimination and You

1. Make a list of five occasions when you have been discriminated against in your life. At least three of these should be based on some biological fact that you can't change about yourself (your race, height, sex, age, sexuality, hair color, body type, etc.). Try, if you can, to list multiple biological facts for which you have been discriminated against.

2. Make a list of five occasions when you have been prejudiced against or discriminated against someone (or a group of people). Make sure that at least three of the five were based on biological facts that the person (or group of people) couldn't change, such as race, sex, sexuality, or physical appearance.

3. Write a two- to three-page essay that discusses (a) your own experiences of being discriminated against, including how it felt and how it made you act and react; (b) why you were prejudiced or discriminated against others; and (c) how a person can face multiple points of discrimination.

4. Make sure to include at least one full paragraph addressing what you might be able to do, in your own life, to be less prejudiced and less likely to discriminate against other groups of people.

EXERCISE 9.4   Gender Differences in Personal Ads

1. Write an advertisement about yourself for an online dating site. In your ad, describe yourself (in at least 40 words) and what you are looking for in a partner (in at least 40 words). Be honest and realistic in what you write, as if this truly were an ad you would submit to find a romantic partner.

(Continued)

(Continued)

2. Get in groups of four (preferably two women and two men), and read your ads to each other. What do these ads tell you about gender and the way we are socialized to maintain and conform to gender roles? Dig beneath the surface in analyzing (a) what is included in the ads and how this reflects gender socialization and (b) what isn't included in the ads and how this reflects gender socialization.

EXERCISE 9.5   Media Images of Women and Men

Women, read the following statement by Lynne Grefe, CEO of the National Eating Disorders Association, and answer the questions below it.

In 1965, the average fashion model weighed just eight percent less than the average American woman.... The average fashion model today is 5'11" and weighs 117 pounds, which makes her thinner than 98 percent of women. Three-quarters of the female characters in TV situation comedies are underweight. Yet the average woman stands 5'4", weighs 140 pounds and wears between a size 12 [and] 16. We know that continued exposure to unrealistic images is linked to depression, loss of self-esteem and the development of unhealthy eating habits in women and girls. Genetics may load the gun, but society pulls the trigger. (National Eating Disorders Association, 2009, para. 5)

1. Do you think the media regularly exposes you to unrealistic images of women? Why or why not?

2. Do you ever find yourself trying to mold your body into one of those unrealistic images? Why or why not?

3. What do you think you and other people can do to (a) counter the effects of and (b) diminish the prevalence of such unrealistic portrayals of women in the media?

Men, read "If Being a Man Means Having Body Hair and Sweating, Why Are the Sexy Guys in Ads Immune to Both?" at http://seedmagazine.com/

(Continued)

(Continued)

content/article/the_media_assault_on_male_body_image, and answer the following questions:

1. Do you think the media regularly exposes you to unrealistic images of men, such as those described in the article? Why or why not?

2. What is your reaction to the findings described in the article? Does your answer relate to the amount of media you tend to consume? Why or why not?

3. What do you think you and other people can do to (a) counter the effects of and (b) diminish the prevalence of such unrealistic portrayals of men in the media?

EXERCISE 9.6   ## A (Gendered) Tour Through a Toy Store

Go to a major (chain) toy store, and try to find a toy (not a piece of sports equipment) that is not marketed specifically toward a boy or a girl. Be sure to take note of the following:

1. What is the layout of the store? Are there distinct boys' and girls' sections?

2. What types of toys are marketed toward girls? What types of toys are marketed toward boys?

3. What types of words and descriptions are used on the toys to market them toward girls or boys?

4. Are there many toys that do not indicate on the packaging (e.g., have pictures of either all girls or all boys on it) the sex of the child for which they are deemed appropriate?

5. How did you find the toy you selected? Was it easy or difficult to find? Where was it located? Based on your experience in the toy store, write a two- to three-page paper that analyzes how toys are a means of gender socialization. What values do they teach boys and girls? Why? For what social roles are these toys teaching and training boys and girls?

EXERCISE 9.7   The Storm

The following videos provide good illustrations of the ongoing struggle over cultural norms about same-sex relationships: "A Gathering Storm" at https://www.youtube.com/watch?v=xGi2r-M_gQ8 and the parody of it, "A Gaythering Storm," at http://www.funnyordie.com/videos/6eddb255b2/a-gaythering-storm.

Watch the videos, and answer the following questions:

1. Did you find yourself agreeing with the message of "A Gathering Storm"? What about your gender socialization led you to feel this way?

2. How did you react to "A Gaythering Storm"? What about your gender socialization led you to feel this way?

3. Fifty years from now, how do you think most Americans will view each of these videos? Why? Does your response provide evidence that gender roles are social constructions? Why or why not?

EXERCISE 9.8   Gender, Politics, and Political Power

Go to the CAWP website at http://www.cawp.rutgers.edu/. Browse through the information on the site, and read some of the research it contains on women and politics.

1. What did you learn about women and the political realm? Does the information you've uncovered surprise you at all? Why or why not?

2. Have you ever thought about running for political office? Why or why not?

3. (Option 1) If you have thought of running, do you think your gender would affect the likelihood of your attaining the political office you sought? Based on the information found on the CAWP website, discuss how you think your gender would (a) affect how you would be portrayed by the media, (b) how the public would perceive you, and (c) your chances of winning.

(Option 2) If you haven't thought of running, do you think gender socialization has affected this decision? Why or why not? Pretend now that you are interested in running, and answer the questions posed in Option 1.

(Continued)

(Continued)

4. Imagine that you are the campaign manager for a female candidate running for president. How would you advise her? What should she stress in her campaign speeches? How should she speak? How should she dress? What issues would you suggest she take on, and what issues would you advise her to stay away from?

5. How might your advice be different if the candidate were a man? What concerns might you have that you wouldn't have if the candidate were a woman? What might you not have to worry about if the candidate were a man instead of a woman?

6. What do your answers to Question 5 tell you about the importance of gender roles in the public imagination? What do they tell you about the social construction of these roles? What do they tell you about the connections between gender and power?

EXERCISE 9.9   Leadership Qualities

This exercise will require three short surveys to be administered in sequence to three different pools of respondents. (The easiest method would be to administer the survey to three of your classes, making sure no student responds to more than one of the surveys.)

1. Create a short form with one question and space for about 10 answers. Ask the respondents to write down their sex (but not their names) on the top of the page. The question on the form should read, "What personal qualities make one a natural leader?" Ask the respondents to write a list of about 10 qualities that make one a natural leader. Collect answers from a class that has at least 20 students.

2. Compile a list of all the answers given by the respondents. Then, order them from the most commonly offered responses to the least common. Finally, select the top 10 responses in terms of frequency.

3. Create a form with a four-column table, and list the top 10 personal qualities from the first survey under the heading "Personal Attributes." Label the other columns "Masculine," "Feminine," and "Equally Masculine & Feminine," as shown on the next page.

(Continued)

(Continued)

Personal Attributes	Masculine	Feminine	Equally Masculine & Feminine
Attribute 1			
Attribute 2			

4. Ask the members of a different class (with at least 20 students) to rate each attribute as fitting best into one of the three categories. Ask the respondents to write down their sex (but not their names) at the top of the page. Collect the forms when they are finished.

5. Summarize how many of the popular leadership qualities are associated with masculine identity and how many are associated with feminine identity.

6. Survey a different class (with at least 20 students), using a new form that lists all of the attributes and asks respondents to indicate their sex and to evaluate each attribute on a scale from least to most desirable as follows:

For each of the following personal attributes, please circle the number that indicates how desirable you find it as a feature of a woman's personality:

Personal Attributes	Most Undesirable	Neutral	Most Desirable
Attribute 1	1 2 3 4	5 6	7 8 9 10
Attribute 2	1 2 3 4	5 6	7 8 9 10

7. Collect the forms, and average the ratings. Overall, how desirable did the respondents find leadership qualities to be in women?

8. Modify the form in Step 6 to measure how desirable those characteristics are in men. Compare the results.

9. Compare the responses of the male and female respondents, and write a two- to three-page paper summarizing and sociologically analyzing your results. What do you believe are the causes and effects of the trends you have identified in your data?

EXERCISE 9.10   Marriage and Babies: Which Comes First?

1. Why does it generally make economic sense to wait to have a baby until after marriage or a legal partnership?

2. Under what circumstances would it not necessarily make economic sense to wait to have a baby until after marriage or a legal partnership?

Answer either 3a or 3b.

3a. For you, personally, does it (or did it) make economic sense to wait to have a baby until after marriage or a legal partnership? Why or why not?

3b. How do you think people's decision to have children (a) with or (b) without first becoming married or legally partnered affects society?

4. How do you think (a) your sex, (b) your race and ethnicity, (c) your religious background, (d) your age, and (e) your social class influenced your answers to Question 3a or 3b?

EXERCISE 9.11   Promoting Gender Equality Throughout the World

Go to the United Nations Development Funds' *State of World Population 2013: Motherhood in Childhood* at https://www.unfpa.org/swp, and watch at least two of the short videos on the site.

Then, answer the following questions:

1. What stories were told in each of the videos?

2. How did the videos reveal the relationship among education, adolescent motherhood, and gender equality?

3. How did they influence your views on gender inequality throughout the globe and the most effective means to address it? Why?

Extra credit: Write a one- to two-page paper that uses your sociological imagination in developing the plan for a program that would promote gender equality worldwide (or in a specific country). Be creative, strategic, and specific.

EXERCISE 9.12   Single and Unequal

Read "Two Classes, Divided by 'I Do'" at http://www.nytimes.com/2012/07/15/us/two-classes-in-america-divided-by-i-do.html?ref=us&pagewanted=all, and watch the "Single and Unequal" video that accompanies it. Then, answer the following questions in a two- to three-page paper.

1. How does the information in the article and video relate to your own life?

2. How does what you learned from the article and video relate to the key three points you learned in this chapter and/or the chapter on social stratification?

3. How has completing this exercise influenced your own perception of the impact of marriage on (a) a family and (b) society? Why?

DISCUSSION QUESTIONS

1. Think about the division of labor along gender lines in the household in which you grew up. Who did what? Why was it like that? Would you want to maintain or change this in your own adult household? Why? If you are cohabitating now (with a spouse, partner, or roommates), discuss how you divide the labor in your current household and if it is similar to the way household chores were distributed in your family of origin (and why or why not).

2. What does "equal rights" mean to you? How much equality is there between men and women in U.S. society?

3. Gender role socialization begins at birth, or before. Friends and relatives want to know the sex of the expected child so that they can purchase gender-appropriate blankets, pillows, bibs, and clothes (blue or pink). The socialization continues and becomes more intense as children get older. Is it possible to raise boys and girls in the same way? Is it desirable? What are some of the obvious ways in which children are taught gender roles? Can people change those to reduce gender-based discrimination? Should we? If so, how? Be specific in outlining some proactive ways to create gender equity through changing gender roles and expectations.

4. How are gender roles related to sex roles? What do they teach us about how to act sexually and with whom to have sex?

5. Why should women in the United States care about the status of women in Bangladesh or Ethiopia or other distant nations? Is there any responsibility for the

U.S. women's movement to participate in the global women's movement? Why or why not? If so, what are some of the ways in which U.S. women can contribute?

6. Why should men be interested in promoting equal rights and opportunities for women? What are some appropriate ways for men to help women gain greater social, political, and economic power?

7. Would you feel (a) more comfortable and (b) more secure with a female or a male president? Why? How do you think gender socialization influenced your answer? How do you think the courses that made you aware of gender socialization influenced your answer? If you answered that you would feel more secure with a man as president, what would need to happen to change your mind?

8. What do you think would be the most effective way to diminish social inequality between the sexes in the United States? Political inequality? Economic inequality?

9. If you were to conduct a study about sex discrimination, how would you go about doing so? What theoretical perspective would best help you make sense of your findings?

10. Describe how women of color are "doubly oppressed" and lesbian women of color are "triply oppressed" in our society. Does your friendship circle include people of various (a) genders, (b) sexual orientations, and (c) races? Why or why not?

SUGGESTIONS FOR SPECIFIC ACTIONS

1. Are you interested in promoting economic equality for women? Go to the website of 9 to 5, National Organization of Working Women, at http://www.9to5 .org. Read about the efforts 9 to 5 is making to fight for the issues of working women. If you want to become part of one of the 9 to 5 campaigns, follow the steps on their "Get Involved" and "Action Alert" pages.

2. Go to http://www.freethechildren.com/get-involved/toolkits/the-power-of-a-girl/, and read "The Power of a Girl." Then, read "Nelly Furtado: Supporting Girls' Education" at http://www.freethechildren.com/nelly. Then, go to http://www .freethechildren.com/international-programming/, and help raise the money to adopt a village!

3. Go to the Human Rights Watch website at http://hrw.org, learn about their campaigns to stop human rights violations against women, and participate in one (write "women" in the search bar).

Please go to this book's website at http://study.sagepub.com/korgen5e to find further civic engagement opportunities, resources, and peer-reviewed articles related to this chapter.

NOTES

1. A very small percentage of the population is born with both male and female sexual characteristics (known as intersexuality). Almost always in these cases, an operation is performed shortly after birth to make the child's sex organs primarily male or female (usually female).

2. Sex change operations, although very painful and expensive, are possible. However, few people choose to go through them, and even fewer have the means and opportunity to have such operations.

3. His comments about making conversations with the other parents (all mothers!) waiting to pick up their children from school are quite amusing. While he can hold his own when the conversations turn to laundry, he says he would much rather be discussing football. Just because people have the power to defy some gender role expectations does not mean that gender socialization has not affected them at all.

4. And boys are taught to distance themselves from "girlish" behavior. The saying "You cry like a girl" is one of the many ways boys are taught to be anything but "like a girl."

5. See the Center for American Women and Politics (CAWP) website at http://www .cawp.rutgers.edu/index.php for more information about women in the political realm.

REFERENCES

Associated Press. (2008, April 4). *Clinton responds to seemingly sexist shouts.* Retrieved from http://www.usatoday.com/news/politics/election2008/2008-01-07-clinton-iron-emotion_N.htm

Aumann, K., Galinsky, E., & Matos, K. (2011, July). *The new male mystique* (Families and Work Institute, National Study of the Changing Workforce). Retrieved from http://www.familiesandwork.org/site/research/reports/newmalemystique.pdf

Bureau of Labor Statistics. (2011, March 16). *Women in the labor force: A databook* (2010 ed.). Retrieved from http://www.bls.gov/cps/wlf-databook2010.htm

Bureau of Labor Statistics. (2012, May 1). *Women as a percent of total employed in selected occupations, 2011.* Retrieved from http://www.bls.gov/opub/ted/2012/ted_20120501.htm

Bureau of Labor Statistics. (2013a, June 2). *American Time Use Survey summary.* Retrieved from http://www.bls.gov/news.release/atus.nr0.htm

Bureau of Labor Statistics. (2013b, October). *BLS reports: Highlights of women's earnings in 2012* (Rep. 1045). Retrieved from http://www.bls.gov/cps/cpswom2012.pdf

Bureau of Labor Statistics (2013c, May 10). *Happy Mother's Day from BLS: Working mothers in 2012.* Retrieved from http://www.bls.gov/opub/ted/2013/ted_20130510 .htm

Center for American Women and Politics. (2012). *Facts: State legislature.* Retrieved from http://www.cawp.rutgers.edu/fast_facts/levels_of_office/state_legislature.php

Child Trends. (2012). *Family structure.* Retrieved from http://www.childtrendsdatabank.org/?q=node/334

Child Trends. (2014). *Non-marital births: Educational differences.* Retrieved from http://www.childtrends.org/non-marital-births-educational-differences/

Commuri, S., & Gentry, J. W. (2005, September). Resource allocation in households with women as chief wage earners. *Journal of Consumer Research, 32,* 185–195.

Confessore, N., & Peters, J. W. (2014, April 28). Gay rights push shifts its focus to south and west. *The New York Times.* Retrieved from http://www.nytimes.com/2014/04/28/us/politics/gay-rights-push-shifts-its-focus-south-and-west.html?hp

DeNavas-Walt, C., Proctor, B. D., & Smith, J. (2011, September). *Income, poverty, and health insurance coverage in the United States: 2010* (U.S. Bureau of the Census). Retrieved from http://www.census.gov/prod/2011pubs/p60–239.pdf

DeParle, J. (2012). Two classes, divided by "I do." *The New York Times.* Retrieved from http://www.nytimes.com/2012/07/15/us/two-classes-in-america-divided-by-i-do.html?ref=us&pagewanted=all

Edin, K., & Kefalas, M. (2005). *Promises I can keep: Why poor women put motherhood before marriage.* Berkeley: University of California Press.

Equal Employment Opportunity Commission. (2009, February 26). *Big Vanilla Athletic Club to pay $161,000 to settle EEOC lawsuit for sexual harassment.* Retrieved from http://www.eeoc.gov/eeoc/newsroom/release/2-26-09.cfm

Equal Employment Opportunity Commission. (2011, November 10). *Amtrak to pay $171,483 to settle EEOC sex/wage discrimination suit.* Retrieved from http://www.eeoc.gov/eeoc/newsroom/release/11-10-11a.cfm

Equal Employment Opportunity Commission. (2012, June 25). *FedEx Freight to pay $115,000 to settle EEOC sex discrimination lawsuit.* Retrieved from http://www.eeoc.gov/eeoc/newsroom/release/6-25-12b.cfm

Ely, R. J., Ibarra, H., & Kolb, D. (2011, September). Taking gender into account: Theory and design for women's leadership development programs. *Academy of Management Learning & Education, 10*(3), 507–527.

Francisco, D. (2012, February 22). *As girls hockey skyrockets, tips to develop players* (NHL.com). Retrieved from http://www.nhl.com/ice/news.htm?id=618378

Gay, Lesbian, and Straight Education Network. (n.d.). *Research (2003–2013).* Retrieved from http://www.glsen.org/cgi-bin/iowa/all/research/index.html

Goldstein, J. (2013, June 14). 5 settle gender bias suit against Fire Department. *The New York Times.* Retrieved from http://www.nytimes.com/2013/06/15/nyregion/women-settle-gender-bias-lawsuit-against-fire-dept.html

Hamilton, B. E., Martin, J. A., & Ventura, S. J. (2011, November 17). Births: Preliminary data for 2010. *National Vital Statistics Report, 60*(2). Retrieved from http://www.cdc.gov/nchs/data/nvsr60/nvsr60_02.pdf

Hatzenbuehler, M. L. (2011, April 18). The social environment and suicide attempts in lesbian, gay, and bisexual youth. *Pediatrics.* Retrieved from http://pediatrics.aappublications.org/content/early/2011/04/18/peds.2010-3020

Heller, K. (2012). The myth of the high rate of divorce. *Psych Central*. Retrieved from http://psychcentral.com/lib/2012/the-myth-of-the-high-rate-of-divorce

Himmelsbach, A. (2012, September 9). Players' support of gay marriage alters N.F.L. image. *The New York Times*. Retrieved from http://www.nytimes.com/2012/09/09/sports/football/players-support-of-gay-marriage-alters-nfl-image.html?_r=1

Hochschild, A. R. (with Machung, A.). (2003). *The second shift*. New York, NY: Penguin Books.

Joyner, J. (2008, January 8). Hillary Clinton "Iron my shirt" stunt. *Outside the beltway*. Retrieved from http://www.outsidethebeltway.com/hillary_clinton_iron_my_shirt_stunt/

Kantor, J. (2013, September 7). *Harvard Business School case study: Gender equity*. *The New York Times*. Retrieved from http://www.nytimes.com/2013/09/08/education/harvard-case-study-gender-equity.html?_r=0

Kosciw, J. G., Greytak, E. A., Diaz, E. M., & Bartkiewicz, M. J. (2010). *The 2009 National School Climate Survey: The experiences of lesbian, gay, bisexual and transgender youth in our nation's schools*. New York, NY: Gay, Lesbian & Straight Education Network.

McGeehan, P. (2013, September 6). Bank of America to pay $39 million in gender bias case. *The New York Times*. Retrieved from http://dealbook.nytimes.com/2013/09/06/bank-of-america-to-pay-39-million-in-gender-bias-case/?_r=0

McKinley, J. C., Jr. (2012, July 6). Hip-hop world gives gay singer support. *The New York Times*. Retrieved from http://www.nytimes.com/2012/07/07/arts/music/frank-ocean-draws-praise-for-declaring-his-homosexuality.html?_r=1

Moss-Racusin, C. A., Dovidio, J. F., Brescoll, V. L., Graham, M. J., & Handelsman, J. (2012, September 17). Science faculty's subtle gender biases favor male students. *Proceedings of the National Academy of Sciences of the United States of America, 108*, 3157–3162.

National Eating Disorders Association. (2009, February 26). *National Eating Disorders Association unveils powerful and provocative ad campaign*. Retrieved from http://www.nationaleatingdisorders.org/press-rom/press-releases/2009-press-releases/national-eating-disorder-association-unveils-powerful-provocative-ad-campaign

Net Income. (2014, February 25). Jason Collins no. 98 top-seller Tuesday. *Netsdaily*. Retrieved from http://www.netsdaily.com/2014/2/25/5445580/jason-collins-no-98-goes-on-sale-tuesday

Pesta, A. (2012, November). The 2012 election brings a stunning array of firsts for women in Congress. *The Daily Beast*. Retrieved from http://www.thedailybeast.com/articles/2012/11/08/2012-election-brings-stunning-array-of-firsts-for-women-in-congress.html

Pew Charitable Trusts. (2010). *Collateral costs: Incarceration's effect on economic mobility*. Washington, DC: Pew Charitable Trusts. Retrieved from http://www.pewstates.org/uploadedFiles/PCS_Assets/2010/Collateral_Costs(1).pdf

Pew Research Center. (2012, April 25). *More support for gun rights, gay marriage than in 2008, 2004*. Retrieved from http://www.people-press.org/files/legacy-pdf/4-25-12%20Social%20Issues.pdf

Pew Research Center for the People & the Press. (2013, June 6). *Section 1: Same-sex marriage, civil unions and inevitability* (LGBT in Changing Times Series). Retrieved from http://www.people-press.org/2013/06/06/section-1-same-sex-marriage-civil-unions-and-inevitability/

Quart, A. (2013, August 17). Crushed by the cost of child care. *The New York Times.* Retrieved from http://opinionator.blogs.nytimes.com/2013/08/17/crushed-by-the-cost-of-child-care/?hp

Sedghi, A. (2012, March, 7). International Women's Day 2012: Women's representation in politics. *The Guardian.* Retrieved from http://www.guardian.co.uk/news/datablog/2012/mar/07/women-representation-in-politics-worldwide

Slaughter, A.-M. (2012, July/August). Why women still can't have it all. *The Atlantic.* Retrieved from http://www.theatlantic.com/magazine/archive/2012/07/why-women-still-can-8217-t-have-it-all/9020

Soares, R., Cobb, B., Lebow, E., Winsten, H., Wojnas, V., & Regis, A. (2011). 2011 Catalyst census: Fortune 500 women executive officers and top earners. *Catalyst.* Retrieved from http://www.catalyst.org/knowledge/2011-catalyst-census-fortune-500-women-executive-officers-and-top-earners

Tannen, D. (2001). *You just don't understand: women and men in conversation.* New York, NY: HarperCollins.

UNFPA (2012, August). *Sex imbalances at birth: Current trends, consequences, and policy implications.* Retrieved from http://www.unfpa.org/webdav/site/global/shared/documents/publications/2012/Sex%20Imbalances%20at%20Birth.%20PDF%20UNFPA%20APRO%20publication%202012.pdf

University of Michigan Institute for Social Research. (2007, January). Time, money and who does the laundry. *Research Update, 4.* Retrieved from http://www.isr.umich.edu/home/news/research-update/2007-01.pdf

U.S. Bureau of the Census. (2011, December 5). *One-third of fathers with working wives regularly care for their children* (Census Bureau Reports). Retrieved from http://www.census.gov/newsroom/releases/archives/children/cb11-198.html

The Washington Post. (2012, November 7). *Exit polls 2012: How votes are shifting.* Retrieved from http://www.washingtonpost.com/wp-srv/special/politics/2012-exit-polls/index.html#United-States

Watt, H., & Newell, C. (2013, October 7). Law "does not prohibit" sex-selection abortions, DPP warns. *The Telegraph.* Retrieved from http://www.telegraph.co.uk/health/healthnews/10360386/Law-does-not-prohibit-sex-selection-abortions-DPP-warns.html

Wood, J. (2009). *Gendered lives: Communication, gender, and culture* (8th ed.). Belmont, CA: Wadsworth.

Zeliker, V. A. (2011, January 27). The gender of money. *The Wall Street Journal.* Retrieved from http://blogs.wsj.com/ideas-market/2011/01/27/the-gender-of-money

10

Social Institutions

Family and Economy

W hat do social institutions have to do with your life? A lot! The makeup of your family, the laws you must follow, your professional career, your schooling, and even whether or not you believe in a higher power (and, if so, what kind of higher power) are all based on the social institutions in your society. You begin your life among family and learn about the world through educational institutions (schools) and perhaps through religious institutions (including rituals surrounding birth, marriage, and death). Much of your education is about preparing for life within structured economic institutions (the labor market).[1] All the while, your public life, and even your private one, is moved and shaped by the workings of political institutions. If the institutions change, so do you. Think about the impact of the Twenty-Sixth Amendment, which lowered the voting age from 21 to 18, on the political power of all young U.S. citizens, and college students in particular.

How do we know an institution when we see one? In everyday language, physical places, for example, a jail, are sometimes referred to as institutions. But in sociology, *social institutions* are patterns of behavior governed by rules that are maintained through repetition, tradition, and legal support. Members of every society create and maintain social institutions to control human behavior and go about meeting their basic needs. How do we know what is a basic need for a society? Try creating your own imaginary society and thinking about what you need to do for it to survive. What means of controlling behavior would you establish to maintain your society? Keep in mind that you can eat what you like at home, but we all share the problem of where the garbage will go when you are done.

Imagine that you and your fellow students are stranded on a distant planet that looks and feels like Earth but has no other human inhabitants. What is the first thing you would do? Almost certainly, you would (a) figure out what you need to do to survive and (b) start assigning people to those tasks you determine need doing. The first thing you would probably need to do is ensure some semblance of order for these undertakings. So the first institution you would set up is some sort of *government*. (We're assuming that there are a lot of other students with you, not just a few classmates.) Second, you would have to start producing some food, finding water, and arranging for some system to distribute these goods. Whether you all share equally or distribute the goods according to some complex system of entitlements, you would be creating a system that includes ownership and "exchange value." In other words, you would be creating an *economic* institution, an institution that organizes how a society generates, allocates, and uses products and services. Because the needs of your group in this imaginary world would be different from the needs of the society in which you currently live, you would not need the same institutions in the same way. But here is the interesting part about ideas and practices that become *institutionalized*: It is hard to imagine them differently. For that reason, you would have a very hard time creating a government or an economy that did not strongly resemble the one you know now (or at least one that you have read or heard about). And yet, when you stop to think about it, there are innumerable ways in which societies *could* choose to organize their governments and economies.

Although not everyone believes in a higher power or practices a religion, every known society has had some form of religious institution (just ask an anthropologist). Would you and your companions adopt a unified system of belief to help you make sense of your new situation? If you were not rescued quickly, you might start trying to establish, in an organized way, a connection between yourselves and a higher power. Organizing a new religion or reestablishing an old one (from Earth) might help you come to terms with your situation, feel that someone (or something) was watching over you, and believe that eventually (even if only when you die) you would be going to a better place, seeing old loved ones, and so forth. If you remained in the distant world for more than a very short period of time, you would also have to set up rules about who could have sex with whom (to avoid nasty fights and to protect physically vulnerable members of the population) and (eventually) who should take care of the offspring of such unions (and how). In doing so, you would be establishing the institution of the *family*.

Finally, if you remain stuck on that planet, you would have to ensure that new members born into your society could learn your culture and the skills necessary to help your society survive. You would have to establish a social institution responsible for educating the members of your society. Once you have done so, you would have established the fifth basic institution found in almost every society, an *educational system*.

As you have probably already noticed, these institutions are all related to one another. A functionalist would maintain that they are also all *interdependent*. Just as a living organism begins to die if a single one of its major organs (e.g., the heart) starts to fail, functionalists maintain that if one institution is not working properly in a society, all the others (and the aggregate society) will suffer as well. For example, if our education system is not carrying out its function properly, young adults will not be prepared to get good jobs and therefore will not be able to support a family, pay taxes, financially support their religious organizations, or buy goods. Eventually, the faulty educational system would harm the family, economic, religious, and political institutions.

Unlike functionalists, conflict theorists examine the manner in which different interests in society work against one another. Karl Marx, for example, famously demonstrated that the worker class and the owner class were necessarily in conflict over just about everything that went on in society, from the organization of work to the proper use of the police and courts to the workings of a free press. But conflict also occurs among social institutions. For example, some religious institutions believe that they should have control over governmental and educational institutions, and throughout the history of the United States, there has been a seesaw power relationship between economic and governmental institutions.

Marx maintained that there was one institution that influences and largely directs all the other institutions. According to Marx (1859/1970), as the type of economic system changes, so does the makeup of the other institutions. The government, the schools, the family, and religion are all tools for those who own the means of production. Marxism, therefore, begins with the assumption of *economic determinism*—that is, that the economic institutions shape the rest. Some political theorists, such as Niccolo Machiavelli (1469–1527), are *political determinists*. (Machiavelli, who is most remembered for his classic text *The Prince* [1909/2001], defined war as an extension of politics, merely another means by which leaders seek to extend their influence.) There are also those for whom religious institutions, or even social institutions (e.g., systems of racial privilege), form the determining institution, with the rest following. Although all the major institutions are tied to one another in some way, in this chapter, we will focus on the social institutions of the family and the economy.

The Family

Marx (1859/1970) maintained that relations among family members and even the average size of families are influenced by changes in the economic system. For example, under an agrarian economic system, in which work is centered on the family, the size of families is large so that they can produce many workers to till the land and produce crops. As societies become industrialized and the work shifts to factories and other centralized locations, families become smaller. The move from farm to city means that families can no longer feed themselves through producing more food in the fields. More children would mean more mouths have to be fed through low-wage work in factories.

According to Marx's writing partner, Friedrich Engels (1884/1942), families maintain the economic system of capitalism and the existing class structure. Legal marriages were created so that men would be able to know clearly who their heirs were so that they could bequeath their wealth to their male offspring. A marriage contract transferred a kind of ownership of the bride from her father, whose name she bore, to the husband, whose name she adopted. The traditional patriarchal family structure also worked to perpetuate the capitalist economic system because it allowed men to devote themselves to making money while their wives took care of them, their children, and their home (for no pay). This system also contributed to the maintenance of gender inequality.

Whereas conflict theorists use a macro-level approach to see connections between families and economic systems, symbolic interactionists use a micro-level analysis to focus on how institutions influence the roles men and women play and the status they assume in the family. As you learned in Chapter 9, even today, and even in the most egalitarian nations in the world, gender socialization within families contributes to inequality between men and women.

Even in Sweden, one of the most gender-egalitarian societies in the world, women still do more of the household labor than do men. Even though both husbands and wives in Sweden are likely to say that they should share their domestic chores equally, women still end up doing more of the work around the house. While most younger Swedes have been taught that gender equality is a good thing, they have also been influenced by the gender inequality they experienced as children and still see around them. Until this disparity in egalitarian goals and outcomes is bridged, there will remain, even in Sweden, "a distinctive gap between the gender values individuals express and the actual gender division of labour they experience" (Lane & Bäck-Wiklund, 2011, p. 221).

However, even though gender inequality remains in societies around the world, the institution of the family is changing. Across the globe, the marriage rate is falling, and the cohabitation rate is rising. For example, whereas the divorce rate in the United States has fallen to 3.6 in 2011 from 4.0 in 2000, the marriage rate also fell during that same period (from 8.2 to 6.8), for every 1,000 people (Centers for Disease Control and Prevention, 2013). In 1960, 72.2% of those 18 years or older in the United States were married, compared with 50.5% in 2012 (Fry, 2014).

The percentage of babies born to unwed parents has increased since the late 1990s. In 2012, 40.7% of all babies in the United States were born to unmarried women (Martin, Hamilton, Osterman, Curtin, & Mathews, 2013), As Stephanie Coontz, the author of *Marriage, a History: From Obedience to Intimacy, or How Love Conquered Marriage* (2005b), puts it, "From Turkey to South Africa to Brazil, countries are having to codify the legal rights and obligations of single individuals and unmarried couples raising children" (quoted in Coontz, 2005a, para. 11). The pattern is clear: Fewer children are being raised by married parents.

Other changes to the institution of the family are now taking place. Same-sex couples and working mothers are becoming increasingly common and influencing the shape of families in the United States and across the globe. For example, as noted in Chapter 9 in this book, a growing number of U.S. states and nations across the globe recognize marriages or civil unions between same-sex adults.[2] Also, most mothers now work outside the home (as well as in it). Today, 75.1% of American mothers with children under 18 years work outside the home. The percentage of employed mothers with children under the age of 6 has also increased dramatically over the past few decades (from 39% in 1975 to 64.8% in 2012) (Bureau of Labor Statistics, 2013; Pew Research Center, 2012). Even children raised by two married parents tend to have working mothers. In 2012, among married couples with children, 59% had both parents in the paid labor force (Bureau of Labor Statistics, 2013).

It's important to note that working both outside and inside the home is not a new phenomenon for women, particularly for women of color (Coontz, 1992). However, the fact that so many women of all races and social classes are now doing so is a relatively new social phenomenon. Today, the options families have, such as keeping one potential breadwinner at home, hiring a caregiver for their children, sending their children to day care facilities, and so forth, all relate to the economic position of the family. With both day care fees and household expenses, such as medical insurance, rising rapidly, parents with limited education and job skills face almost impossible choices when trying to both support their families financially and supervise and care for their children.

Family life can be even more expensive and stressful for parents who are part of the "sandwich generation," meaning they have both dependent children and elderly parents who need care. While grandparents can be of great help to their adult children, they can also need assistance from them. As life expectancies rise and the baby boomers age, their adult children are often faced with figuring out how to assist their parents while raising their own children. Limits on prescription and health care coverage can leave many elderly people unable to pay for their medical needs or afford nursing assistance when they need care. Adult children, often with children of their own, must frequently face tough family and economic choices. The situation is even bleaker if they are uninsured. If that is the case, it is likely that they cannot even afford to take care of themselves! Fortunately, the numbers of the uninsured has declined since the rollout of the Affordable Care Act in 2014 and should continue to fall as the act goes into full effect over the next couple of years. From a high of 18% in 2013, the uninsured rate among those 18 to 64 years of age had dropped to 14.7% in March 2014 (Levy, 2014).

The Economic System

Economies organize how a society creates, distributes, and uses its goods and services. Today, we all live in a global economy in which the economic system of capitalism dominates. As Max Weber described it, the rational capitalism that arose in the West and that has spawned globalization requires paid (not slave) labor, free movement of goods, and sound legal and financial institutions. It also requires a bureaucratic system that hinges on educated administrators, accurate record keeping, and the technology to allow for long-distance communication and transportation (Collins, 1980). Goods and services are created and sold, for profit, across national borders at an increasingly rapid pace.

Inequality among nations is related to what each contributes to and takes from the global economy. "Global north" nations (most postindustrial nations, such as the United States, Western European nations, and Japan) primarily contribute service work in the knowledge economy, with high-skilled workers (Odeh, 2010). In contrast, "global South" nations (e.g., most Latin American, African, Middle Eastern, and Asian nations) tend to produce raw materials or provide cheap labor to produce the goods consumed in global North nations. While some global South nations, such as India and China, are becoming increasingly competitive (in 2012 alone, China graduated 16.8 million college students [FlorCruz, 2012]), most global South nations are far from equal competitors to nations in the global North. In addition, corporations based in global North nations often control the resources of global South nations, and this makes it difficult for the poorer nations to build the infrastructure needed to create stronger economies. The nations with strong educational, banking, legal, and military systems have benefited the most from the globalization process and have used their economic advantage to increase their power in determining global governance and the future of the global economy. Other sectors of the world have not benefited as much from globalization. The World Trade Organization (WTO), which oversees the terms of global trade; the International Monetary Fund, which manages global financial markets; and the World Bank, which provides loans for economic development, are primarily controlled by global North nations and influenced by the concerns of global corporations, further disadvantaging the world's poorer nations.

Today, more than a third of the world lives on less than $2 a day and 22% on less than $1.25 a day (Phelps & Crabtree, 2013). Contrary to the oft-spoken retort that "that's a lot of money 'over there,'" the result is that there are nearly 842 million hungry people in the world (FAO, IFAD, & WFP, 2013), 748 million people lack access to clean water (World Health Organization & UNICEF, 2014), 2.5 billion people live without basic sanitation (World Health Organization & UNICEF, 2014), and 1.2 billion people have no electricity (Plumer, 2013). Almost half of the world's wealth is held by just the top 1% of wealthy people, and this 1% of the wealthiest has 65 times as much wealth as the bottom 50% of the world combined (Fuentes-Nieva and Galasso, 2014). In fact, the wealthiest 85 individuals in the world have more wealth than the bottom 3.5 billion people combined (Fuentes-Nieva and Galasso, 2014).

Growing levels of economic inequality can also be seen *within* global North nations. In the United States, inequalities have steadily increased over the past 20 years, as the middle and lower classes have lost income and the very wealthy have gained greater income. In 2012, the *median* household income (meaning that half of all households made more and half made less) of all Americans was $51,371. Adjusted for inflation, this was a 6.6% drop from the median income in 2000 (Noss, 2013). On the other hand, the top earners have done very well. Today, the average CEO makes 273 times as much as the average worker (Mishel & Sabadish, 2013).

One of the most drastic outcomes of these trends in wealth and poverty is that one in five two-parent households and almost one in three single-parent households struggled to afford food in the first 6 months of 2013 (Stutzman & Mendes, 2013). Many of the hungry are the working poor. For example, Winsome Stoner works full-time at a food pantry in her neighborhood in New York City. Her husband also works. Their combined income, though, still leaves them relying on food stamps (or SNAP benefits, as they are now called) and struggling to feed their seven-person household. One in seven Americans now relies on food stamps to feed his or her family (Seversen & Hu, 2013). Winsome says that food stamps do "cushion me a bit, it helps. But we still run out of food by the end of the month. The middle, sometimes." Their food stamp allowance of $640.00 a month provides $1 per meal for each member of their household. In November 2013, Congress cut the food stamp budget and, therefore, the food stamps given to Winsome and all others who rely on them (Resnikoff, 2013, para. 15).

As the quote above illustrates, workers on the low end of the global economic spectrum toil for very little compensation. The result is often hunger and deprivation for the workers and their families. Some work for even less than the minimum wage. Although sweatshops are most common in global South nations because of lack of unions and inadequately enforced (or non-existent) labor laws, there are also pockets of sweatshops in global North nations, including many right here in the United States. The study described in Bernhardt et al.'s (2009) *Broken Laws, Unprotected Workers: Violations of Employment and Labor Laws in America's Cities* revealed that "many employment and labor laws are regularly and systematically violated" (p. 2) in the United States. The authors of this report surveyed workers in low-wage industries in Chicago, New York, and Los Angeles. They discovered that more than one out of four low-wage workers were not paid even the minimum wage during the previous week and more than three out of four of those who worked longer than 40 hours the week prior to the survey were not paid overtime wages as required.

However, even workers who do not have their wages stolen from them can feel the pain of being on the bottom end of a global society in which inequality is increasing. For example, in Virginia in recent years, workers in an Ikea factory were forced to work overtime with little or no notice. They were all paid much less than workers who reside where the parent company is located (Sweden). Workers in Sweden were paid $19.00 an hour with generous benefits, compared with the American workers' hourly rate of $8.00. Approximately one third of the American workers were temporary hires and made even less. In response, the workers voted to join a union (Eidelson, 2011; Popper, 2011). And seeing the gains the Ikea employees made with their union contract in Virginia, workers in the Ikea factory in Maryland voted to join the same union the following year (Jamieson, 2012).

Organized people have pressured their government to take action to address wage theft and other labor violations, such as those described above. As more and more organized citizens demand that their elected leaders do something to curb the abuse of workers, anti-sweatshop legislation has become increasingly common. Seven states and 44 cities have adopted sweat-free policies[3] (see http://www.sweatfree.org/policieslist).

College students have been some of the most powerful opponents of sweatshops. On campuses across the nation, undergraduates have been striving to make sure that the apparel sold on their campus is made in sweat-free factories. As noted in Chapter 1 (this book), 180 colleges and universities (such as The College of the Holy Cross, Bridgewater State University, Beloit College, Indiana University, California State University at San Bernardino, and Miami University) have joined the Worker Rights Consortium (WRC) "to combat sweatshops and protect the rights of workers who make apparel and other products" (WRC, 2013, para. 1).[4]

Sociologist in Action: Alan Ashbaugh

In the following paragraphs, Alan Ashbaugh, a recent college graduate, describes how he uses the sociological tools he gained as a sociology major at Colby College in Maine in working to bring about social justice locally, nationally, and globally.

Studying sociology greatly influenced the course of my life, giving me the tools to examine the social world, the skills and inspiration to effect positive change, and the direction to use my sociological training meaningfully and effectively.

In my sociology classes at Colby College, Waterville, Maine, I learned about the nature of society; about the harsh and complex realities of social issues; and, most important, that change toward a more just world is possible. A sociological truth that I will always remember is that society is not a static, unstoppable force, as it is so often referred to in popular media, but it is instead a constantly emerging and shifting combination of individuals making decisions and taking action. Thus, the world is already changing; we need only to guide it in the right direction by taking effective social action.

Of the many issues we explored in my introductory sociology course, the one that stood out for me is the vast economic inequality in my own community and internationally, as well as the social classes that create and perpetuate these inequalities. A subsequent sociology course on globalization broadened my sociological perspective to focus on the global issues of poverty, inequality, and justice, and the impact of each individual's actions on people worldwide. Examining these issues led me to a more vivid understanding of the social world; a stronger grasp of issues in my local and international communities; and a better sense of my place in Colby, Waterville, and society as a whole. This newfound understanding inspired me to get involved on and off campus, using my sociological training to move toward change. I became a founding leader of the Colby South End Coalition, which addresses the social and economic divide between Colby and its hometown of Waterville by encouraging volunteerism, dialogue, and a coming together of the two communities. I also took on the role as head of Colby Habitat for Humanity, which tackled economic inequality locally by connecting low-income families with decent, affordable housing. Moving beyond Waterville in scope, I helped to organize the Voter Coalition to "get out the vote" for the upcoming presidential election, and I traveled to Chile to investigate the social promise of the emerging concept of corporate social responsibility.

When I graduated from Colby, I did not have a set career path. I only knew that I loved raising awareness of social issues and bringing students together to take action, and that I wanted to continue to be socially active beyond college. My senior year, I had the good fortune of learning about a job opportunity at an organization called Free The Children through an inspiring, socially involved professor in my sociology department. Free The Children was founded in 1995 by a 12-year-old boy named Craig Kielburger, who was so appalled at the practice of child labor he had read about in the newspaper that he gathered a group of his friends and classmates to raise awareness and take action to effect change—exactly what I was passionate about. In the past 10 years, Free The Children has grown to become the largest network of children helping children through education, having built over 400 schools, educating more than 35,000 children every day, having sent more than $9 million worth of medical supplies, and having implemented alternative income projects benefiting more than 20,000 people in developing countries. Free The Children's mission and the work they do matched my own personal goals and beliefs, so I applied for the position just prior to graduation and was hired! Today, as an International Youth Coordinator at Free The Children, I provide youth with the tools to make a difference in the world, such as information on social issues, effective fundraising and awareness-raising techniques, and the public speaking skills to powerfully communicate their passion to their peers. I use my sociological training each day in my work at Free The Children in examining the social issues that we are working to address, discovering the best ways to encourage and enable young people to effect positive change and "become agents of change for their peers around the world." The image of society I formed from my sociology classes of a constantly emerging collection of individual actions, in conjunction with the social issues we studied, help me to remember every day the power that each individual has to make a huge difference and the tremendous importance of doing so.

SOURCE: Courtesy of Alan Ashbaugh.

EXERCISE 10.1   Functions of the Economy

Imagine that you live in a society in which the economic institution is not work-ing properly (e.g., there is high unemployment or high inflation). According to the functionalist theoretical perspective, how might the decline in the economic insti-tution affect the other institutions in society? Specifically, how would it affect the (a) family and (b) educational, (c) religious, and (d) governmental institutions?

Now imagine that you live in a society in which the economic institution is strong and thriving. According to the functionalist theoretical perspective, how might the thriving economic institution affect the other institutions in society? Specifically, how would it affect the (a) family and (b) educational, (c) reli-gious, and (d) governmental institutions?

EXERCISE 10.2   The Changing American Family

There are multiple structural and cultural causes for the changes in the insti-tution of the family that are noted above. There is also ongoing debate as to whether these changes are more positive or negative for society. Write a one- to two-page essay that examines these changes in the family from either (a) a conflict perspective or (b) a functionalist perspective. (If need be, refer back to the descriptions of these perspectives in Chapter 2.)

When writing your essay, be sure to

1. provide an overview of how society operates according to the theoretical perspective you have chosen and then apply that perspective to the changes in the social institution of the family and

2. discuss whether someone coming from the theoretical perspective you have chosen would approve or disapprove of the changes in the family (and why or why not).

EXERCISE 10.3   When a Family Breaks Down

What happens when a family breaks down? What does our society do to strengthen families and make sure that children are protected? Listen to "'Hope's Boy,' a Memoir of Childhood in Foster Care" at http://www.npr.org/

(Continued)

(Continued)

templates/story/story.php?storyId=68349288, and then answer the following questions:

1. What is the position in the economic institution of most people who experienced foster care? Do they tend to be economically successful?

2. Use Cooley's concept of the looking-glass self (Chapter 5) and/or the theories covered in the deviance chapter (Chapter 6) to make sense of why foster children tend not to succeed.

3. Using the theories you discussed and the information in the story to which you listened, what policy recommendations would you make to improve the foster care system in the United States?

EXERCISE 10.4   The World Trade Organization

1. Go to the Global Exchange website, and read about the World Trade Organization (WTO) at http://www.globalexchange.org/resources/WTO, and then go to the WTO's own website and read "What Is the WTO?" at http://www.wto.org/english/thewto_e/whatis_e/whatis_e.htm.

2. Read the descriptions of the WTO on both websites.

3. Write a paper that answers either Questions a to c or Questions d and e below.

   a. What groups or organizations are represented in each document?

   b. As a sociologist, which documents do you think are most convincing? Explain why.

   c. Did you know very much about the WTO before reading this chapter and these documents? If yes, what gave you that knowledge? If not, why do you think you didn't know much about the WTO?

   d. How would a conflict theorist describe the function of the WTO?

   e. How would a functionalist theorist describe the function of the WTO?

Extra credit: Answer all five of the above questions (a–e). Then, outline what you and your classmates could do to create better awareness on campus and in your local community about the WTO in an effort to help put pressure on it to operate in a more transparent and equitable manner.

EXERCISE 10.5	**When It's American Workers Who Are Exploited**

Read "Ikea's U.S. Factory Churns Out Unhappy Workers" at http://articles.latimes.com/2011/apr/10/business/la-fi-ikea-union-20110410, and write a two- to three-page paper in which you answer the following questions:

1. How does the information in the article relate to the material in this chapter?

2. How does it make you feel to read about how a Swedish corporation treats workers in the United States far worse than its workers in Sweden?

3. Do you think that these inequities should be addressed and, if so, by whom? If not, why not?

4. Would you hold American corporations to the same standards when they employ workers in foreign countries as you are suggesting we hold Ikea to when employing American laborers? Why or why not?

5. How did this article and the chapter influence your perspective on global inequality? Why?

EXERCISE 10.6	**Why Are We Cutting Food Stamps?**

Read and watch the related video "Cut in Food Stamps Forces Hard Choices on Poor" at http://www.nytimes.com/2013/11/08/us/cut-in-food-stamps-forces-hard-choices-on-poor.html?pagewanted=2&_r=0&src=rechp, and read "Food Stamp Cut Backed by Republicans With Voters on Rolls" at http://www.bloomberg.com/news/2013-08-14/food-stamp-cut-backed-by-republicans-with-voters-on-rolls.html and "The Insanity of our Food Policy" at http://opinionator.blogs.nytimes.com/2013/11/16/the-insanity-of-our-food-policy/. Then answer the following questions. Can you relate to the lives of the people described in these articles and the video? Why or why not?

1. Were you aware that one in seven Americans relies on food stamps? What is your reaction to that fact? Why?

2. How does cutting the federal budget for food stamps negatively affect the economy, as described in the articles and the video? Who benefits from such cuts?

(Continued)

(Continued)

3. What theoretical perspective described in this book best explains why some poor people, who rely on food stamps, vote for members of Congress who support cutting food stamp benefits? Why?

4. Describe what steps you can take to curb hunger in (a) your local community, (b) your state, and (c) your nation.

EXERCISE 10.7	**Students Creating Change: The Anti-Sweatshop Movement**

Go to the United Students Against Sweatshops website at http://usas.org.

Write a two-page paper that describes (a) one campaign on which United Students Against Sweatshops is currently working, (b) whether or not you could see yourself joining that campaign, and (c) why you could or could not see yourself participating in the campaign.

EXERCISE 10.8	**Work, Unemployment, and Our Changing Economy**

Go to the website for the U.S. Department of Labor's Mass Layoff Statistics page at http://www.bls.gov/mls/home.htm#overview%20htm, click on "Mass Layoffs (Monthly)," and read the "Mass Layoffs Summary." Read the most recent summary, and answer the following questions:

1. What were the top three reasons (in order) for the most recent mass layoffs?

2. Which metropolitan area was the most affected by the recent mass layoffs?

3. How does the most recent quarterly report on mass layoffs compare with those of the previous 4 years?

Now go to http://www.google.com. Search for "Unemployment Insurance and [name of your state]," and answer the following questions:

1. What percentage of their salary do unemployed people receive in unemployment insurance (assuming that they met the eligibility requirements

(Continued)

(Continued)

for maximum unemployment insurance coverage in your state)? What is the maximum rate?

2. For how long can they collect unemployment insurance?

3. If the head of your household were unemployed, how well do you think the individual could support his or her family on unemployment insurance? Elaborate.

EXERCISE 10.9   Immigration and Citizenship

Select two nations outside the United States (one in the Western Hemisphere and one in the Eastern Hemisphere), and go to the U.S. Citizenship and Immigration Services home page at http://www.uscis.gov/portal/site/uscis.

Write a two-page paper, using the information on the website to figure out how you might successfully emigrate from each respective nation to the United States. Be sure to include the factors that would ease your path to American citizenship (being a highly skilled worker, being wealthy, having a family member here, etc.).

Conclude your paper by describing what you learned from the exercise and how it affected your perspective on the immigration process. (If you did not learn anything new, explain why you did not.)

DISCUSSION QUESTIONS

1. What role do you think economic globalization plays in legal and illegal immigration to the United States?

2. How do you think the changes in our economic institution (e.g., inflation, fewer jobs that pay a "family" wage, the growing need for a college education) are affecting the social institution of the family?

3. Why is it in the interest of global North workers to organize with global South workers for higher wages?

4. What families might be most vulnerable to the negative impacts of the Great Recession? Why? Do you feel that your family has been affected by the recession? If not, why not? If yes, why and in what ways?

5. Which theoretical perspective, conflict theory or functionalism, would you choose to best make sense of how the economic institution operates in U.S. society? Why?

6. Imagine that the institution of the family suddenly disappeared. How might U.S. society be different without this primary institution? Do you think U.S. society could survive without it? Why or why not?

7. If you marry or begin a domestic partnership, do you think you will share domestic chores equally with your spouse? Why or why not? Be sure to discuss how your gender socialization, your family of origin, and your place in the economic institution affect your answer. Or if you are already married or have begun a domestic partnership, how do these factors affect whether or not you share domestic chores equally?

SUGGESTIONS FOR SPECIFIC ACTIONS

1. Research the family-related personnel policies at your college. Do you think they provide adequate benefits for employees who must care for a sick family member? If not, come up with a reasonable suggestion for policy reform, and work with your student government leaders to present your ideas (and advocate for them) to the administration.

2. Research the policies that your college has for providing benefits to partners of lesbian, gay, bisexual, transgender, or intersexed (LGBTI) employees. Are they the same as for the partners of heterosexual employees? If not, why not? How do your findings, in either case, reflect the values of your college (your institution!) and of the greater society? If you find inequalities and believe that they need to be changed, what steps would you take to ensure that the partners of all employees receive equal benefits?

3a. Review the information on the U.S. Immigration and Customs Enforcement's Students and Exchange Visitors webpage at http://www.ice.gov/sevis/students.

3b. Interview the administrator on your campus who is in charge of international students. Ask him or her how your school assists international students through the process of becoming students on your campus.

3c. Interview five international students at your school. Ask them about the steps they went through to become students there. Be sure to note any differences in their experiences and why these differences may have occurred (the year of their matriculation, the nation from which they came, their economic status, etc.).

3d. Use this information to create a resource for international students that could be put on your school website (if approved by your college or university administration).

4. Research the salaries and benefits of the cafeteria workers and custodial professionals on your campus. Do they receive a living wage? Do some research to learn more about how students on other campuses have advocated for cafeteria workers and custodial professionals and how you might do so as well. As a starting place, you can find information at www.jobswithjustice.org.

5. Go to Free The Children's website at http://www.freethechildren.com. After browsing through it, read the information provided on child labor (http://we .freethechildren.com/learn-facts?issue=child-labour). One of the most powerful ways to fight against child labor is to ensure that children have schools to attend and the resources (funds for school fees, books, uniforms, etc.) to afford to go to school. Now that you know about child labor and how important education is, you can start a campaign to raise money to build schools in regions known for child labor. Check out the resources at http://www.freethechildren.com/whatwedo/international/aav/education, and begin a school-building campaign at your college.

Please go to this book's website at http://study.sagepub.com/korgen5e to find further civic engagement opportunities, resources, peer-reviewed articles, and updated web links related to this chapter.

NOTES

1. Of course, some students leave high school and join the military institution. Many do this in the hope of receiving the training and experience they need to succeed economically once they leave the military.

2. The Internal Revenue Service now recognizes same-sex marriages.

3. For example, the city of Bangor, Maine, passed legislation stating, "All clothes available on local store shelves should be made according to established international standards of ethical production" (see para. 2 at http://ihscslnews.org/view_article.php?id=127).

4. For more information about the campaign, go to the WRC website at http://workersrights.org.

REFERENCES

Bernhardt, A., Milkman, R., Theodore, N., Heckathorn, D., Auer, M., DeFilippis, J., . . . Spiller, M. (2009). *Broken laws, unprotected workers: Violations of employment and labor laws in America's cities*. Retrieved from http://www.nelp.org/page/-/brokenlaws/BrokenLawsReport2009.pdf?nocdn=1

Bureau of Labor Statistics. (2013, April 26). *Employment characteristics of families—2012*. Retrieved from http://www.bls.gov/news.release/archives/famee_04262013.pdf

Centers for Disease Control and Prevention. (2013, February 19). *National marriage and divorce rate trends*. Retrieved from http://www.cdc.gov/nchs/nvss/marriage_divorce_tables.htm

Collins, R. (1980). Weber's last theory of capitalism: A systematization. *American Sociological Review, 45,* 925–942.

Coontz, S. (1992). *The way we never were: American families and the nostalgia trap.* New York, NY: Basic Books.

Coontz, S. (2005a, May 1). For better, for worse: Marriage means something different now. *The Washington Post.* Retrieved from http://www.washingtonpost.com/wp-dyn/content/article/2005/04/30/AR2005043000108_pf.html

Coontz, S. (2005b). *Marriage, a history: From obedience to intimacy, or how love conquered marriage.* New York, NY: Viking.

Eidelson, J. (2011, Aug. 5). *Union victory at Virginia IKEA plant: Resistance grows against race-to-bottom wages* (AlterNet). Retrieved from http://www.alternet.org/story/151909/union_victory_at_virginia_ikea_plant%3A_resistance_grows_against_race-to-bottom_wages

Engels, F. (1942). *The origin of the family, private property, and the state* (F. L. Morgan, Trans.). New York, NY: International. (Original work published 1884)

FAO, IFAD, & WFP. (2013). *The state of food insecurity in the world 2013. The multiple dimensions of food security.* Rome, Italy: Food and Agriculture Organisation. Retrieved from http://www.fao.org/docrep/018/i3434e/i3434e.pdf

FlorCruz, J. A. (2012, June 12). School's out: Chinese graduates fight to be heard (CNN.com). Retrieved from http://www.cnn.com/2012/06/12/world/asia/china-college-graduates-florcruz/index.html

Fry, R. (2014, February 6). *New census data show more Americans are tying the knot, but mostly it's the college-educated* (Pew Research Center). Retrieved from http://www.pewresearch.org/fact-tank/2014/02/06/new-census-data-show-more-americans-are-tying-the-knot-but-mostly-its-the-college-educated/

Fuentes-Nieva, R., & Galasso, N. (2014, January 20). *Working for the few: Political capture and economic inequality* (Oxfam Briefing Paper 178). Retrieved from http://www.oxfam.org/sites/www.oxfam.org/files/bp-working-for-few-political-capture-economic-inequality-200114-en.pdf

Jamieson, D. (2012, January 19). Ikea workers in Maryland vote to unionize. *The Huffington Post.* Retrieved from http://www.huffingtonpost.com/2012/01/19/ikea-workers-maryland-unionize_n_1217391.html

Lane, L., & Bäck-Wiklund, M. (2011). Perceived work-life conflict among Swedish dual-earner families. In E. Addis, P. de Villota, F. Degavre, & J. Eriksen (Eds.), *Gender and well being: The role of institutions* (pp. 221–240). London, England: Ashgate.

Levy, J. (2014, April 7). *In U.S., uninsured rate lowest since 2008* (Gallup). Retrieved from http://www.gallup.com/poll/168248/uninsured-rate-lowest-2008.aspx

Machiavelli, N. (2001). *The prince* (Vol. 36, Pt. 1; N. H. Thomson, Trans.). New York, NY: Collier. (Original work published 1909)

Martin, J. A., Hamilton, B. E., Osterman, M. J. K., Curtin, S. C., & Mathews, T. J. (2013, December 30). *Births: Final data for 2012* (National Vital Statistics Report, Vol. 62, No. 9). Retrieved from http://www.cdc.gov/nchs/data/nvsr/nvsr62/nvsr62_09.pdf#table16

Marx, K. (1970). *A contribution to the critique of political economy* (M. Dobbs, Trans.). New York, NY: International. (Original work published 1859)

Mishel, L., & Sabadish, N. (2013, June 26). *CEO pay in 2012 was extraordinarily high relative to typical workers and other high earners* (Economic Policy Institute). Retrieved from http://www.epi.org/publication/ceo-pay-2012-extraordinarily-high/

Noss, A. (2013, September). *Household income: 2012* (American Community Survey Briefs). Retrieved from https://www.census.gov/prod/2013pubs/acsbr12-02.pdf

Odeh, L. E. (2010). A comparative analysis of global North and global South economies. *Journal of Sustainable Development in Africa, 12*(3), 338–348. Retrieved from http://www.jsd-africa.com/Jsda/V12No3_Summer2010_A/PDF/A%20Comparative%20Analysis%20of%20Global%20North%20and%20Global%20South%20Economies%20(Odeh).pdf

Pew Research Center. (2012, April 19). *A gender reversal on career aspirations.* Retrieved from http://www.pewsocialtrends.org/2012/04/19/a-gender-reversal-on-career-aspirations

Phelps, G., & Crabtree, S. (2013, December 23). *More than one in five worldwide living in extreme poverty* (Gallup World). Retrieved from http://www.gallup.com/poll/166565/one-five-worldwide-living-extreme-poverty.aspx

Plumer, B. (2013, May). Here's why 1.2 billion people still don't have access to electricity. *Washington Post.* Retrieved from http://www.washingtonpost.com/blogs/wonkblog/wp/2013/05/29/heres-why-1-2-billion-people-still-dont-have-access-to-electricity/

Popper, N. (2011, April 10). *Ikea's U.S. factory churns out unhappy workers.* Retrieved from http://articles.latimes.com/2011/apr/10/business/la-fi-ikea-union-20110410

Resnikoff, N. (2013, October 30). *America's new hunger crisis* (MSNBC.com). Retrieved from http://www.msnbc.com/all/americas-new-hunger-crisis

Severson, K., & Hu, W. (2013, November 7). Cut in food stamps forces hard choices on poor. *The New York Times.* Retrieved from http://www.nytimes.com/2013/11/08/us/cut-in-food-stamps-forces-hard-choices-on-poor.html?pagewanted=all&_r=0

Stutzman, J., & Mendes, E. (2013, July 17). *In U.S., single-parent households struggle more to buy food* (Gallup). Retrieved from http://www.gallup.com/poll/163544/single-parent-households-struggle-buy-food.aspx

Worker Rights Consortium. (2013). *About us.* Retrieved from http://www.workersrights.org/about/as.asp

World Health Organization, & UNICEF. (2014). *Progress on drinking water and sanitation: 2014 update.* Retrieved from http://www.wssinfo.org/fileadmin/user_upload/resources/JMP_report_2014_webEng.pdf

11

Social Institutions, Continued

Education, Government, and Religion

S hould students in U.S. public schools be required to "pledge allegiance to the flag of the United States of America and to the Republic for which it stands, one nation under God, indivisible, with liberty and justice for all"?[1] This question reveals the connection among educational, political, and religious institutions in the United States. How is our nation connected to God? Which God? Whose God? Are you less of an American if you don't believe in God? These questions have been debated by politicians, religious leaders, and educators across the United States. In this chapter, we examine the institutions of education, government, and religion and their relationships to one another and to the other primary institutions in U.S. society.

Educational Institutions

Educational institutions teach young members of society the basic and (in some cases) advanced skills needed to function effectively in our society. In turn, educated citizens enable societies to run smoothly and to become more technologically advanced, more productive, and more prosperous. The educational level of a nation's population is directly related to its level of income equality and overall economic health.[2] As other key institutions in society change, the functions of the educational system must adjust accordingly. For example, as economies change, so do the skills needed by citizens and those taught in the educational systems. As institutions become increasingly complex and bureaucratized, they need an increasingly well-educated workforce. As Max Weber (1970) pointed out, "Trained expertness is increasingly indispensable for modern bureaucracies" (p. 240).

A 2013 Organisation for Economic Co-operation and Development (OECD) study shows, however, that the United States has fallen behind most other developed nations in teaching its population the technical and mathematical skills needed in the workplace today and is only average in literacy. The tests, in literacy, basic math, and "problem solving in technology-rich environments," were given to people of ages 16 to 65 in 22 OECD nations, Cyprus, and the Russian Federation. Young Americans scored lower than older Americans on the tests, and test takers in Japan and Finland earned the highest scores on all three tests (OECD, 2013; Pérez-Peña, 2013).

There were also more high *and* more low scores among American test takers than among those from other nations. So it appears that the U.S. education system is polarized, with a large divide between those at the top and those at the bottom, and with those in the middle learning fewer skills than students from most other developed nations. This does not bode well for the economic or social health of the United States or its individual residents. As the OECD (2013) report notes, "If there is one central message emerging from this new Survey of Adult Skills, it is that what people know and what they can do with what they know has a major impact on their life chances" (p. 6). Educational institutions must teach students information *and* how to use that information in the modern workplace, and they must do so for *all* citizens and not just those at the top of the educational ladder.

Educational institutions are also connected in a variety of ways to the institution of government. Those who score higher on the OECD Survey of Adult Skills are also more likely to trust others, engage in volunteer activities, believe that they have an impact on political processes, and be employed and make above-average salaries (OECD, 2013). Schools teach students how government functions and their obligations as citizens to participate in public life. An educated citizenry also provides the skills and brainpower a nation needs in an increasingly competitive global society. To provide such a workforce, our educational system must be effective and properly funded.

State and local governments supply most of the funding for public schools. States provide 43.5% of the funding, local communities 44%, and the federal government 12.5% (Dixon, 2012). In most states, primary and secondary public schools receive funding based largely on local property taxes. Both state and federal governments create educational goals. State governments and education experts across the nation developed the Common Core Standards, which 45 states and Washington, D.C., have now begun to implement. For the first time, almost every state will expect students to achieve the same standard of achievement in English and mathematics. In recent years, the federal government has also played a larger role in regulating the function and operation of public schools. For example, the federally mandated No Child Left Behind Act of 2001 (NCLB) established, for the first time, test-focused goals and timetables that public schools must adhere to in order to receive federal funding. The NCLB Act came under criticism for narrowing the curriculum, lowering standards to increase the numbers of passing scores, and focusing on test scores rather than overall educational growth (U.S. Department of Education, 2011). In response to this critique, the secretary of education in the Obama administration, Arne Duncan, has granted states flexibility on NCLB requirements "in exchange for rigorous and comprehensive state-developed plans designed to improve educational outcomes for all students, close achievement gaps, increase equity, and improve the quality of instruction" (U.S. Department of Education, n.d., para. 1).

Despite the Common Core Standards and the NCLB Act, though, most of what occurs within our schools is still determined or administered by local government. School boards, whose members are locally elected or appointed, oversee the operation of schools and create goals at the local level that are consistent with state and federal laws. Even private schools, although they do have greater freedom in determining the curriculum, are bound to abide by U.S. laws, such as those that protect against discrimination. In short, government fingerprints can be found at all levels of the institution of education, in school curricula, school buildings, and teaching approaches.

All three of the institutions examined in this chapter—education, government, and religion—are evident when we look at the NCLB Act,[3] and the school boards that are working to put this legislation into action. For example, one aspect of this federal law allows religious organizations to receive federal education grants to run after-school programs for students in the public education system. The merits of forming or sustaining other connections between religious organizations and public schools are fought over, in many areas of the country, among local school board members and their supporters.

One of the most heated school board battles has centered on whether to teach "intelligent design" or evolution in science classes. Proponents of the faith-based idea of intelligent design—the notion that some intelligent, supernatural force was responsible for the creation of the world—have tried to influence the composition of school boards in their efforts to have this belief represented in the public school curriculum. The elected State Board of Education in Kansas, for example, changed that state's science curriculum to include the Christian notion of intelligent design in science classes along-side the teaching of evolution, whereas residents of Dover, Pennsylvania, voted to oust all eight of their local school board members after the board proposed to do the same thing there.[4]

In 2013, a physics professor at Ball State University who had been teaching intelligent design in his classes was prohibited from doing so. In making the decision, the president of the university, Jo Ann Gora, said,

> Teaching intelligent design as a scientific theory is not a matter of academic freedom—it is an issue of academic integrity. The scientific community has overwhelmingly rejected intelligent design as a scientific theory. Therefore, it does not represent the best standards of the discipline as determined by the scholars of those disciplines. Said simply, to allow intelligent design to be presented to science students as a valid scientific theory would violate the academic integrity of the course as it would fail to accurately represent the consensus of science scholars. (Quote found in Kingkade, 2013)

Science, rather than religion, must determine what is taught in science classes at Ball State University.

Fundamentalist religious sources, however, have had a tremendous impact on what is taught in high schools. A 2011 poll of high school science teachers revealed that just 28% consistently follow the National Research Council's recommendations "to describe straightforwardly the evidence for evolution and explain the ways in which it is a unifying theme in all of biology" (Bakalar, 2011, para. 2), and 13% teach their students through the lens of creationism (e.g., intelligent design). The other 60% tend to teach both evolution and creationism and/or try to avoid the topic of evolution (which is at the heart of all biology!) in order to avoid controversy (Bakalar, 2011). According to a 2013 Pew Research Center poll, just 60% of Americans believe that "humans and other living things have evolved over time" (para. 1). No doubt, this stems in large part from the fact that so few people learn the facts about evolution in their high school biology class.

Many young people have joined the effort to move religion out of science classrooms. For example, one high school student from Louisiana, Zack Kopplin, used his senior project to start a drive to repeal the 2008 Louisiana Science Education Act, which allows for the teaching of creationism in Louisiana public schools. Now a college student at Rice University, Zack is widely known as a highly respected advocate for science. Zack's efforts have been endorsed by 78 Nobel laureates, the American Association for the Advancement of Science, and the New Orleans City Council (Dvorsky, 2013; Quenqua, 2013).

Government

The U.S. Constitution sets the framework for governance in the United States. As anyone who has ever taken a U.S. government or history course (or watched *Schoolhouse Rock*) knows, the Preamble to the Constitution describes what the founders of this nation hoped to gain from establishing their government under the Constitution.

> We, the people of the United States, in order to form a more perfect Union, establish justice, insure domestic tranquility, provide for the common defense, promote the general welfare, and secure the blessings of liberty to ourselves and our posterity, do ordain and establish this Constitution for the United States of America. (See a transcript of the Constitution of the United States at http://www.archives.gov/exhibits/charters/constitution.html.)

As the Preamble indicates, the government regulates a wide range of interactions and processes in our society. Government is responsible for the smooth functioning of society. This broad mandate includes ensuring public safety, from personal safety in neighborhoods, to making sure that levees are properly built and maintained to protect citizens from flooding,[5] to overseeing public commerce (everything from an efficient transportation system to stable financial markets), to running fair and democratic elections. The government, in short, is responsible for overseeing the well-being and social welfare of the nation's citizens.

However, the majority of Americans do not actually exercise the power they have to elect their governmental representatives. Many do not even know who their elected representatives are, never mind whether or not they are actually "promot[ing] the general welfare." Just over half of all Americans who are eligible to vote exercise that right in presidential elections. Far fewer tend to vote in nonpresidential, local elections. Less than 40% of eligible voters vote in nonpresidential-year state elections (U.S. Bureau of the Census, 2012), and even fewer tend to vote in elections when only local government representatives or initiatives are on the ballot.

Many Americans feel disconnected from the political process and turned off by the huge amounts of money spent on the campaigns they see covered on television. However, unlike national or statewide elections, which involve millions of dollars and depend in great part on who can raise the most money, local elections are more open to people who commit the resources of time and energy to cultivating local contacts and to urging people personally and in small groups to vote for them. While many state and national politicians spend much of their energy focused on potential large donors, most local political hopefuls spend their energies trying to persuade community leaders to convince their own followers to vote for them. Therefore, whereas organized money is more important in state and federal elections, in local elections, organized people can propel someone into office. However, in all cases, those running for election or reelection to political posts can safely ignore people who do not involve themselves in politics and who are not likely to vote.

Religious Institutions

Approximately 75% of Americans identify as Christian. The term *Christian* encompasses a plethora of religions, ranging from mainstream Protestant to Evangelical Protestant to Catholic. Following the umbrella group of Christians, the second largest group related to religion is the unaffiliated. The percentage of unaffiliated has doubled in the past couple of decades and continues to rise, with a full one third of adults under 30 falling into this category (Table 11.1; Pew Forum on Religion & Public Life, 2012).

Analyses of religious institutions differ rather dramatically among the three primary theoretical perspectives in sociology. These theories help us understand the different roles religions play in society, how religions adapt to changes in society, and how they influence society and the individuals in it. It is important to note that sociologists are interested in the interaction between religion and society rather than in the veracity of the teachings of a particular religion.

Table 11.1   Religious Affiliation in the United States

Protestant/other Christian	51.9
Catholic	23.3
Mormon	2.1
Jewish	1.7
Muslim	0.6
Other non-Christian	2.6
No religious identity	15.6
No response given	2.2

SOURCE: Gallup (2012).

Following Durkheim's famous writings in this area, functionalists maintain that religion serves several functions for society: It unites its followers, helps establish order by providing a "correct" way of living, and gives people a sense of meaning and purpose in their lives. Of course, this particular functional analysis of religion assumes that there is only one religion in the society and does not consider societies with multiple religions, such as the United States. However, even in societies such as the United States, where there are multiple religions, those who belong to religious organizations feel more positively about their society and their ability to influence it, are more trusting of others, and spend more of their time in organized groups in their community than those who do not belong to religious organizations. Religious organizations provide volunteer opportunities for members and socialize them into a lifestyle that includes volunteering and active involvement in their communities (Jansen, 2011; Johnston, 2013).

Conflict theorists argue that religions tend to distract oppressed people and prevent them from concentrating on the inequities of their societies. Marx once described religion as "the opiate of the people" (as quoted in Bottomore, 1964, p. 27). He argued that religion helps maintain the status quo by encouraging workers to ignore their sufferings here on Earth, thus acting as an "opiate" by keeping the oppressed subdued and uninterested in rising up against their oppressors. The clergy, financially supported by the owning class, counsel their followers not to protest the inequality that led to their poor conditions but rather to be docile and "good" here on Earth so that they may receive their reward for their earthly suffering and forbearance in Heaven.[6]

Symbolic interactionists point out that religions are socially constructed, created, and re-created by followers through the use of symbols and rituals. They agree with functionalists that religion gives order to our lives. However, they also stress that individuals have agency (the ability to create and change institutions) and play active and consistent roles in the design and maintenance of their religion. Just as societies change and people create, adjust, and discard symbols, religious institutions change as well. For example, the change in symbols and attitudes within the Catholic Church brought about by the Second Vatican Council (1962–1965) changed the outlook of the church and many of its rules. The language of the Mass changed from Latin to the tongue of the parishioners, the priest no longer faced away from his parishioners when saying Mass, and guitars and folk groups replaced many organs and choirs, respectively. These symbolic shifts changed how members of the church related to one another and saw their roles within the church. Just changing certain symbols helped foster a rise in status of the Catholic laity and created a Catholic Church that Catholics who lived 100 years ago would scarcely recognize.

The Relationships Among Educational, Governmental, and Religious Institutions

Like all other major institutions in society, educational, governmental, and religious institutions must find a way to coexist. Depending on one's theoretical perspective, the grounds of this coexistence can vary widely. For example, functionalists maintain that they can cooperate for the good of the whole society, whereas conflict theorists argue that the educational, governmental, religious, and family institutions merely carry out the desires of those who control the economic institution.

No matter the theoretical perspective, it is clear that social institutions must interact with one another in a variety of ways. However, *how* they interact with one another differs from one society to the next. For example, the influence of religion on government and educational systems varies widely from society to society. The laws of some societies are based on religious doctrines. In other societies, religions are not even officially acknowledged by the government.

The Relationship Among Religion, Government, and Education: Comparing the United States and France

Due in part to the fact that there was no one dominant religious organization at the time of the founding of the United States, the First Amendment to the U.S. Constitution states that "Congress shall make no law respecting an establishment of religion, or prohibiting the free exercise thereof." There is an inherent tension between the two clauses in this phrase. Some people stress the separation between church and state, whereas others emphasize the First Amendment's declaration that government cannot prohibit the exercise of religion.

Although there is no officially state-sponsored religion in the United States, there are obvious examples of the influence of religion on U.S. government. From the words "In God We Trust" on our money to the routine inclusion of Biblical scripture in speeches by our presidents, the imagery prevalent throughout the United States is Christian. France, on the other hand, has a constitution that does not even mention religious differences among its people. The French people are free to practice whatever religion they would like to, but they must do so in a private manner. In the United States, religious organizations are given tax-exempt status and are frequently recognized and honored by political leaders, whereas the French government's only official relationship with religious organizations is to make sure they do not infringe on the liberty of others. Unlike in the United States, where some advocate bringing back compulsory prayer in schools and where there is an ongoing debate about requiring students to say a pledge that includes the word *God* in it, France expressly forbids religion in its public schools. In keeping with French laws that prohibit public displays of religion, not only are students forbidden to pray publicly, but they also may not wear religious garb (such as head coverings) in school, even if their religion mandates that they wear such things in public.

Although U.S. law prohibits the government from endorsing or sanctioning one religion over another, it does not in any way prevent citizens from invoking religious grounds as a basis for their voting or other political participation, even to the point of forming national social movements to change the law. For example,

> in the 1830s, temperance and antislavery [movements] mobilized hundreds of thousands of Americans in a wave of confessional protests. In these protests, men and women gathered together to bear witness against what they deemed as the sins of drinking and slavery to pledge fellowship with reform societies, and to demand that religious and civil institutions repent. They were met with fierce resistance, and much of it was violent. (Young, 2002, p. 661)

However, the goals of both of the movements mentioned above were eventually adopted as law. What is significant here is that Christian activists, believing that drinking or slavery was morally wrong, led movements to change the laws concerning drinking and slavery but not to change the laws concerning the role of religion in society.

In the United States, public schools are educational institutions mandated by law, funded and regulated by government, and answerable to all citizens. Is it possible to have religious practices within a public school system without violating the laws mandating the separation of church and state? Consider the case described in Exercise 11.4 below.

Of course, not all those who say that they are members of a religion actually attend religious services. As noted in Chapter 5, an estimated 37% of Americans attend religious gatherings regularly (once a week or more), far more than most Europeans (*The Economist*, 2010; Manchin, 2004; Newport, 2010). On the other hand, it is possible to believe in a God or Universal Spirit to whom you feel connected without attending religious services. For example, while fewer than 4 out of 10 Americans attend weekly religious services (Newport, 2010) and 20% are not affiliated with a religious organization (Pew Forum on Religion & Public Life, 2012), 92% say that they believe in God (Newport, 2011).

The Hijab Debate

The debate about religious garb in schools reveals how the relationships among government, religion, and education vary from society to society and over time. As noted above, since 2004, France has prohibited all religious forms of dress, including hijabs (head scarves worn by Muslim girls and women), in schools. In 2011, Azerbaijan imposed a similar ruling, as increasing numbers of its citizens began to embrace Islam after the nation emerged from the forced secularism of the Soviet era (Abbasov, 2011). Meanwhile, in Saudi Arabia and Iran, women and girls *must* wear the hijab or face punishment from the government for not doing so (Talley, 2011), and Turkey has recently lifted its ban on the hijab in state institutions (Reuters, 2013). In each of these cases, government officials recognize schools as the socializing agents they are.

In states such as Saudi Arabia and Iran, where religious leaders have a strong influence over government, schools are used to promote the dominant religion. Likewise, the recent lifting of the hijab ban in public institutions in Turkey reflects the Islamist-based political party now in power in that nation. However, in nations with secular governments, such as France and Azerbaijan, that fear the rising influence of religion in society, schools are used to dampen the influence of religion. Meanwhile, in the United States, with our declaration of religious freedom and separation of church and state, we continue to debate whether creationism can or should be taught in public schools. As these examples illustrate, the social institutions of religion, education, and government—like all major social institutions—are interdependent and continually interact with and influence one another in every society.

Sociologist in Action: Tim Woods

Dr. Tim Woods grew up in a small farming community in Oklahoma. As an undergraduate majoring in sociology at Southwestern Oklahoma State University, he joined a group of two sociology professors and a handful of students who volunteered at a local prison. In the prison, the faculty and students served as associates and advisers to the Lifers' Club, an organization of prisoners who were serving life sentences. While the prison volunteer program had no formal ties to the sociology curriculum, this experience left a lasting impression on Woods's work and teaching.

Interacting with the inmates forced Woods to question some fundamental ideas he held, especially those concerning the roles of individual responsibility and self-efficacy. A key event concerned a very religious inmate Woods had befriended. While many inmates joked that no one in the prison was guilty, this particular inmate vociferously and continually proclaimed his innocence, explaining that God had sent him to prison to help the other inmates. Wary of the inmate's stories, Woods understood these proclamations to be psychological dissonance, either a denial of individual responsibility or mental illness. However, some 2 years after he left the prison for graduate school, Woods received word that new evidence had been discovered establishing the inmate's innocence. He was released from prison. This became an important example to Woods of the real-world connections among social structure, power, and the lived experiences of individuals.

Dr. Woods is now the chair of the Department of Political Science and Sociology at Manchester Community College in Manchester, Connecticut. Wishing that his students have the same type of opportunity to learn and contribute to their community that he had had at the prison, Woods began embedding community engagement into the formal coursework in sociology. He wanted students to develop a sociological imagination through their interaction with the community. As they served in and reflected on life in their community, students began to connect first their own and then others' personal troubles to social issues in their community and the larger world. This experience also advanced students' understanding of broader sociological concepts and theories by visibly connecting those concepts to their own lived experiences and those of others in the community.

Initially, Woods's students simply volunteered at a variety of community nonprofit organizations and related their experiences there to the course material. Over time, Woods and his students' roles grew from merely volunteering to publicly advocating for structural community change. Their sociological imagination enabled them to recognize the need for and potential of collective action to address the social needs of the community. Joining forces with the local homeless shelter, religious organizations, and town officials, they helped establish the Manchester Initiative for Supportive Housing and have taken a leading role in advocating for supportive housing as a long-term solution to homelessness. Their strategy for community awareness has become a topic of discussion among supportive housing advocates as far from Connecticut as California.

Woods believes that community colleges provide a unique opportunity for sociologists interested in teaching about and engaging in public sociology and community change. Unlike most students in 4-year colleges and

(Continued)

(Continued)

universities, community college students are more strongly embedded in their communities, where they live, work, worship, and go to college, and as a result, they have long-term stakes in the community. While it is certainly possible for professors and students at 4-year schools to make a positive impact on the communities surrounding their campus, they must often make extra efforts to know and be accepted by members of the local community. Tim Woods's students, similar to Jane Addams and the other Hull House researchers and activists, live in the community they are trying to improve. Also, community college students are usually more representative of the diversity (in terms of race and ethnicity, class, age, religion, etc.) that one finds in a community. These factors increase the legitimacy and success of student projects in the community and make the connection between classroom and community more authentic and enduring.

EXERCISE 11.1   How Are Your Local Schools Funded?

Find the official webpage of your local school board by going to an Internet search engine (e.g., Google.com, Yahoo.com, etc.) and searching for the name of your town or city and the phrase "school board." Write a one- to two-page paper that answers the following questions:

1. How are your local schools funded?

2. Has funding increased or decreased over the past few years (and why)?

3. How do people become school board members? Are they elected? Are they appointed (and if so, by whom)?

4. Are the school board members nonpartisan, or are they affiliated with a political party? If they are politically affiliated, how many are Democrats? How many are Republicans? Any independents or other party affiliations?

5. According to the school board website, what are the key challenges facing your local public schools? How does the board claim to be addressing these challenges?

(Continued)

(Continued)

6. Now, imagine that you are an official member of the school board. What two key challenges do you want to focus on? These may be similar to the ones that the board has identified, or they may be your own, based on the research you have done. Outline these challenges, and then describe several ideas you would suggest to address them. For at least one of these suggestions for change, elaborate on your plan, and discuss in detail how your skills as a sociologist can help create this change.

EXERCISE 11.2 Education for All?

Read about the Education for All movement at http://www.unesco.org/new/en/education/themes/leading-the-international-agenda/education-for-all/. Then, go to http://www.un.org/millenniumgoals/pdf/MDG_FS_2_EN.pdf, and read the information about inequality in education across the globe. Then, answer the following questions:

1. Why do you think education was established as a basic right under the 1948 Universal Declaration of Human Rights?

2. Why should you care about whether or not people in other nations have access to education?

3. What do you think that you, working with others, can do to promote the goal of universal education by 2015?

EXERCISE 11.3 How Does Your Representative Vote?

1. Go to the website for the U.S. House of Representatives, http://www.house.gov.

2. Look up your state representative by entering your zip code under "FIND YOUR REPRESENTATIVE" in the top left corner of the page and clicking on the "GO" button.

(Continued)

(Continued)

3. When the page opens, click on the representative's name, and look at his or her website by clicking on the pull-down menu "Representatives' Web sites A–Z by last name" at the top of the page.

4. Find information on the positions your representative is taking on five issues.

5. Answer the following questions:

   a. Do you agree with the votes? (In other words, do they represent you?) Why or why not?

   b. Will you vote in the next (i) local, (ii) state, and (iii) national elections? Why or why not?

   c. Does reading about how your representative has voted recently make you more or less interested in voting for or against him or her in the next election? Why?

   d. If you do not agree with his or her vote on one or more issues, what actions can you (as a citizen) take to express your dissatisfaction?

   e. What actions can you take toward having your representative vote more to your liking on future issues?

EXERCISE 11.4   School Sports and Prayer

The Bill of Rights Institute's website (http://billofrightsinstitute.org/religiousliberty/cases) lists the landmark Supreme Court cases that deal with the tension between the separation of church and state and freedom to worship clauses in the First Amendment. *Santa Fe Independent School District v. Doe* (2000) is one of the more recent decisions. For this case, Justice Stevens wrote what follows below for the majority opinion of the Court (three justices dissented).[7]

> Prior to 1995, a student elected as Santa Fe High School's student council chaplain delivered a prayer over the public address system before each home varsity football game. Respondents, Mormon and Catholic students or alumni and their mothers, filed a suit challenging this practice and others under the Establishment Clause of the First Amendment.

(Continued)

(Continued)

While the suit was pending, the petitioner school district (referred to as "District" below) adopted a different policy, which authorizes two student elections, the first to determine whether "invocations" should be delivered at games and the second to select the spokesperson to deliver them. After the students held elections authorizing such prayers and selecting a spokesperson, the district court entered an order modifying the policy to permit only nonsectarian, nonproselytizing prayer. The fifth circuit court held that, even as modified by the district court, the football prayer policy was invalid.

Held: The District's policy permitting student-led, student-initiated prayer at football games violates the Establishment Clause. Pp. 9–26.

The Court's analysis is guided by the principles endorsed in *Lee v. Weisman*, 505 U.S. 577. There, in concluding that a prayer delivered by a rabbi at a graduation ceremony violated the Establishment Clause, the Court held that, at a minimum, the Constitution guarantees that government may not coerce anyone to support or participate in religion or its exercise, or otherwise act in a way that establishes a state religion or religious faith, or tends to do so, *id.,* at 587. The District argues unpersuasively that these principles are inapplicable because the policy's messages are private student speech, not public speech. The delivery of a message such as the invocation here—on school property, at school-sponsored events, over the school's public address system, by a speaker representing the student body, under the supervision of school faculty, and pursuant to a school policy that explicitly and implicitly encourages public prayer—is not properly characterized as "private" speech. (See http://www.law.cornell.edu/supct/html/historics/USSC_CR_0530_0290_ZS.html)

1. Do you agree with this opinion? Why or why not?

2. What might a symbolic interactionist say about the use of symbols by those carrying out these prayers? What do these symbols convey to the students and other fans attending the games? In particular, what do they imply about the appropriateness of public praying at football games?

3. What might a conflict theorist say about the Court's decision?

EXERCISE 11.5   The Role of Religion in the Lives of Individuals

Survey 10 people about their religion. In the survey, include questions about (a) their religious affiliation (if they have one), (b) how often they go to religious services, and (c) if they think their belief in God or a Higher Power guides their actions during an average day.

Then interview them, asking them to provide examples to illustrate their answers. Compare the results of your surveys and interviews. Were the findings consistent? Why or why not? How might a symbolic interactionist interpret your findings? Why?

EXERCISE 11.6   Racism in a "Color-Blind" France

Since the 2005 riots and more recent episodes of public racism, some French citizens have questioned the government's practice of ignoring racial and religious differences among French citizens and advocated for the establishment of racial and religious statistical categories so that the government can discern patterns of discrimination.

Listen to "Diverse Marseille Spared in French Riots" at http://www.npr.org/templates/story/story.php?storyId=5044219, and read "The Justice Minister and the Banana: How Racist Is France"? at http://www.newyorker.com/online/blogs/comment/2013/11/the-justice-minister-and-the-banana-how-racist-is-france.html.

Write a two- to three-page paper that answers the following questions:

1. What did you learn about the reasons for the 2005 riots in France and French attitudes toward race and religion? How do these differ from American attitudes?

2. What are three reforms that the French government could enact to diminish the current racial outbreaks in France and prevent riots like those in 2005 from breaking out again?

3. What strategies would you use to try to convince the French public to support these reform measures? How would your tactics to garner support for these reforms take French attitudes toward race and religion into consideration?

EXERCISE 11.7   Secularism, Religion, and Democracy

Listen to the following stories:

"Hijab Bridges Faith and Fashion for US Muslim Women" at http://www .fashionfightingfamine.com/blog/npr-hijab-bridges-faith-and-fashion-for-us-muslim-women

"A Tale of Two U.S. Muslim Women: To Cover or Not?" at http://www.npr .org/templates/story/story.php?storyId=6556263

"Debating the Burqa: Sarkozy Proposes Ban" at http://www.npr.org/ templates/story/story.php?storyId=106198806

Then, answer the following questions:

1. What do you believe are the best arguments for supporting a ban on women wearing (a) a hijab or (b) a burqa?

2. What do you believe are the best arguments for allowing women to wear (a) a hijab or (b) a burqa?

3. Which of the arguments you have laid out are the most sociological (taking into account the impact on society as well as on individuals)? Why?

4. Which of the arguments do you agree with most strongly? Why?

DISCUSSION QUESTIONS

1. Before you read this chapter, did you know the names of your U.S. senators and representative? Did you know their party affiliations? Why or why not? Why is it important to know who they are and how they vote?

2. What do you think the purpose of public schools should be? Do you think your education fulfilled that purpose? Why or why not? Did you go to public schools to get your primary and secondary education? Why or why not?

3. Do you think religious symbols should be allowed in public schools in the United States? Why or why not?

4. Do you ever wonder why the word *God* is used so often by public officials in their public statements? Discuss why you think this happens.

5. Do you think students in U.S. public schools should be required to "pledge allegiance to the flag of the United States of America and to the Republic for which it stands, one nation under God, indivisible, with liberty and justice for all"? Why or why not?

6. Do you think the French government needs to officially recognize the religious, racial, and ethnic diversity within France? If yes, why? (And how might the government go about doing so?) If not, why not?

7. How might you go about studying the influence of religion at your school? What methodology would you use to collect your data? What theory would you use to make sense of your data?

8. What role do you think the federal government should play in improving the public education system in the United States? Why? If you think funding for schools should be increased, from where do you think the money should come? Why?

9. Describe the relationship between the economic, family, and educational institutions in your own life. What do you think would happen to you if you did not have access to a college education? How would that lack of access affect your economic position and your ability to support a family?

SUGGESTIONS FOR SPECIFIC ACTIONS

1. Go to the website http://www.house.gov. Find one issue up for debate in the House of Representatives that interests you. Research the issue, and write a letter to your representative to encourage him or her to vote your way.

2. Attend two different types of religious services in your local community. Observe and compare what kinds of people are in positions of authority (their gender, race, and age). Think about how these different religious groups might influence society if they were the "official" national religions.

3. Research a religious organization that is working on a social justice issue. Write a two-page essay outlining the scope of the issue, why the organization is addressing it, and how it is carrying out the campaign (i.e., what methods it is using). Include at least one paragraph analyzing the power that religious groups can have in organizing citizens toward a more just society and an additional paragraph that discusses the possible negative consequences of religiously motivated social justice. Finally, determine how you can help with the campaign, and follow through with at least one action to do so.

Here are some campaigns that might interest you:

Bread for the World campaign to end hunger (http://www.bread.org)

Interfaith Worker Justice's campaign against wage theft (http://www.iwj.org/issues/wage-theft)

MAZON's fight to combat hunger (http://www.mazon.org)

American Friends Service Committee's work on justice and peace issues (http://afsc.org/AfricaLifeOverDebt)

Catholic Relief Services' efforts to fight AIDS in Africa (http://crs.org)

These are just a few examples; feel free to come up with your own as well.
Please go to this book's website at http://study.sagepub.com/korgen5e to find further civic engagement opportunities, resources, peer-reviewed articles, and updated web links related to this chapter.

NOTES

1. The pledge, originally written in 1892, was amended in 1923, 1924, and 1954. The phrase "under God" was the most recent addition, added during the Cold War in part to distinguish the United States from the USSR, which had outlawed religious practice.

2. See Gary Becker's article "Human Capital and Poverty" at the Acton Institute website, http://www.acton.org/pub/religion-liberty/volume-8-number-1/human-capital-and-poverty.

3. See the federal government's No Child Left Behind Act website at http://www.ed.gov/nclb/landing.jhtml.

4. A U.S. district court ruled in 2005 that the school board's decision to mandate the teaching of intelligent design violated the constitutional separation between church and state (see Associated Press, 2005).

5. The government's failure to fulfill this responsibility during and after Hurricane Katrina in 2005 was (and continues to be) painfully displayed. Hundreds of Americans lost their lives, and thousands more lost their homes, livelihoods, and neighborhoods, due to the breach that occurred in the levees protecting New Orleans.

6. It is important to note that Marx was not exposed to religions that actively promoted social justice, as many have done in the past century. In fact, in recent years, some religious leaders (such as Liberation Theologians) have been accused of being Marxists!

7. To see the Supreme Court's full opinion for this case, go to the Legal Information Institute's Supreme Court Collection, found at http://www.oyez.org/cases/1990-1999/1999/1999_99_62.

REFERENCES

Abbasov, S. (2011, January 6). *Azerbaijan: Hijab ban in schools fuels debate in Baku on role of Islam* (EURASIANET.org). Retrieved from http://www.eurasianet.org/node/62670

Associated Press. (2005, December 20). Judge rules against intelligent design. *MSNBC.* Retrieved from http://www.msnbc.msn.com/id/10545387

Bakalar, N. (2011, February 7). On evolution, biology teachers stray from lesson plan. *The New York Times.* Retrieved from http://www.nytimes.com/2011/02/08/science/ 08creationism.html?_r=0

Bottomore, T. (Trans. & Ed.). (1964). *Karl Marx: Early writings.* New York, NY: McGraw-Hill.

Dixon, M. (2012, June). *Public education finances: 2010* (U.S. Bureau of the Census). Retrieved from http://www2.census.gov/govs/school/10f33pub.pdf

Dvorsky, G. (2013, January 15). How 19-year-old activist Zack Kopplin is making life hell for Louisiana creationists. *Io9.* Retrieved from http://io9.com/5976112/how- 19-year-old-activist-zack-kopplin-is-making-life-hell-for-louisianas-creationists

The Economist. (2010, August 9). *Europe's irreligious.* Retrieved from http://www .economist.com/blogs/dailychart/2010/08/religious_attendance

Gallup. (2012, December 24). *In U.S., 77% identify as Christian.* Retrieved from http://www.gallup.com/poll/159548/identify-christian.aspx.

Jansen, J. (2011, December 23). *The civic and community engagement of religiously active Americans* (Pew Internet & American Life Project). Retrieved from http:// www.pewinternet.org/Reports/2011/Social-side-of-religious.aspx?src=prc-headline

Johnston, J. B. (2013). Religion and volunteering over the adult life course. *Journal for the Scientific Study of Religion, 52*(4), 733–752.

Kingkade, T. (2013, August 1). Ball State University bans teaching intelligent design in science classes. *The Huffington Post.* Retrieved from http://www.huffingtonpost .com/2013/08/01/ball-state-intelligent-design_n_3688857.html

Manchin, R. (2004, September 21). *Religion in Europe: Trust not filling the pews* (Gallup.com). Retrieved from http://www.gallup.com/poll/13117/Religion- Europe-Trust-Filling-Pews.aspx

Newport, F. (2010, June 25). *Americans' church attendance inches up in 2010* (Gallup.com). Retrieved from http://www.gallup.com/poll/141044/americans- church-attendance-inches-2010.aspx

Newport, F. (2011, June 3). *More than 9 in 10 Americans continue to believe in God* (Gallup.com). Retrieved from http://www.gallup.com/poll/147887/Americans- Continue-Believe-God.aspx

Organisation for Economic Co-operation and Development. (2013). *Skilled for life? Key findings from the Survey of Adult Skills.* Retrieved from http://skills.oecd. org/SkillsOutlook_2013_KeyFindings.pdf

Pérez-Peña, R. (2013, October 8). *U.S. adults fare poorly in a study of skills.* Retrieved from http://www.nytimes.com/2013/10/08/us/us-adults-fare-poorly-in-a-study- of-skills.html

Pew Forum on Religion & Public Life. (2012, October 9). *"Nones" on the rise: One- in-five adults have no religious affiliation.* Retrieved from http://www.pewforum .org/uploadedFiles/Topics/Religious_Affiliation/Unaffiliated/NonesOnTheRise- full.pdf

Pew Research Center (2013, December 30). *Public's view on human evolution.* Retrieved from http://www.pewforum.org/2013/12/30/publics-views-on-human- evolution/

Quenqua, D. (2013, September 2). Young students against bad science. *The New York Times*. Retrieved from http://www.nytimes.com/2013/09/03/science/young-and-against-bad-science.html

Reuters (2013, October 8). Turkey lifts decades-old ban on Islamic head scarf. *The New York Times*. Retrieved from http://in.reuters.com/article/2013/10/08/turkey-headscarf-ban-idINDEE99706920131008

Santa Fe Independent School District v. Doe. (2000). *Certiorari to the United States Court of Appeals for the Fifth Circuit. No. 99–62. Argued March 29, 2000—Decided June 19, 2000* (Legal Information Institute). Retrieved from http://straylight.law.cornell.edu/supct/html/99-62.ZS.html

Talley, J. (2011, April 19). *Banning hijab: Anti-veil laws around the world* (NakedLaw). Retrieved from http://nakedlaw.avvo.com/2011/04/banning-hijab-anti-veil-laws-around-the-world

U.S. Bureau of the Census. (2012). Table 397: Participation in elections for president and U.S. representatives: 1932–2010. In *Statistical abstract of the United States: 2012*. Suitland, MD: Author.

U.S. Department of Education. (2011, September 23). *Obama administration sets high bar for flexibility from No Child Left Behind in order to advance equity and support reform*. Retrieved from http://www.ed.gov/news/press-releases/obama-administration-sets-high-bar-flexibility-no-child-left-behind-order-advanc

U.S. Department of Education. (n.d.). *Elementary and secondary education: ESEA flexibility*. Retrieved from http://www2.ed.gov/policy/elsec/guid/esea-flexibility/index.html

Weber, M. (1970). *From Max Weber* (H. H. Gerth & C. W. Mills, Eds.). Oxford, England: Routledge.

Young, M. P. (2002). Confessional protest: The religious birth of U.S. national social movements. *American Sociological Review, 67*(5), 660–688.

12

The Engaged
Sociologist in Action

Congratulations! After reading this book and completing the exercises
in the earlier chapters, you have no doubt developed a sociological
eye and can make use of your sociological imagination. Now there's no turning back. With a toolbox packed full with *sociological* tools, you cannot help
but perceive social patterns that affect all of us but are often unnoticed by
those without your sociological training. The best news is that you have also
acquired the means to be an effective agent of social change!

Through this sociology class (and perhaps through other means as
well), you have developed the skills you need to become an informed and
effective citizen who can help shape our society. But as any good super-
hero knows, with great power comes responsibility. Your sociological
training allows you to understand how society works. It is your obligation
now to use that knowledge to influence society in ways that will make it
better. And just as a carpenter must not only purchase tools but also learn
how to use them properly, so must a sociologist in action learn how to use
his or her tools. So now it is time for you to practice using your sociological tools to research and address social issues by completing one of the
projects we outline below.

The Basic Steps of Social Science Research

No matter what topic you choose to research, you will need to remember and to follow the basic steps of all social science research:

1. Choose a research topic.

2. Find out what other researchers have discovered about that topic.

3. Choose a methodology (how you will collect your data).

4. Collect and analyze your data.

5. Relate your findings to those of other researchers.

6. Do something with your findings!

Select one of the projects below. Then, use the detailed research directions that follow to plan and carry out your chosen project.

Project 12.1 Civic Engagement and Higher Education

In recent years, many educators and leaders in society have talked and written about the obligation of colleges and universities to educate citizens.[1] However, it is still not clear (a) how many *students* think civic engagement should be a part of college education and (b) how many students are actually civically engaged. Your task will be to seek answers to these questions from students on your campus and to devise ways to encourage them to play an active role in shaping society.

Project 12.2 Social Responsibility on Campus

Is your college or university a "socially responsible" institution? In this project, you will (a) use different indicators of social responsibility to measure how socially responsible your school is and (b) use your findings in an effort to make your school more socially responsible.

Some of the questions to consider are the following: Does everyone on campus have equal access to education and other resources? Are campus faculty and staff paid and treated fairly? Do athletes wear, or does your campus store sell, apparel made in sweatshops? Does your university recycle everything that it can? Has your university invested in any corporations that are cited for human rights violations? Are female and male professors compensated equally? Would students know if your school was not acting in socially responsible ways? If students did know, would they organize to create change?

Project 12.3 Connecting the Campus to the Community

What are the needs of the community around your college? Are they being met? Does your college or university actively seek input from local leaders on how it might help the community in which it resides? Do student groups and clubs connect the student body with the local community? Is there a chasm (social or status) between the college community and the larger community? Do students have prejudices toward the local community, or does the local community have prejudices toward students? Does your college contribute to the economic well-being of the greater community? This project will examine the social and economic environment of the community of which your school is a part and determine to what extent your school is working to improve the vitality of that community.

Step 1: Research Preparation

A. What You (Think You) Know

Before you start your research, it is important to take stock of what you *think* you know about the topic and *why* you think you know it. This will help focus your thinking and make you aware of some of the potential biases you may have toward the issue. In a one-page paper, (a) describe what you hypothesize (think) will be the answer to your research question and (b) support your hypothesis with examples from your own life, previous research you have done, and your "best guess" sociological analysis (utilizing, of course, your sociological imagination and sociological eye!).

B. Reviewing the Literature

The next step is to examine previous research on your topic. Go to your school library, and locate the databases of academic articles in the social sciences. We recommend Sociological Abstracts, JSTOR, or Academic Search Premier. Conduct several searches for articles using any combination of key words or phrases, such as the following:

For Project 12.1, "student activism," "student apathy," "college and activism," "civic engagement and college," "educating students," and "student attitudes"

For Project 12.2, "civic engagement and colleges," "student activism," "students and social responsibility," "colleges and social responsibility," and "student movements"

For Project 12.3, "poverty," "hunger," "homelessness," "unemployment," "town and gown," and "campus and community"

If you are having problems with your searches or the search terms are not producing the desired results, please ask a reference librarian at your school for assistance. Reference librarians are amazing resources and can be a huge help to you as you proceed.

Choose four or five recently published articles available in your library that appear relevant to your research question.

Of course, none of the articles will answer the research question completely. However, each may contribute a piece of related data or way of thinking about the question. For each article, note the following:

- Which of your major concepts (e.g., student attitudes, social responsibility, campus and community relations) is discussed?
- What did the researchers find that adds to your knowledge about the question?

Write a two-page summary of the articles you have read. Then, write a one-page paper summarizing what you have learned from the articles that influences your thinking on the question you are addressing. Have your expectations changed at all? Why or why not? If yes, revise your hypothesis.

Step 2: Obtain Your Data

You have developed a research question and conducted some background work. No doubt your thoughts about what you will find from your research have changed since you first thought about the research question. Now, it is time to obtain the data to test whether your present expectations are on target. In each of the three guided exercises below, we present a research design appropriate for one of the research projects. Be sure to continue with the project you selected when you began Step 1 (i.e., if you chose Project 12.1 in Step 1, you should continue with Project 12.1 throughout the chapter). You can work individually or in small groups, depending on your professor's preference.

Project 12.1 Civic Engagement and Higher Education: Data Collection Exercise

In this exercise, you will survey at least 30 students to determine (a) how interested students at your school are in learning how to become active, effective members of society and (b) the extent to which students on your campus are socially active.

1. Go to this book's website (http://study.sagepub.com/korgen5e). Select "Research Tools," and download "Survey for Research Project 12.1"; also, download the "Scoring Guide" for Research Project 12.1.

2. Determine where and when to find respondents. Do not just haphazardly hand out forms to people. Rather, select a large general education class that will provide a fairly representative sample of the student body (representing students from different years, majors, races, ethnicities, sexes, etc.). Be sure to secure prior permission from the professor teaching the course before you hand out your survey at the beginning of one of the class meetings.

3. Ask the students to take a 5- to 10-minute survey. Read them the instructions, and then hand out the survey. Instruct the students not to sign their names, and tell them to put the completed surveys face down in a pile in a specified place in the classroom. (That way they know that you will not be able to connect them with their individual responses.)

4. Follow the instructions in the scoring guide to analyze the results. You may want to try grouping your data with those of other students who are also carrying out this project. (This will enable you to have a larger sample on which to base your findings.) Write a three- to four-page paper that presents and analyzes your results and relates them to the previous research you found on the topic.

Project 12.2 Social Responsibility on Campus: Data Collection Exercise

In this exercise, you will interview at least 10 students about how socially responsible they believe your school is. You will ask them questions that address both specific indicators of social responsibility and their overall impression of the social responsibility of the school.

1. Go to this book's website. Select "Research Tools," and download the interview guidelines, the coding guide, and the informed consent statement for Research Project 12.2.

2. Determine where and when to find respondents. Be sure to interview students who are most likely to know (and care) about your topic (e.g., leaders in student government, club officers, members of student-activist groups, student representatives to the Board of Trustees, etc.).

3. Ask the students you select for permission to interview them. Give them the informed consent sheet to read and sign. Ask permission to tape-record the interview. (If they won't allow you to record, you will need to take detailed notes.)

4. Ask them the questions you devised after reading and following the instructions in the interview guidelines. Start with your own questions, but let the respondent guide the conversation. Do not try to force all of your respondents to answer the same questions in the same way. However, do make sure they each cover all of the questions you have prepared. The point is to get their individual perspectives and then compare them with one another. A good interviewer asks probe questions throughout the interview. These are very short and simple questions such as "Can you expand on that?" or "Interesting. What else might you add?" Probe questions give a cue to the person being interviewed to talk more on the subject, while not pushing the interviewee toward your own biases.

5. Follow the instructions in the coding guide to analyze the results. If possible, group your data with those of other students carrying out the same project. (This will enable you to have a larger sample on which to base your findings.)

6. Write a three- to four-page paper that presents and analyzes your results and relates them to the previous research you found on the topic.

Project 12.3 Connecting the Campus to the Community: Data Collection Exercise

Note: For this project, you can collect data through *either* interviews *or* surveys.

Interviews. You will interview leaders in the local community about the relationship between your school and the community.

1. Go to this book's website. Select "Research Tools," and download the interview guidelines, the coding guide, and the informed consent statement for Research Project 12.3.

2. Identify at least three leaders in the local community who would have reason to know the extent and nature of the connection between your school and the community (e.g., the mayor, deputies to the mayor, the city manager, city

council members, directors of local nonprofit agencies). You can find local nonprofit organizations in your area by using World Hunger Year's Grassroots Resources Directory (http://www.whyhunger.org/findfood), which includes organizations that deal with various issues related to poverty, in addition to hunger. Simply fill in the information, and the database will give you a list of organizations in your area. You can also find such organizations by using the database at http://idealist.org.

3. Ask each community leader for permission to do the interview. If he or she agrees, provide a copy of the informed consent sheet to read and sign. Ask permission to tape-record the interview. (If he or she won't allow you to record it, you will need to take detailed notes.)

4. Ask the community leaders the questions you devised after reading and following the instructions in the interview guidelines. Start with your own questions, but let the respondent guide the conversation. Do not try to force all of your respondents to answer the same questions in the same way. However, do make sure they each cover all of the questions you've prepared. The point is to get their individual perspectives and then compare them with one another. A good interviewer asks probe questions throughout the interview. These are very short and simple questions such as "Can you expand on that?" or "Interesting. What else might you add?" Probe questions give a cue to the person being interviewed to talk more on the subject, while not pushing the interviewee toward your own biases.

5. Follow the instructions in the coding guide to analyze the results. If possible, group your data with those of other students carrying out interviews for this project. (This will enable you to have a larger sample on which to base your findings.)

6. Compare your findings with those of your classmates who collected survey data for this project.

7. Write a three- to four-page paper that presents and analyzes your results (and, if possible, the results of your classmates' interviews), relates them to the previous research you found on the topic, and compares them with the findings of your classmates who conducted surveys on this topic.

Surveys. You will survey at least 30 students to measure the (a) attitudes of students toward the local community and (b) degree of interaction between students and the community.

1. Go to this book's website. Select "Research Tools," and download "Survey for Research Project 12.3"; also, download the "Scoring Guide" for Research Project 12.3.

2. Determine where and when to find respondents. Do not just hand out forms to people haphazardly. Select a large general education class that will provide a fairly representative sample of the student body. Be sure to secure prior permission from the professor teaching the course before handing out your survey at the beginning of one of the class meetings.

3. Ask the students to take a 5- to 10-minute survey. Read them the instructions, and then hand out the survey. Instruct the students not to sign their names, and tell them to put the completed surveys face down in a pile in a specified place in the classroom. (That way they know that you won't be able to connect them with their individual responses.)

4. Follow the instructions in the scoring guide to analyze the results. If possible, group your data with those of other students carrying out the survey for this project. (This will enable you to have a larger sample on which to base your findings.)

5. Compare your findings with those of your classmates who conducted interviews for Research Project 12.3.

6. Write a three- to four-page paper that presents and analyzes your results (and, if possible, the results of your classmates' interviews), relates them to the previous research you found on the topic, and compares them with the findings of your classmates who conducted interviews on this topic.

Step 3: Do Something About It

Now that you have personally investigated an important social issue, you are in a strong position to address it. The following exercises will help you use your sociological knowledge to make a difference in the lives of people in your community.

Project 12.1 Civic Engagement and Higher Education: Civic Engagement Exercise

From your research, you have some data that indicate how many students think civic engagement should be a part of college education and how many students are socially active. For this exercise, you will prepare a *talking points* document designed to change the minds of those students who do not think civic engagement should be a part of college education. You will then organize a campus panel with other students at which you will present your talking points.

A talking points document is a brief summary of relevant issues to help you put things into perspective, to establish a context for your concerns, and to focus on what is most important in your argument. It is also a fact sheet that provides evidence to support your position.

1. Drawing on your knowledge of the topic (through your background reading), list the five most important reasons why students should want civic engagement to be a part of their college education.

2. Using information from your survey data, this book, or published research on the topic, identify the specific reasons why students might not want civic engagement to be a part of college education, and then counter their arguments. (For example, if you think students will say that they don't have time to be socially active, mention the fact that many schools have included civic engagement activities within courses. If students don't understand how they can benefit from becoming socially active, describe to them the connection between social activism and social power.)

3. Write a one-page summary of the talking points that is designed to help you communicate your five points to a group of students.

4. Try it out. Bring your talking points to a few friends or relatives, and ask them if they will let you briefly discuss why you think civic engagement should be a part of the college experience. Think about their responses, criticisms, and suggestions, and then make changes in your document in ways that will strengthen it.

5. Prepare a 5-minute presentation based on what you have learned. Consider the reasons why rational and thoughtful people might not want civic engagement to be a part of college education, and think carefully about what you might say that will address and possibly overcome their hesitation. You can find great guides to help you with putting together and delivering your speech at http://www.pbs.org/standarddeviantstv/transcript_public.html and http://www.enotes.com/topics/how-write-speech.

6. Work with other students who carried out this project to organize and participate in a student panel presentation for the campus community about the connection between civic engagement and higher education.

Project 12.2 Social Responsibility on Campus: Civic Engagement Exercise

Based on your preparation work, you should have a fairly good idea about what social issues students believe your college or university should be addressing on campus (e.g., sweatshops, right to a living wage, health care benefits, sex discrimination, racism).

1. Write a two-page summary of the issue that most concerns you. Include in it a simple description of (a) what the social issue is, (b) who (which group or groups) is suffering as a result of it, (c) who has the power or authority to change it, and (d) what makes you feel that there is a need to address the social issue in the first place.

2. Rewrite your statement in the form of a two-paragraph letter to the editor of your school paper. Begin the letter with the phrase "We the undersigned . . . ." Work and rework this document until you feel confident that you have included your major points and presented them in a clear and powerful manner.

3. Ask people around campus if they would be willing to join you in signing the letter. Provide a signature list form where they can sign their names, print their names, and (optionally) identify themselves (student, professor, staff, etc.). Also, ask them if they wish to become more active in resolving the injustice. If they do, take down their contact information (including their phone numbers and e-mail addresses).

4. If you find that most people do not agree with your letter, stop and rethink it. Have you represented the issue fairly? What are their objections? Are they right? If so, you might want to consider a different issue or a different approach and start again. If you feel that they are wrong, you should consider what you could do differently that might convince them to join your cause.

5. After you have collected at least 20 signatures (hopefully more!), send the letter to your school newspaper, to the president of your college, and to any other key people on campus whom you have identified as having the power to affect this issue.

6. Call a meeting of the people who want to act on the issue. Discuss what to do, and do it. That is, devise an action plan and strategy to take action on your issue. On the following websites, you can find some excellent resources compiled by other student groups that will help you write letters, organize meetings, and gain all of the tools you need to work for your issue:

http://www.campusactivism.org/displayresource-471.htm

http://www.thetaskforce.org/reports_and_research/campus_manual

http://www3.thestar.com/static/PDF/060217_jrjour_guide.pdf

http://www.campusactivism.org/uploads/FireItUp.pdf

You may also want to consult books such as *Take More Action* by Marc and Craig Kielburger and Deepa Shankaran (2004) or *Organizing for Social Change: Midwest Academy—Manual for Activists* by Kimberley Bobo, Jackie Kendall, and Steve Max (1999) for some guidelines on how to organize effectively. Michael Gecan's book *Going Public* (2004) is also an excellent overview of how to build power through organizing people. Dave Beckworth and Cristina Lopez's *Community Organizing: People Power From the Grassroots* (n.d.) gives the basics of good organizing.

Project 12.3 Connecting the Campus to the Community: Civic Engagement Exercise

Identify a few nonprofit groups in your area that are working on poverty-related issues. There may be an office on campus that can help you find one, such as the Community Service Office. If you are an active member of a church, mosque, synagogue, or other civic organization, find out how it is addressing poverty in the community. Call your local mayor's office, and ask if there are community groups that the city or town works with on poverty-related issues, such as hunger, homelessness, and housing. You should also search World Hunger Year's Grassroots Resources Directory (http://www.whyhunger.org/connect). As we noted above, you can simply fill in the information, and the database will give you a list of organizations in your area.

You can also find such organizations through the Idealist website at http://idealist.org.

1. Visit the organization you have chosen (or visit several if you are having trouble choosing). Speak with the people there, pick up their literature, and look over their website if they have one. Identify and summarize what their basic work is, how it is organized, and what they want from volunteers. Given your knowledge of the issue, make note of how well the organization's work relates to your area of interest.

2. Get to know the organization better. Attend a meeting, or volunteer for an event. Speak with other volunteers about their experiences.

3. If you are excited by the work of the organization, get a group of students together to volunteer their time and talents to work with the people there. Tell the other potential volunteers what you know about the issue and what this organization is doing. Try to get a meaningful sense of what kind of commitment other students are willing to make so that you don't promise too much, and then offer your group's services to the organization as volunteers.

Two notes of caution should be added before you recruit too many volunteers. First, make sure that you have spoken to the people coordinating the efforts of the organization to find out what they need. They may need help with staffing, clerical work, building repairs, fund-raising, or a variety of other tasks. It is very important that they are part of your process! Second, many organizations prefer to start their volunteers off with clerical tasks, like faxing or filing. The point of this exercise is to get your hands dirty and do something about an ongoing social problem, even if the work you are doing may seem mundane. However, make sure you have a clear sense of what the organization wants from you before you commit to doing it.

Sociologist in Action: You!

(Place a brief biography here and a description of the class project you just completed or any other social change exercise you undertook as part of this course.) You've now joined the ranks of the other "sociologists in action" highlighted in this book. Like their work, your efforts can inspire others to become knowledgeable, engaged, and effective citizens. Although these sociologists may not look like superheroes, they have all managed to harness the power of sociology to make society better. Congratulations on becoming one of them! Please e-mail us your Sociologist in Action piece (korgenk@ gmail.com), and let us know if we can use it on our website or in future editions of *The Engaged Sociologist: Connecting the Classroom to the Community* or our other books, *Sociologists in Action: Sociology, Social Change, and Social Justice* and *Sociologists in Action on Inequalities: Race, Class, Gender, and Sexuality*.

CONCLUSION

You now have sociological tools, skills, and knowledge. You do not have to be a professional sociologist to use them. Just keep your eyes open to how society is working (the sociological eye), make connections between personal troubles and public issues (the sociological imagination), and always look for multiple perspectives. Ask questions, and find your own answers. Question your answers, and always dig deeper. Change is always happening all around us. Whether or not we choose to help direct it is up to us. We don't know what social problems or issues you will confront in your life, but we do know that you can make a difference. The anthropologist Margaret Mead once said, "Never doubt that a small group of thoughtful, committed citizens can change the world. Indeed, it's the only thing that ever has." Using your sociological tools, *you* can help change the world!

NOTE

1. The Campus Compact and American Democracy Project efforts are a direct result of this growing realization among academic and government leaders. You can find many sources and links to articles about this topic on the websites for these organizations (http://www.compact.org and http://www.aascu.org/programs/adp, respectively).

REFERENCES

Beckworth, D., & Lopez, C. (n.d.). *Community organizing: People power from the grassroots.* Retrieved from http://comm-org.wisc.edu/papers97/beckwith.htm

Bobo, K. A., Kendall, J., & Max, S. (1999). *Organizing for social change: Midwest Academy—manual for activists.* Santa Ana, CA: Seven Locks Press.

Gecan, M. (2004). *Going public.* New York, NY: Random House.

Kielburger, M., Kielburger, C., & Shankaran, D. (2004). *Take more action.* Toronto, Ontario, Canada: Thomson/Nelson.

Index

About the Authors

Kathleen Odell Korgen, PhD, is a professor of sociology at William Paterson University in Wayne, New Jersey. Her primary areas of specialization are race relations, racial identity, and public sociology. Professor Korgen's work on public sociology includes coediting (with Jonathan White and Shelley White) *Sociologists in Action: Sociology, Social Change, and Social Justice* (2014) and *Sociologists in Action on Inequalities: Race, Class, Gender, and Sexuality* (2015). She has written or edited the following books on race relations and racial identity: *Race Policy and Multiracial Americans* (forthcoming), *Multiracial Americans and Social Class* (2010), *Crossing the Racial Divide: Close Friendships Between Black and White Americans* (2002), and *From Black to Biracial: Transforming Racial Identity Among Americans* (1999). Professor Korgen works as a consultant for other sociology departments as a member of the American Sociological Association Departmental Resources Group. She has received William Paterson University's Award for Excellence in Scholarship/Creative Expression and the university's Award for Excellence in Teaching.

Jonathan M. White, PhD, is director of the Bentley Service Learning Center and associate professor of sociology at Bentley University in Massachusetts. His primary areas of specialization are inequality, poverty, globalization, human rights, and public sociology. Dr. White has received numerous teaching and humanitarian awards. He is the founding director of Sports for Hunger, the Hunger Resource Center, and the Halloween for Hunger, We are Silent, and Pass-the-Fast campaigns. He serves on the board of directors for Free The Children, Peace Through Youth, Me to We, and the Graduation Pledge Alliance. Dr. White has authored several articles in the fields of inequality and globalization. His work on public sociology includes coediting (with Kathleen Korgen and Shelley White) *Sociologists in Action: Sociology, Social Change, and Social Justice* (2014) and *Sociologists in*

Action on Inequalities: Race, Class, Gender, and Sexuality (2015). He is also currently writing a book titled *Hungry to Be Heard: Voices From a Malnourished America.* Dr. White lives in Waltham, Massachusetts, with his wife, Shelley, and is the very proud uncle of his 13 nieces and nephews, Jarred, Kyle, Tyler, Arielle, Cameron, Brianna, Mikayla, Joshua, Jack, Logan, Tyler, Joey, and Brookelyn.

⑤SAGE research**methods**

The essential online tool for researchers from the world's leading methods publisher

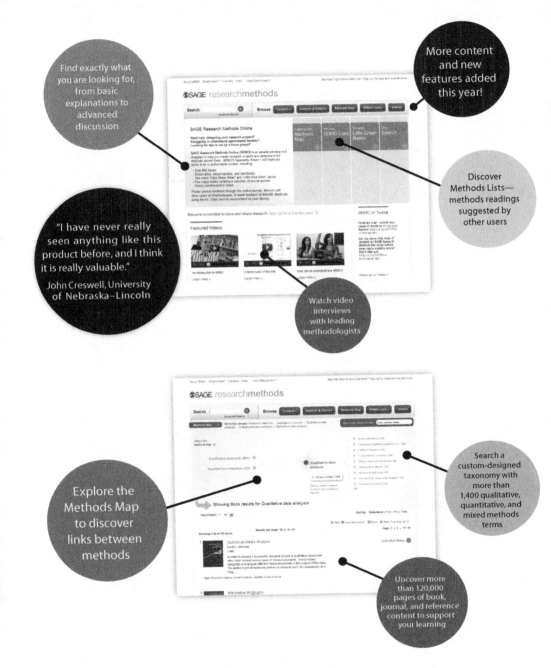

Find exactly what you are looking for, from basic explanations to advanced discussion

More content and new features added this year!

Discover Methods Lists— methods readings suggested by other users

"I have never really seen anything like this product before, and I think it is really valuable."

John Creswell, University of Nebraska–Lincoln

Watch video interviews with leading methodologists

Explore the Methods Map to discover links between methods

Search a custom-designed taxonomy with more than 1,400 qualitative, quantitative, and mixed methods terms

Uncover more than 120,000 pages of book, journal, and reference content to support your learning

Find out more at
www.sageresearchmethods.com